Warwick University Caribbean Studies

The Powerless People

An analysis of the Amerindians of the Corentyne river

Andrew Sanders

MACMILLAN CARIBBEAN

For my Mattie Buckpeople them, with apologies

Soc
F
2379
S26
1987

First published 1987

Published by *Macmillan Publishers Ltd*
London and Basingstoke
*Associated companies and representatives in Accra,
Auckland, Delhi, Dublin, Gaborone, Hamburg, Harare,
Hong Kong, Kuala Lumpur, Lagos, Manzini, Melbourne,
Mexico City, Nairobi, New York, Singapore, Tokyo*

ISBN 0-333-45096-5

Printed in Hong Kong

British Library Cataloguing in Publication Data
Sanders, Andrew
    The powerless people: an analysis of
    the Amerindians of the Corentyne river.
    — (Warwick University Caribbean studies).
    1. Indians of South America —
    Courantyne River Region (Guyana and
    Surinam) — Social conditions
    I. Title II. Series
    305.8′98′08817   F2380.1.S6
ISBN 0-333-45096-5

Acknowledgement
Publication of this book has been made possible by a
generous grant from the Muir-Hanna Trust, University of
Ulster

Cover based on a painting by Aubrey Williams presented to
The Centre for Caribbean Studies, University of Warwick.

Preface

The Centre for Caribbean Studies at the University of Warwick was founded in 1984 in order to stimulate academic interest and research in a region which, in spite of its creative vitality and geopolitical importance, has not received the academic recognition it deserves in its own right. In the past, the Caribbean has tended to be subsumed under either Commonwealth or Latin American Studies. The purpose of the Centre is to teach and research on the region (which includes those circum-Caribbean areas sharing similar traits with the islands) from a comparative, cross-cultural and inter-disciplinary perspective. It is intended that this Pan-Caribbean approach will be reflected in the publication each year of papers from the Centre's annual symposium as well as in other volumes.

Each year it is planned to include among these a study of a small community as the Caribbean cannot be fully understood without considering its many micro societies. Andrew Sanders' analysis of an Amerindian village on the Corentyne river in Guyana is the first of such studies. It is too often forgotten that the history of the region did not commence with Columbus and that descendants of the original inhabitants did not entirely disappear in spite of decimation by disease, exploitation and absorption through miscegenation. In the circum-Caribbean, and especially in the Guyanas many communities, although small and isolated, survived as 'powerless people', marginalized and forgotten except by anthropologists and, to their credit, colonial officials. The Guyanas, unlike the islands, share a continental destiny and as power abhors a vacuum, expanding frontiers of settlement are encroaching on scarcely populated interiors. In this process, Amerindians will be the major casualties as in neighbouring Brazil. Although in one sense this is an historical study and the community studied has since become a victim of 'progress' it should serve to alert us to the threat faced by the descendants of the indigenous inhabitants of the Americas and to remind us of Lévi Strauss's remark that every time a native society disappears humanity is impoverished.

Titles in this series

Labour in the Caribbean   M. Cross, G. Heumann
Land and Development in the Caribbean   J. Besson, J. Momsen

Contents

CHAPTER 1 | Introduction

1

This work is concerned with an aspect of race relations in Guyana. It analyzes the relationship between the descendents of Guyana's aboriginal population, the Amerindians (American Indians)[1], and the national society at the time Guyana achieved independence. Much of the analysis remains relevent to the nineteen-eighties, and a short Afterward examines developments in Amerindian relations since the end of the nineteen-sixties.

The analysis proceeds by an examination of how the Amerindians of the Corentyne river, and in particular the inhabitants of Orealla village, saw their social world. It discusses the meanings of concepts they used to create their picture of their world, and the assumptions and beliefs about different categories of persons revealed by their use of these concepts.

Many Orealla folk concepts were called by terms used in conventional English, such as 'families', 'shame', 'respect', and 'nation'. Although the terms were the same the concepts to which they applied often were different, sometimes markedly so. Consequently it is necessary to indicate in the text which usage is being employed. One way of achieving this might be to place the Orealla term in quotes but this has proved cumbersome. Instead the Orealla usage is indicated by beginning it with a capital letter, as in Families, Shame, Respect, Nation, Advantage, Mattie and Eyepass. It is hoped that this will cause a minimum of confusion.

Oreallans were typical of Guyana's Coastal Amerindians and the concepts they employed were used widely throughout Coastal Amerindian communities. They may also have been used in many Interior Amerindian communities, as a consequence of creolization. They, or similar concepts with the same terms, were used by non-Amerindian lower class Guyanese. Jayawardena has examined Mattie and Eyepass among Guyanese 'East Indian'[2] sugar workers[3], and differences between his interpretation and the one given here will be discussed.

Notes are placed at the end of each chapter.

1

Central to the analysis is an examination of four important folk concepts used by Oreallans to interpret relations between individuals and between categories of persons. These were Manners and Respect; Mattie; Advantage; and Eyepass. Respectively they symbolised social status and social hierarchy; common identity; exploitation and inequality of power; and competition for social standing.

An understanding of the meanings of these concepts provides important insights into much Orealla behaviour. Such an understanding involves more than knowing what Oreallans said about the concepts. It involves their application to behaviour; the way they were used to explain, justify, and criticize behaviour. From their application can be deduced meanings implicit in their use. For example, that Mattie meant a certain kind of belonging and therefore a certain kind of equality; and that it both implied the existence of a boundary between categories of persons and at the same time negated such boundaries between the parties applying the concept to each other. It is possible to deduce such meanings because the concepts were used in a structured manner and not at random. They were associated with particular contexts.

From such meanings, stated or implied, can be deduced relationships between the concepts themselves[4], enabling further statements to be made about the meanings of concepts and giving further insights into the way Oreallans saw their world. For example, it is deduced that Advantage was the antithesis of Mattie because the meanings of Advantage, explicitly stated by Oreallans, contravened all the meanings of Mattie, some of which were explicit while others were implied. From this it is suggested that Mattie effectively would end with the boundaries of the category 'Buck' (Amerindian), since other racial categories were believed to Advantage Bucks. Consequently the non-Amerindian would never be accepted as a member of the community because Mattie was the idiom through which people were incorporated into common categories. It is then postulated that Amerindians who were thought consistently to Advantage their fellows, such as Amerindian shopkeepers, would be thought of as acting in ways which were un-Buck and accused of considering themselves to be above their social position. This process of building up a pattern of inter-related meanings is an example of what Geertz, following Dilthey, characterizes as the hermeneutic cycle[5].

As with all interpretive anthropology — anthropology concerned with 'what being (a particular people) is really like[6]'; with understanding 'from (their) point of view[7]' — the examination goes beyond the everyday perceptions of the people themselves to deduce connections between meanings that they normally would not make and suggest meanings of which usually they would be unaware[8]. I have said that some of the meanings of Oreallans' concepts were implicit in their use. By this I do not intend to suggest that Oreallans were incapable of deducing them, or that everyone was unaware of them. They were not unconscious meanings in the sense in which the term is used by structuralists[9]. They were meanings implicit in the logic of the use of a concept, and Oreallans were less aware of them than they were of meanings which were communicated more formally. Oreallans did not analyze their concepts to any depth of abstraction and work out their inter-relationships. They learned how to apply them to individuals and social categories and were unconcerned about the detailed meanings implied in the manner of their use. For example, Mattie was the term used to describe the relationship between close friends. An Oreallan might address a non-Amerindian, towards whom he was likely to feel hostile, as 'Mattie' if he wished to obtain something from him. He did so to suggest that the relationship between them was like that between friends. This was part of a pattern of uses of the term in situations involving group identity which suggests that equivalence, an aspect of friendship, was the specific factor being stressed. But the Oreallan might be unaware of this, regarding his action simply as a false statement of friendship.

From what Oreallans said about the concepts they used, and from deductions based upon the way they were applied, a picture has been built up of the way they saw their world. It is made up of inter-related meanings, of inter-relationships between folk concepts. Oreallans would not have produced such an account. It is a model of meanings which is more sophisticated and systematic than the models used by Oreallans themselves. It is couched in terms which are more analytical than those used by Oreallans. It gives a more total picture of their concepts than any held by Oreallans, and consequently enables inferences to be made from the relationships between them. The degree of structured inter-relationship between the concepts is a product of the model. It is greater than that which appeared to exist in the Amerindians' models from which it was deduced, but this enables inferences to be made about social relationships. For example, that Oreallans' association of Advantage with race and Mattie with the Indian Right, a body of rights unique to Amerindians as a protected group in Guyana, caused them to attempt to apply a definition of Amerindian in terms of phenotype, in spite of significant miscegenation and of their belief that all persons with an Amerindian parent were Amerindians; and that this made the position of the mixed Amerindian an equivocal one. From the model deductions can also be made about the nature of the folk concepts themselves, for example, that Eyepass is basically an offence against individuals whereas Advantage is basically an offence against groups, or persons as members of groups. These are inferences of an analytical kind that Oreallans would not make.

Analysis and presentation of data on Orealla folk concepts is done through examination of the different folk models Oreallans held of their community. These consisted of sets of beliefs and assumptions about relationships between categories of persons. They were composed of folk concepts such as Mattie, Eyepass, Nation, Respect, Advantage, Families and Buck in a degree of ordered inter-relationship. Oreallans perceived their concepts through their positions in the structure of models they held of their community, of themselves, and of the wider society. The models defined the contexts to which concepts were applied, and people sought to justify or criticize their use by appealing to folk models they shared with other persons. Application of particular folk models to particular situations revealed the assumptions behind their use. It also revealed the inter-relationships between the concepts which comprised them, and their implicit meanings.

From the ways Oreallans spoke of their village, and of themselves as members, I deduced that they held five significant models of the community. As a residential unit composed of persons with certain kinds of common rights and obligations by virtue of membership (Oreallans). As persons related to each other as holders of kinship statuses carrying reciprocal rights and obligations (Families). As members of two tribes (Nations). As Amerindians, members of a particular racial group (Bucks). And as persons who were jealous of each other's success and sought to do one another down. Each was organised around a particular theme or idiom, a concept in terms of which inter-personal and inter-group relations were defined. Oreallans around the Indian Right. Families around Manners and Respect, the norms of proper behaviour between statuses. Nation and Buck around Mattie, the belief that persons belonging to the same grouping should have certain obligations towards each other in consequence. And competitors around Eyepass, the belief that Amerindians continually sought to assert moral superiority over one another. Undoubtedly the models held by different individuals varied in their structure. What I have created is my model of the 'standard' model in each of the five cases, of which each person's model might be viewed as a variant. One consequence of their use of these folk models was to impress upon Oreallans the powerlessness of Amerindians as a racial group in Guyanese society.

In creating an analytical model of the meanings of Oreallan's concepts, inter-relationships between concepts have been defined more precisely than their use would suggest. This is justified on the grounds that it gives an understanding of Amerindian relationships. However, the account of each folk model indicates the degree of systematic inter-relationship between concepts which was demonstrated in their use. It also seeks to relate the beliefs and assumptions contained in the models to the situation on the ground — to the general pattern of relations which existed betwen Amerindians, and between Amerindians and non-Amerindians.

This part of the analysis is an interpretation, based on observed behaviour, of the way Oreallans saw themselves, their community, and their world. It is not a description of life in an Amerindian village. Nor is it simply an account of what Oreallans said about their community. It is an account of the way I believe Oreallans perceived their community and their social world, and of what I believe the meanings of important Orealla concepts to have been. It is possible that other anthropologists, dealing with the same communities, would have made other interpretations. They might have deduced other meanings for Mattie or Eyepass; or deduced fewer, more, or different folk models of the community.

To support my interpretation I contend that the deduction of these folk models and these meanings enabled me to interact with Corentyne Amerindians, and other Coastal Amerindians, at a significant level of understanding. That they enabled me to understand much of their behaviour and to predict their behaviour in many situations[10]. That the inferences which could be drawn from the meanings, and from their application to categories of persons, give analytically useful insights enabling hypotheses to be proposed concerning Amerindian behaviour. For example, it is suggested that the non-Amerindian could never be accepted into the community because he could never become Mattie, and that this resulted in constant professions of Mattie by non-Amerindians living in the community. It also caused villagers to make a distinction between mixed Amerindian insiders and mixed Amerindian outsiders and to try to place them in different racial categories.

Among interpretive anthropologies this work has some affinities with that of David Schneider[11]. Schneider's concern is with systematic inter-relationships between cognitive elements, between sets of symbols and their associated meanings[12]. This contrasts with the interpretive anthropology of Geertz, who takes primarily an actor-oriented perspective and is concerned with the ethos of a culture. Geertz seeks to elucidate key themes of a culture; value orientations revealed through the operation of symbols in human behaviour. For Geertz symbols have their meaning through action. They organize meanings, emotions, concepts and attitudes[13].

Like Schneider I am concerned with a pattern of logical relations between meanings, a degree of formal integration between cognitive elements — symbols and meanings — which make up a world view. However Schneider's conception of the inter-relationship between culture and behaviour is problematic, whereas I follow the view enunciated by Hanson that although culture and behaviour are different aspects of social life culture is expressed in behaviour and should be studied in behaviour[14]. I believe meanings must be examined through their use in interaction. Like Geertz, but for different purposes, my starting point for interpretation is human beings interacting.

However the examination seeks to go beyond interpretation to explain why Oreallans saw their world in this way; why they used their inter-related concepts to create a particular perception of the world. It is concerned particularly with trying to explain why Oreallans' opposed ideas of race and mankind operated in the manner it suggests they did. It argues that this was a consequence of the incorporation of Amerindians as a group into Guyanese society at the base of a system of stratification in which ideas about race and culture were important elements, in a position which many sociologists, and psychologists, would term socially marginal. The analysis examines the historical development of Amerindian relations with the West Indian society of Guyana and the incorporation of the Amerindian group within it as a protected group towards whom different social classes, identified by Amerindians with different racial groups, held different attitudes.

It examines the consequences for relations with non-Amerindians, and for the behaviour of the Amerindian group within the national context, of what I believe was the most significant feature of the world view of Guyanese Amerindians, Coastal and Interior. This was their perception of their social world as divided by a fundamental dichotomy between Amerindians and non-Amerindians, the non-Amerindian part being powerful and the Amerindian powerless, and the powerful half divided between protectors and exploiters who were identified in racial terms.

The analysis examines Amerindian relations with the national society by focusing on the community, rather than by taking the Amerindian category as the initial unit for analysis. One reason for this is pragmatic. Fieldwork was carried out within Amerindian communities, so I am familiar with the working of the community. But communities often were relatively isolated, and consequently they were the context of much social life. Studying the application of concepts within the community, by persons acting as members of the village, enabled me to deduce meanings and to understand attitudes and behaviour in a wider social context.

The fieldwork on which this analysis is based was undertaken in Guyana between March 1965 and July 1968. It was financed by the Research Institute for the Study of Man; the Nuffield Foundation; and the Royal Anthropological Institute, to all of whom I express my thanks for their generous assistance. I also wish to thank the University of Guyana for study leave from my duties as lecturer in sociology in order to live on the Corentyne river from July 1966 until September 1967, and for various kinds of assistance with my research.

I wish to record my thanks to the University of Ulster, who provided a grant towards the publication of this work.

I also wish to express my thanks to the many Guyanese and Surinamers, Amerindian and non-Amerindian, officials and others, who generously gave me their assistance, and often their companionship.

During earlier periods on the Corentyne river I was accompanied by my wife, who proved invaluable as a co-worker. Much of the material pertaining to women in this work was either collected by her directly or could not have been obtained without her help.

My main debt of course is to the Amerindians of Guyana, and particularly to those of Orealla village. To them this book is dedicated, and I hope sincerely that it causes them no embarrassment.

Basically this is an analysis of the Amerindian position in Guyana as of 1968. A short Afterward attempts to deal with their situation since then. However, much of the material remains relevent to the present day, and I believe the work makes a useful contribution to the study of Amerindians in the Guianas. It fills a gap by examining relations between contemporary creolized Amerindians and other racial groups. Whereas Drummond has examined the problem of ethnic identity[15], there has been little work on Amerindian race relations and on Amerindian conceptions of the wider society and of the various racial groups which comprise its population.

Because the body of the work is concerned with the Amerindian situation in the 1960s I have chosen to write in the past tense rather than in the ethnographic present. Although this means many statements of fact which remain true today are written as in the past I believe this to be less misleading than putting the account in the present tense.

In various forms this work has been read by Dr Audrey Butt Colson, Pitt Rivers Museum, Oxford; Professor Raymond Smith,

University of Chicago; Professor John Blacking, Queens University
of Belfast; Dr Kay Milton, Queens University of Belfast; Mr Nicholas
Dodge, University of Ulster; Mr Michael Lamb, University of Ulster;
Mr Ronnie Moore, University of Ulster; and Dr John Offer,
University of Ulster. I wish to thank them all for their helpful
comments and suggestions. They bear no responsibility for any of the
statements herein.

2

Population distribution in the Guianas is extremely uneven, with the
great majority of the population living in densely populated regions
along the Atlantic coast. In Suriname more than eighty per cent of the
population lives along or near the coast, occupying four per cent of
the land area of the country[16]. The main areas of population
concentration are the Suriname shore of the Corentyne estuary and
east of the Corentyne port of Nickerie; the capital city of Paramaribo,
which has forty per cent of the country's population; and the region
between Paramaribo on the Suriname river and Albina on the Moroni
river. In Guyana the disproportion is even greater, with approximately
ninety-five per cent of the population living in four per cent of the
country, overwhelmingly along the coast and in a few inland towns
such as Linden on the Demerara river and Bartica on the Essequibo
river. The main area of concentrated settlement stretches from the
Guyana shore of the Corentyne estuary west to Charity on the
Pomeroon river, and includes the two cities of Georgetown and New
Amsterdam.

In December 1964 the population of Guyana, then British Guiana,
was estimated at 683,030 persons[17]. This was in the country's last years
as a British colony, Guyana becoming independent in May 1966. The
estimated racial composition of the colony is given in Table 1.1.

Table 1.1 *Racial composition of Guyana in December 1964* [18].

Guyana census categories	Percentage of population
East Indian (i.e. Indian)	50.2
African	31.3
Mixed Races[19]	11.9
Portuguese[20]	1.0
Chinese	0.6
European	0.4
Amerindian	4.6

Amerindians are the descendents of the aboriginal population and their number was estimated at 29,430[21]. At that time a commonly quoted figure for the Amerindian population of Guyana was 40,000[22], but this was probably too high. The report of the Amerindian Lands Commission[23], published in 1969, estimated a total population of 32,203 for 138 Amerindian communities. This excluded a few communities the commissioners were unable to visit and did not include the small number of Amerindians living in coastal villages and towns.

Anthropologists[24] and administrators[25] have classified Guyana s Amerindians into two categories, Coastal and Interior, of approximately equal numbers. The Coastal category consists of Arawaks, Waraos, and coastal Caribs. As their name indicates, they are the groups in closest proximity to the Atlantic coast, where approximately ninety per cent of Guyana's population lives.

The population of the Atlantic coast of Guyana consists of the descendents of immigrant populations, and shares a West Indian culture which contains much cultural and racial variation[26] and consequently is often designated as Creole or creolized[27]. The society of the Atlantic coast which carries this heterogeneous West Indian culture I designate the Coastal society. Coastal Amerindians have a long history of contact with the Coastal society. Their communities are all within a hundred miles by river of areas of Coastal Guyanese settlement, and communication with these areas is relatively easy. Most are in areas of tropical forest or savannah. In forest areas they are usually situated where physical features create natural breaks in the forest. In the Moruka river area, just west of the Pomeroon river, many Amerindians live on Bush islands in pegasse[28] swamp.

Interior Amerindians live mainly in the far west along the border with Venezuela and Brazil, and in the Rupununi savannahs in the southwest. They are classified into seven tribes: Akawaio in the upper Mazaruni; Arekuna on the upper Kamarang river; Patamona in the valleys of the Ireng and its tributaries and the tributaries of the Potaro; Macusi in the north savannahs of the Rupununi; Wapisiana in the south savannahs of the Rupununi; Carib at the headwaters of the Barama river; and Waiwai at the headwaters of the Essequibo river [29].

With the exception of the Barama river Caribs[30] and the Waiwai[31], all Amerindian communities have undergone marked change as a result of contact with the Coastal society and its agents. They have come to share many of the attitudes, institutions, and aspirations of other lower-class Guyanese. This change has been most marked among Coastal Amerindians, of whom the people of Orealla village may be taken as typical. Coastal Amerindians also exhibit a high degree of miscegenation, especially with persons of African ancestry [32]. West of the Pomeroon river, among the so-called 'Spanish Arawak'[33], there has also been much miscegenation with Spanish and Portuguese.

In the 1960s Amerindians provided much of the labour for all Bush industries, and were particularly important in three minor Guyanese industries — the lumber industry; balata production; and cattle ranching in the Rupununi savannahs of southwestern Guyana.

During the period of fieldwork Suriname was an internally autonomous part of the Kingdom of the Netherlands, a political status held since 1954 [34]. The 1964 census gave a population of 324,211. The racial composition of the population is given in Table 1.2.

Table 1.2   Racial composition of Suriname in 1964 [35].

Suriname census categories[36]	Percentage of population
Creole (i.e. Negro; Negro–White mixtures)	35.5
Bush Negro[37]	8.5
Hindustani[38]	34.7
Javanese (i.e. Indonesian)	14.9
Chinese	1.6
Amerindian	2.3
European	1.3
Other and Unknown	1.1

The census gave 7,287 persons who classified themselves as Amerindian. Of these 2,979 (41 per cent) were classed as 'non-tribal' individuals, mainly living in Paramaribo and its immediate vicinity. 'Tribal' Amerindians lived in Amerindian villages. Of these, 43 per cent were Caribs and 49 per cent were Arawaks, living on rivers and creeks near the Atlantic coast[39].

In a review of Amerindians in Suriname[40] Kloos states that their status is higher than that of Amerindians in Guyana. Although as a group they have low racial status they are not as despised as they are in Guyana. The general attitude towards them is one of sentimentality, as the aboriginal inhabitants of the country[41]. Tribal Amerindians have fundamentally a subsistence economy, with those living near the Atlantic coast participating in the Suriname economy by selling their produce or labour. Amerindians living in and around Paramaribo are found in many occupations. While they rarely hold high status occupations, they are rarely found in the poorest section of the society[42].

As are their Guyanese counterparts, Suriname Amerindians are citizens, and with the exception of tribal groups of the far Interior[43] they participate in Suriname elections. Unlike Guyanese Amerindians they have no special legal status[44]. There are no special administrative arrangements for dealing with Amerindians and no Amerindian reserves on which their communities might be located[45]. Most villages are situated on Crown land (*domeingrond*), to which they have no legal title. The government has the right to dispose of this land, but should pay attention to the claims of third parties such as Amerindians and Bush Negroes. Kloos states that at the time of his writing this situation had produced few conflicts with the authorities, but had become a source of uncertainty and anxiety in some villages[46]. Because of their small numbers Amerindians had little political influence in Suriname, but Kloos reports that Amerindian political awareness was growing[47].

3

In Guyana the distinction between the Coast and the Interior is more than merely a geographical one. It dominates the Coastal society's conception of its country. Its members differentiate between the Coast and the Interior or 'the Bush'. All Amerindian communities, including Coastal Amerindian ones, are in the Interior. In Guyana a distinction is implicit between 'town', 'country', and 'Bush'[48]. Coastal Guyanese ascribe to them differing degrees of attraction. The town (Georgetown and New Amsterdam) is a bright, exciting place, full of interesting people. At the other extreme the Bush is a dark, dangerous, uninteresting place, inhabited by fierce animals and backward, furtive Amerindians.

Notes

1 Amerindian is the official term used in Guyana for American Indian. It is also the anthropological term for American Indian.
2 Guyanese of Indian ancestry.
3 C. Jayawardena, (1963); C. Jayawardena, (1968). See also A. Mayer, (1967), pp. 176–80.
4 Meanings deduced from these inter-relationships, for example that to Advantage a fellow Amerindian was to behave like an outsider, are of the type which Hanson terms implicational - meanings 'in the logic or structure of institutions (sic)'. (F.A. Hanson, (1975), p. 71). In this particular case they are in the relationship between sets of meanings, and individuals may be aware of them to varying degrees.

5 C. Geertz, (1977), p. 491; W. Outhwaite, (1975), pp.32–7; P. Shankman, (1984), p. 267.
6 C. Geertz, (1979), p. 186.
7 C. Geertz, (1977); G.E. Marcus, and M.J. Fischer, (1986), p. 25.
8 C. Geertz, (1973), p. 5.
9 E.R. Leach, (1973).
10 F.A. Hanson, (1975), pp. 59–69; K. Milton (1981).
11 D.M. Schneider, (1968); D.M. Schneider, (1977).
12 R. Feinberg, (1979), p. 547; F.A. Hanson, (1975), pp. 99–103; G.E. Marcus, and M.J. Fischer, (1986), pp. 149–51; S. Ortner, (1984), p. 130.
13 C. Geertz, (1973); C. Geertz, (1979), p. 218; S. Ortner, (1984), pp. 129–30.
14 R. Feinberg, (1979), pp. 542–4; F.A. Hanson, (1975), pp. 99–103.
15 L. Drummond, (1974); L. Drummond, (1981).
16 N. Van Renselaar and H. Hoetinik, (1968), p. 312.
17 *International Commission of Jurists*, (1965), p. 32.
18 Ibid.
19 The Mixed category is a bureaucratic classification including any form of mixture. A significant element in this category is that category which is colloquially known as 'Red'. This is mixed Afro-European, and is more formally described as Coloured.
20 In Guyana, Portuguese are differentiated from 'Europeans' because of the manner of their introduction into the society, as indentured labourers performing menial work (E.P. Skinner, (1960), p. 904; R.T. Smith, (1962), pp. 49, 104–5; R.T. Smith, (1982), pp. 113–4).
21 *International Commission of Jurists,* op.cit.
22 e.g. *Amerindian Lands Commission,* (1969), p. 20.
23 *Amerindian Lands Commission,* (1969).
24 A.J. Butt, (1965), pp. 81–9.
25 P.S. Peberdy, (1948).
26 R.T. Smith, (1976), p. 207. See also L. Drummond (1974), p. 19; L. Drummond, (1981); E.P. Skinner, (1960); R.T. Smith, (1962), pp. 134–43; R.T. Smith, (1966); R.T. Smith, (1967). But contrast Despres, who claims Guyana is a plural society and that the concept of a common culture is not useful (L.A.Despres, (1967); L.A. Despres, (1970); L.A. Despres, (1975).)
27 L. Drummond, (1974), p.19; L. Drummond, (1981); R.T. Smith, (1967), pp. 233–45.
28 Areas of acidic peat soils.
29 A.J. Butt (1965). The Amerindian Lands Commission estimated the following population figures for the communities it visited - Akawaio and Arekuna, 3013; Patamona, 2094; Makusi, 5330; Wapisiana, 5600; Barama river Caribs, 650; Waiwai, 700 (*Amerindian Lands Commission,* (1969)).
30 J. Gillin, (1936).
31 N. Fock, (1963).
32 L. Drummond, (1974); L. Drummond, (n.d.).
33 E. Im Thurn, (1883); E. Im Thurn, (1884).
34 N. Van Renselaar and H. Hoetinik, (1968), p. 313.
35 E. Dew, 1978, p. 5.
36 These are not the same as the categories in the Guyanese census,

Guyanese and Suriname racial terms are not the same. I attempt to correlate them in Table 1.2 and the following footnotes.

37 Bush Negroes are the descendents of escaped slaves who live largely in tribal forms of organization in the interior of Suriname (A.J.F. Kobben, (1976)).
38 In Guyanese terms, East Indian.
39 P. Kloos, (1971), p. 11.
40 P. Kloos, (1972).
41 Ibid., p. 352. I must point out that Kloos' evaluation is based upon my accounts of Amerindians in Guyana, especially A.Sanders, (1972).
42 P. Kloos, (1972) op.cit.
43 The Trio, Wayana, and Akuliyo. These are groups whose contacts with Suriname society, in the form of missionary activity, are recent (P. Kloos, (1972)).
44 P. Kloos, (1972), p. 352.
45 Ibid.
46 Ibid. For the political situation of Amerindians in Suriname in the 1970s and 1980s see S. Hira, (1983).
47 P. Kloos, (1972) p. 353.
48 L. Drummond, (1974), pp. 36–42.

CHAPTER 2 | Amerindians in Guyana

1

Although it is indisputable that 'race' bears an important relationship to the social structure of West Indian societies, the nature of this relationship is the subject of much contention. In the case of Guyana this is demonstrated by the variety of terms used in recent analyses. Despres writes of cultural sections, ethnic groups, and ethnic collectivities[1]. Drummond uses the terms racial and ethnic categories, Creole culture, ethnic stereotypes, and ethnicity[2]. R.T. Smith has decided that racial group is most apposite[3]. Different terms reflect differing interpretations of Guyanese society and culture.

For Despres Guyana is a plural society, using the term in the sense in which it has been developed by M.G. Smith[4]. A plural society is one into which institutionally diverse groups are incorporated differentially in terms of status and power, and it depends ultimately for its maintainence upon the regulation of inter-group relations by a dominant group organised as a 'corporate group'[5]. Despres uses the term corporate group in the particular sense in which it is used by M.G.Smith, its defining characteristic being possession of the organization and ability to carry out action as a collectivity[6]. While Guyana was a colony this was the European group.

Despres' analyses are concerned with Guyana's two largest racially identified social categories, African and East Indian. These, he claims, are almost co-terminous with discrete groups which have their own institutions but which cut across social classes. For Despres, institutions are patterns of belief and behaviour that both organize activity and express cultural values[7]. The operation of their differing values has caused Africans and East Indians to develop different local institutions — institutions which organize activity within the context of the local community[8] — and has resulted in a significant degree of segregation between the two populations[9]. Value differences also have resulted in their developing, or supporting, different broker institutions — institutions that link local activities to the national level of social activity[10] — so that they are incorporated into the national structure as separate groups, with the result that at the national level structural segmentation mirrors cultural differences[11]. These groups Despres has chosen to term ethnic groups. Ethnic groups are cultural groups. (In his 1967 work Despres uses the term cultural section instead of ethnic group.) Within ethnic groups relationships are complex and diffuse, based upon value consensus. Between them they are highly segmented and specialised. Ethnic groups, and not socially differentiated persons, are the basic units of Guyanese society[12].

When Despres is speaking of the social structure of Guyana as a whole he presents some confusion as to the relationship between racial categories and cultural groups. At times he hints that not only Africans and East Indians, but also Europeans, Portuguese, Chinese and Amerindians form separate ethnic groups in this sense[13]. This interpretation results from his belief that different institutional arrangements are by definition expressions of differences in cultural values, as sometimes he appears to believe that where different racial categories tend to support different examples of institutions of the same structural type, such as political parties, *ipso facto* this indicates fundamental value differences between them. At other times he suggests that Afro-Guyanese and Portuguese share a common culture — 'Western (as distinct from South Asian), Christian, urban, and fundamentally anti-communist[14]'. In this case the political opposition between Afro-Guyanese and Portuguese, of which he makes much in his 1967 analysis, cannot be explained in terms of cultural pluralism.

Despres combines a plural society interpretaton with a cultural-ecological approach[15]. Culture is a set of ways for occupying and utilising an environment[16]. Populations entered Guyana with different cultural beliefs and practices. Their differential adaptation to Guyanese micro-environments, and competition between them, generated culture change and further cultural differentiation. This perpetuated the categorical identity of populations and resulted in their monopoly of some broker institutions and their competition for others.

Differential success in resource competition produced a situation of unequal status and power between categorically identified populations. This further strengthened ethnic identity, and made it the basis for corporate political organization. Because of the increasing size and occupational success of the East Indian population — a consequence of its culturally-based ability to exploit more effectively many available resources — Africans came to see East Indians as a collective threat to their well-being. This promoted competition between them, as groups, for control of national governmental institutions, and because of the racial diacritica associated with ethnic identities most of the Mixed population had little choice but to identify with African interests. While government remained under the control of the metropolitan power it attempted to accommodate this inter-sectional conflict by according East Indians and Africans consociational status — corporate but equal entitlements in the public domain[17].

Some aspects of Despres' interpretation of the operation of pluralism in Guyana have changed significantly since his earlier analyses[18]. He no longer regards plural societies as basically stable due to restriction of competition between ethnic groups resulting from ecological adaptation. Instead he stresses the influence of cultural factors in promoting competition, and consequently gives a lesser role to external political interference in promoting inter-racial conflict in British Guiana in the 1950s and 1960s[19].

In contrast to Despres, R.T. Smith argues that racially defined categories of persons do not correspond to social groups. They are cognitive categories. The relationship between 'race' and social structure is not rooted in differences in institutions, but in cultural beliefs concerning race which are maintained because of their past and present use in social behaviour[20]. The basic assumption behind West Indian ideas about race is that there exist pure races which can be mixed[21]. In Guyana these 'pure races' are European or White; African or Black; East Indian; Chinese; Portuguese; and Amerindian. Each is thought of as possessing a particular physical type, characterized by a particular 'blood'. Races can mix, and hence blood can be mixed, but this does not produce a new race. Races and types of mixtures are often attributed their own cultures and patterns of behaviour as a consequence of their blood. Different races consist of different types of person.

The basic elements of this system of beliefs concerning race — for example, the assumption that pure races exist and can be mixed; and that different races consist of different types of person — Smith terms cultural conceptions — 'elements which define the nature and com-ponents of the world, the units of which it is made up, and the meaning of those units'[22]. Whereas the valuation of racial difference and the characteristics ascribed to different races and mixtures can vary with time, place, and the social group applying the stereotype, and can change over relatively short periods of time, the conceptions themselves persist because of their continuous past use, which makes them available for the interpretation of present reality. As they can be used to explain and interpret situations they can provide a rationale for action. In the West Indies they have their origin in the development of an early capitalist mode of production under a particular set of historical circumstances[23], and their persistence has been reinforced through their association with social stratification and social mobility. But while conceptions and their use are conditioned by the social, economic, and political contexts in which they operate they are not determined by them[24]. They exist alongside and in opposition to other cultural conceptions which are also available for the interpretation of social reality[25]. They are used because individuals and groups choose to use them.

The recognized 'pure' races and those categories of mixture that are given social significance R.T. Smith terms racial groups[26]. Racial groups are not organized or bounded entities[27]. They are categories of identity that overlap, enabling many individuals to change their racial identity, and Guyanese talk about, define, and manipulate their racial categories in a bewildering variety of ways[28].

Guyanese, as other West Indians, have a tendency to identify 'races' with cultures[29], but in fact there is often considerable cultural diversity among members of the same racial group. Throughout the colonial period social mobility was possible for some members of all racial groups[30] and consequently racial groups cut across cultural, occupational, and class differences.

In contrast to Despres, for R.T. Smith racial categories do not form the basic units of Guyanese society. These are individuals and small groups; organizations; local communities and economic units such as villages, sugar estates, and bauxite towns. Because of the importance of conceptions of racial difference major social units are often perceived and described in racial terms, such as 'African villages' or 'the Coloured (Afro-European) middle class', labels which support racial interpretations of Guyanese reality but which obscure complicated situations of inter-racial and inter-cultural mixing[31]. Smith argues that in everyday life relations between Guyanese of all racial backgrounds are conditioned by personal, neighbourhood, and associational ties rather than by conceptions of race. There has been much inter-racial mixing, creating acknowledged kinship ties between members of different racial groups[32]. But conceptions of race are always present and can be invoked as explanations for, or tools to be used in, conflicts of all kinds[33].

For R.T. Smith Guyana is a class society in which, as a result of its colonial history, conceptions of race influence behaviour and are important elements of social structure. He argues that a common Guyanese culture exists and is an important factor in social integration[34]. Guyanese share many values and aspirations and there is a common Guyanese way of life in which existing cultural variations have come to be recognized as alternatives and not regarded as deviations. The idea of cultural difference can be a mechanism for integration as can shared cultural conceptions about race. But they can also be used in such a way as to promote or support conflict.

Guyanese society stresses the importance of racial and cultural differences because it is the product of the incorporation of immigrant populations which were racially and culturally differentiated into a common social system under the domination of a European, metropolitan-oriented, power-holding group. Ideas concerning the differential value of physical and cultural characteristics became a part of the culture and were associated with social status, and in colonial Guyana the idea of racial difference became an important factor in social integration.

Of the Despres and R.T. Smith interpretations of the relationship between 'race' and Guyanese social structure, I believe the latter to be the more valid. It accords with my material on Guyanese Amerindians, as I hope the following chapters will demonstrate. It accords with my experiences of Guyanese society between 1965 and 1968. I believe R.T.Smith's model of Guyanese social structure to be a better constructed and more dynamic model, which fits better the facts of Guyanese social life. I believe it provides a more plausible explanation of Guyana's recent and contemporary political history, which is the main purpose for which such models have been used.

With the exception of Amerindians, Guyanese racial categories are not groups in any corporate sense. They are statuses; categories of identity. In practice there is often a marked correlation between racial categories and cultural values, institutions, social groups, occupations and social classes, and many Guyanese believe an even greater degree of correspondence to exist. But racial categories are not themselves groups with their own beliefs, values, or institutions. Nor are they occupational groups or social classes. They cross-cut cultural and institutional differences, social groupings, and social classes. They lack defined boundaries. Many individuals can identify, or be identified, with more than one category, and their racial identities may change.

Racial categories have their present social importance as a consequence of their history of continuous use and manipulation as status indices and explanatory concepts, a result of their asssociation with relative power and status throughout the colonial period. But they do not merely persist because of their historical association with Guyanese social structure. Guyanese commonly use them as reference groups of various kinds[35], although the characteristics, standards, and situations which they associate with racial categories bear varying degrees of correspondence to the reality. They exist because they continue to be used and manipulated, including in the field of competition for power.

Because I believe R.T. Smith's interpretation of the nature of Guyanese racial categories to be correct I intend to adopt his term 'racial group' throughout this work. Although in reality racial groups do not correspond to discrete groups, they are often thought of by Guyanese as distinct groups whose members share common interests. They are perceived in racial terms, but it is a culturally defined conception of race and does not correspond with the biological facts, and as the data on Amerindians demonstrates, the allocation of an individual to a racial group may be influenced by factors such as behaviour, or the self-identification of the individual concerned. Different groups in Guyanese society may have different ideas of what constitutes a particular racial group. For example, Amerindians often ascribe to the 'Black' (African) group many persons whom other Guyanese would ascribe to the Coloured (Afro-European) group.

Drummond's work has been concerned particularly with the relationship between Guyanese racial categories and the cultural classification of particular patterns of behaviour. It focuses upon his concept of ethnicity[36]. By this he means the folk belief that the social setting is populated by distinct kinds of people, who derive their character from inborn qualities or deeply held beliefs which are difficult or impossible to renounce and which are expressed in their everyday behaviour[37]. In the Guyanese context it is the identification of certain patterns of behaviour with such racially defined identities as 'English', 'Coolie' (East Indian), and 'Black' (African). It is a symbolising process enabling the interpretation of people's actions and providing the basis for action. But ethnic categories are ambivalent, a quality of all symbols, and consequently are employed in inconsistent or ambivalent ways.

Drummond defines Guyanese society as Creole society. Its members share common institutions and often common concerns, but perceive themselves as belonging to diverse racial categories[38]. They also share in a common culture, whose basis is ethnicity or 'the ethnic myth'. But they share in Creole culture in a particular sense. Creole culture is a continuum, a range of meanings organised around variable concepts of ethnic identity. It is a set of transformations – mechanisms for allocating variable meanings to acts and beliefs – operating behind the myth that the society consists of discrete groups of racially and culturally distinct persons. Guyanese are aware of all or much of the continuum, although they do not need to behave as others do. Consequently persons can identify and comprehend much of the belief and behaviour they associate with membership of other racial categories. This accords with my own observations in Guyana.

Because ethnicity is ambivalent the interpretation of an act varies with the situation in which it occurs and with who is doing the interpreting. An action could be interpreted as, for example, English in one context and Buck (Amerindian) or Coolie in another. Just as the same act may be accorded different ethnic meanings according to circumstances, so the same individual can act in ways he considers typical of members of other racial categories; behave the same way in different circumstances and accord his acts different ethnic meanings; and have his behaviour interpreted on different occasions as that typical of different categories. What is considered behaviour characteristic of any particular racial category changes over time.

Because East Indians are the main element of the population popularly associated with the idea of a non-'English' culture, interpretation is often governed by a dialectic between concepts of 'English' and 'Coolie' customs. But in fact constant changes, synthesis, and re-interpretation of patterns of behaviour have resulted in the boundary between what is English and Coolie being modified until it has become a continuum. The cultural continuum is the product of centuries of cultural and racial mixing and is able to operate because at any time there is widespread agreement concerning what the meanings of actions can be[39].

Drummond argues that the existence of the continuum and the transformational nature of Guyanese culture vitiate the hypothesis that Guyana is a plural society consisting of discrete cultural groups[40]. If it were, one would expect the concepts of ethnicity to lack their variable, shifting quality. Allocation of ethnic meanings would have to correspond with membership of racial categories. Emphasizing the ambivalence of symbols, Drummond stresses the ability of individual racial identities to change. This is a consequence of his research among the mixed Amerindians of the Pomeroon river, who frequently change their identity from Amerindian to Black[41]. While recognizing that this is an important aspect of race relations in Guyana, in the following account I wish also to discuss the limitations placed upon changing identity. An important limiting factor is the ideology that identity is linked to ancestry, which is associated strongly with cultural conceptions of phenotypes.

Despres, Drummond, and R.T. Smith all stress that some form of plural society model is one of the folk models Guyanese have of their society and often use to interpret situations and order activity. All agree that cultural differences are given social importance and stress that they are continuously changing adaptations to Guyanese circumstances, not simple retentions of traditional cultures as many Guyanese believe. Smith and Drummond stress the ambivalence of ethnic or racial categories. Smith and Despres postulate a dialectical relationship between race and class and the co-existence of universalistic values alongside particularistic values associated with race or ethnicity[42], and believe competition between East Indians and other groups played an important role in the development of East Indian–Black conflict in the 1950s and 1960s.

Drummond points out the variability and ambiguity in the behaviour attributed to different racial groups and the range of ethnic interpretations which can be placed on behaviour. He stresses that identities are not fixed but can change and oscillate. These are crucial points, but the ascription of racial statuses operates within certain cultural constraints. I believe that R.T. Smith's interpretation of the role of 'race' in Guyanese social structure draws attention to some of the limits upon identity changes. Conceptions of race set some of the parameters within which persons effectively can change their identity.

2

Members of the Amerindian category are those persons regarded as descendents of the aboriginal inhabitants of the Guianas who are socially identified as Amerindian. Historically the category has had a long contact with the institutions of the Coastal society, for most of which its members have been subject to special policies and accorded a unique status. Both status and policies changed over the 350 years of Guyana's colonial history. Initial relations were based upon alliance and the fostering of dependence. This was followed by rejection by government cloaked by a professed policy of civilization, which was replaced by the combined policies of protection and gradual integration into Guyanese society. Policies usually were implemented by members of the higher, White, strata of the society, who often were expatriates, and consequently throughout Guyana's colonial history Amerindians had a unique relationship with the European racial group.

The pre-colonial aboriginal population of Guyana consisted of fairly typical South American tropical forest tribes[43], living in a forest environment and practising shifting cultivation with cassava as staple. In the Rupununi savannahs populations were culturally tropical forest with some modifications to adapt to a savannah environment. Tribes were linguistic and cultural entities only. The largest political units were small villages with a maximum size of about 70 persons. (Because of the availability of sea foods villages on the coast sometimes were larger). They consisted of one or two extended families, which were economically self-supporting and politically autonomous. Village leadership was achieved and depended upon personal ability and influence. Heads of extended families competed for leadership by providing community feasts with the help of their dependents. A village leader organized communal activities, but lacked authority to enforce his decisions. Settlement of disputes and redress of grievances was a matter for the individuals and families concerned. A combination of factors, including competition for leadership, operated to generate frequent village fission and the realignment of families and extended families to form new communities. Temporary alliances might be formed between villages, with mutual co-operation and visiting to attend dances and drinking festivities, but inter-village warfare was endemic and relations frequently were hostile. A village leader might also be a shaman — a piaiman. Piaimen conducted a few village ceremonies, but mainly operated as seers, advisers, and doctors. Their role was to combat evil, which they did through the aid of spirit helpers contacted during seances. It was the piaiman's duty to discover responsibility for death by sorcery, which was blamed on members of other villages and resulted in reprisal magic, revenge killings, and feuding.

In the sixteenth century the Dutch began the colonisation of what is now Guyana. They established friendly relations with the Amerindians in order to obtain their assistance against the Spanish west of the Orinoco and to trade for tropical forest products such as annatto (a dye made from the fruit of *Bixa orellana*) and letter wood (*Brosimium aubletii*)[44]. Relations were with the Carib and Arawak of the coastal region in particular, and to a lesser extent with the Akawaio of the northwest and Warao of the Orinoco Delta. They established trading posts on rivers into the Interior, as far south as the junction of the Rupununi and Essequibo rivers. Posts were controlled by postholders appointed to regulate trade and maintain friendly relations with the Amerindians[45]. Although seeking to control the actions of Amerindians the Dutch acknowledged their independence, and the Dutch West India Company instructed that all attempts be made to avoid giving them offense[46].

The multi-racial character of Guyanese society began in earnest in the eighteenth century with the development, along coastal rivers and the Altantic coast, of a plantation society based upon European, White, free, ownership and African, Black, slave, labour[47]. As the social system developed racial and cultural factors were made important elements of stratification, as a consequence of, and in order to buttress, the basic correlation between an economic and a racial dichotomy. Racial and cultural factors became associated with social status. Although race was never made the sole determinant of status it was accorded a major influence on occupational opportunities and social mobility, and this continued to be the case after emancipation, when opportunities for upward mobility increased. Inter-mating between the European and Black categories produced a rapidly increasing category of Coloured persons which occupied a status between the low status Black and the high status White racial groups.

This situation was further complicated by the presence of a significant Amerindian population, although it remained largely outside the plantation society. By the eighteenth century the main aspect of its relationship with the colonies was to assist in maintaining internal security. Amerindians were paid to capture runaway slaves, destroy villages of escaped slaves, and help put down slave revolts[48]. Villages often moved into the vicinity of Interior posts or established themselves behind plantations, to be close to supplies of European goods and ready to take action against the slaves. Amerindians played a vital role in the preservation of plantation society while remaining socially peripheral to that society. They continued to regard themselves as free and independent peoples and were treated as such by the colonists and the Dutch West India Company, and in 1793 an ordinance was passed prohibiting enslavement of Amerindians or the children of Amerindian women[49]. They considered themselves racially superior at least to the darker skinned and slave members of the society, and were regarded as such by its higher strata[50].

Dutch Amerindian policy was based upon three cornerstones: treaties of friendship and alliance with Amerindian 'chiefs'; a system of annual presents and allowances to retain the allegiance of Amerindians and pay for services rendered; and the employment of postholders to foster good relations with Amerindians, attach them to posts, and muster them for operations against escaped or revolting slaves. Postholders offered themselves as mediators in inter-tribal relations and attempted to curtail conflicts which interfered with trade and the smooth functioning of Dutch:Amerindian relations. Amerindian leaders were given official recognition, presented with hats and staves as symbols of their status, and given special presents[51].

European contact created a demand for many kinds of goods such as guns, metal tools, cloth and spirits, which were obtained as payment for political services or by trade[52]. Decrease in self-suffiency was greatest among communities near the coast, where contact was most intensive, but in the Interior demands were created as a result of contacts with trading posts and through inter-tribal trade. The Caribs, until their decline at the beginning of the nineteenth century[53], and the Akawaio[54] were important agents in inter-tribal trade with more distant Interior tribes, but even members of remote tribes occasionally travelled great distances to the coast to trade[55]. By emancipation, in

1833, the long period of contact with the society of the coast had produced significant changes in the customs and appearance of the inhabitants of some Coastal Amerindian communities[56]. The influence of the Coastal society had many deleterious consequences. The population of groups living near the coast declined drastically as a result of epidemics, warfare, and rum[57]. In the Interior the population was disrupted by epidemics, warfare, and a slave trade dominated by the Carib and Akawaio; while the Rupununi tribes were subjected to Brazilian slave raids[58].

When the British obtained the Dutch colonies of Berbice and Demerara-Essequibo they found it expedient to continue the Amerindian policy instituted by the Dutch, and the Amerindians recognised them as heirs to the Dutch and claimed from them the same protections and privileges[59]. In 1808 the British government republished the 1793 ordinance forbidding enslavement of Amerindians[60], and the policy of distributing goods and rations was continued until 1837[61]. The British government also defined the duties of postholders, and appointed Protectors of Indians to supervise postholders in different districts of British Guiana[62]. Protectors were chosen from local merchants and planters and were often members of the Court of Policy — the local legislative and executive body. Chiefs became known as 'Captains' and were issued with Certificates of Commission, but unlike the Dutch British officials did not nominate candidates for the office[63].

With emancipation the Amerindians' usefulness to the colonies ceased. The local legislature was primarily concerned with the need to find new sources of immigrant labour and Amerindians were largely ignored and left to their own devices[64]. This abrupt lack of interest in the concerns of Amerindians by the planter elements of the society is dramatically illustrated by Rodway's classic history of British Guiana, published in 1891–4. Amerindians are prominent in volumes I and II, largely in connection with their assistance against slaves. In volume III, which is concerned almost solely with the vicissitudes of the new system of 'free' labour, they are mentioned twice and do not appear at all in the index![65].

The Combined Court[66] opposed further expenditure on Amerindians and the policy of distributing gifts and rations was terminated by the close of the 1830s[67]. In 1838 the Combined Court abolished the unpaid offices of Protectors of Indians and replaced them with the salaried offices of Superintendents of Rivers and Creeks, in the hope that they would be able to supervise the postholders more closely, but almost immediately it sought to abolish the new offices to save expenses. It was prevented from doing so only by opposition from the Colonial Office. The Court compromised, merging under the office of Superintendent the previous offices of postholder, Commissary of Taxation, and Superintendent[68]. Abolition of Superintendents became a matter of annual debate in the Combined Court, and in 1873 they were replaced by Special Magistrates whose main concern was the protection of Crown lands[69].

On the coast the racial and cultural situation became more complex after emancipation, with the introduction of new populations as indentured workers for the sugar estates. These were Portuguese, Chinese, and Indians. The latter, who came to be termed East Indians, ultimately provided the bulk of indentured labour. Although Europeans, Portuguese were introduced to perform work degrading to 'proper' Europeans, and consequently became a distinct racial group. Emancipated slaves derided them as 'white niggar'. After their indenture many took to retail trading and became hucksters and small shopkeepers, occupations which were again non-'European'. On the proceeds of these occupations succeeding generations elevated their occupational position, and social mobility was assisted by possession of the high status physical characteristics[70]. The Chinese followed the same path as the Portuguese[71]. For a long time the Indians remained on the estates and in their villages, out of the mainstream of Guyanese life and culture. After the First World War they began to be incorporated into the mainstream of the colonial society and its system of stratification by taking up rural occupations such as peasant rice farming and acquiring education for their children. Incorporation progressed particularly rapidly in the mid-twentieth century, with the consequence that many members of the middle class and of other racial groups came to regard East Indian competition as a political and economic threat.

After emancipation there was a deliberate, and largely successful, attempt by the metropolitan power to create a unitary society through common laws, compulsory education, and an open labour market[72]. A new body of Europeans appeared in the colony. They included missionaries, doctors, magistrates, and Colonial Office officials. Largely British expatriates, their task was to civilize the ex-slaves. They attempted to create a common set of values for the whole society which stressed Christianity, the value of education, respect for law, morality, 'good' behaviour, and the importance of correct language. Elementary education was very successful in disseminating the values of colonialism and Christianity[73].

There were greater opportunities for upward mobility, particulary through education. Members of different racial groups became upwardly mobile and there developed a system of social classes based on occupation and similarity of lifestyle. However, because of differential prestige accorded different racial and cultural types and the differential access of racial groups to resources necessary for upward mobility, it was easier for members of some racial groups to rise than it was for others[74]. In the developing class system race and class were intimately related[75]. They were not however co-terminous. Because of social mobility race cut across class[76].

The developing middle class, consisting of a local intelligentsia, professionals, non-metropolitan businessmen and farmers, provided the major dynamic of post-emancipation society. It operated to integrate the society around the dominance of metropolitan culture, by stressing 'English' culture and values. Particularly important in this process was the middle class elite, whose members came to call themselves 'the intelligentsia' and regarded themselves as qualitatively different from other non-Europeans because of their refinement. The dominant Coloured section of the middle class defined themselves in racial terms as different from the Blacks, and upwardly mobile Blackpeople had to undergo a process of cultural whitening in order to be accepted into the middle class. All racial groups except Amerindians were represented in this developing class, but with Europeans, Portuguese, Chinese, and Coloured people over-represented because of their historical socio-economic advantages and the desireability of their phenotypes for certain kinds of valued occupation, and with Africans and East Indians under-represented. Its members developed a common style of life and experienced a common education, and increasingly they became discontented with the social restrictions imposed by membership of a colonial West Indian society[77].

The other main class consisted of the low income earners, semi-employed, and unemployed, who constituted the bulk of the population[78]. In the twentieth century, exposed to mass market media designed originally for high consumption societies, they came to feel progressively more deprived. Elements of the professional and commercial middle class harnessed the economic and social discontent of the lower class in the nationalist movement in order to achieve their own social and political ends, mobilizing the population in an effort to achieve full political and social status for inpatriates and generating new values[79]. The nationalist movement, in the form of the People's Progressive Party, by identifying with an ideology of socialism repudiated Whiteness and colonialism without making a racial appeal to any of the different racial groups among its supporters[80].

R.T. Smith initially termed the type of social structure that developed in colonial British Guiana 'Creole society'[81], because racial and cultural differences were integrated around the dominance of metropolitan culture. In his more recent work he follows Edward Braithwaite in defining Creole society as a social structure in which all races are integrated around the development of a local culture and local values, as was the case in Jamaica prior to 1865, and uses the term 'colonial society' for the type which developed in British Guiana[82].

By stressing the value of metropolitan culture and characteristics the ideology of colonial society was also stressing the existence and social importance of other characteristics seen as non-metropolitan and ranked inferior in the colonial status order. In stressing Whiteness it was stressing the existence of non-White social groups and allocating significance to physical differences. The lower classes, with less chance of mobility, maintained a stronger identification with cultures regarded as non-European, while recognising that 'English' culture was accorded superior status within the national system of stratification. But 'African' cultures and 'Indian' cultures were local adaptations to Guyanese conditions, and much of their content became socially acceptable alternatives within a frame of values set by conceptions of English culture. Similarly, local examples of English culture and institutions were local variations on English culture[83], and the interpretation of what constituted 'English' varied between the city and the remoter parts of the colony[84].

Race was always only one of a number of status markers[85]. Occupation and lifestyle and race provided different, though inter-related, categories of identity and claims to status. But racial stratification was an essential feature of the colonial value system and racial categorization continued as an important element in Guyanese culture. However, during the colonial period the development of unifying institutions influenced the development of liberal ideologies stressing universalistic values and individual achievement[86]. These existed simultaneously with, and in contradiction to, ideologies stressing racial difference. Consequently colonial society not only contained a dialectic between class and race, but also between universalistic values stressing individual accomplishment and the particularistic values contained in the ideology of racial difference[87]. The struggle between classes and status groups was influenced by the idea of race, and the concept of achievement often was assimilated to it.

In the twentieth century, continuing development of modernizing institutions heightened the contradictions in colonial society, generating new attitudes and aspirations[88]. Frustration with an ostensibly universalistic achievement system which defined achievement in terms of racial ranking and the superiority of metropolitan institutions and culture produced social movements aimed at removing the colonial value system. But because of the ideology of racial and cultural difference which supported the structure of colonial society, in the process of rejecting Whiteness it was necessary and inevitable that racial groups should stress their own racial identity in order to redefine it, and assert their own racial solidarity. Tragically this positive process of racial assertion was an important factor in defining the developing conflict in British Guiana from the mid-1950s as inter-racial conflict between the East Indian and African groups[89].

To return to Amerindians. After emancipation their status underwent a rapid and drastic change. Where previously they had held a relatively high racial status, now all other racial groups came to recognize them as possessing the lowest racial status of all[90], despite the fact that many of their physical characteristics approximated the high status European ones more than the low status Black ones. This was justified on the grounds that they were uncivilized savages, lacking any culture of value[91]. They continued to live outside the area of Guyanese settlement, but during the nineteenth century they were subjected increasingly to its influence and drawn economically and administratively into its orbit.

In the mid-nineteenth century, while the Combined Court's concern with Amerindians was reduced to attempts to cut expenditure, religious bodies and representatives of the metropolitan government saw it as their vocation or humanitarian duty to provide protection and civilization for the aborigines. In the immediate pre-emancipation period missionary activity had begun to penetrate the Interior. In 1829 the English Church Missionary Society established a mission at Bartica, at the junction of the Mazaruni and Potaro rivers with the Essequibo, a strategic point on the river routes into the Interior. By 1866 missions had been established on the lower reaches of all major coastal rivers, and during the second half of the century and in the early twentieth century they were established in the more remote Interior and in the Rupununi savannahs[92].

In the metropolis and the colony the function of missions was seen as civilizing the Amerindian through Christianization, and this was regarded as payment to the Amerindians for their past services and for occupation of their lands — a payment held to operate to the Amerindians' gain. However the Combined Court believed attempts to civilize Amerindians were largely futile and voted only meagre sums to support missions, which were maintained by missionary societies in London and by the Guiana Diocesan Church Society. Thus the legislature of British Guiana said it was doing its duty to the

Amerindians through the churches, which it claimed were civilizing the aborigines on its behalf, while making only a small contribution towards their operations[93].

The nineteenth century period of mission expansion was a time of stress and anxiety in Amerindian communities. Coastal Amerindian population continued to decline dramatically, largely due to a series of devastating epidemics. In the more remote Interior population decline and disruption was being caused by epidemics, warfare, attacks by mountain tribes on the savannah tribes, and by Brazilian slaving expeditions. These conditions made missions attractive to Amerindians as centres which offered physical security and spiritual protection, as well as medicines and vaccines. Groups of Amerindians who lived at great distances from the missions travelled many weeks to hear the missionaries' message, and earliest converts were often prominent members of their communities, and included piaimen and persons who had worked on the coast[94].

The susceptibility to new religious ideas which these conditions induced in the Interior tribes is demonstrated by the development of native religious movements in areas remote from the missions. Often their generation was influenced by the diffusion of mission teachings. The most famous of these occurred in 1845, when an Arecuna piaiman, Awacaipu, who had lived in Georgetown and learned to speak English, preached the millenium in the valley of the Kukenaam river, at the foot of Mount Roraima. He proclaimed the Amerindians would be made equal with the Whites and attracted about a thousand followers from all tribes. When the millenium did not materialise he told them they must kill each other, when they would be resurrected and descend from Roraima as Whitepeople. Some four hundred disciples died, and when their resurrection did not take place the enraged survivors killed their prophet. This dramatic example illustrates how strongly the Amerindians of British Guiana had come to associate power and prestige with Whiteness[95].

The first act of the missionaries was to induce the Amerindians to wear European clothing[96]. They instituted a sustained attack on polygamy and taught the sanctity of monogamous Christian marriage. Missions carried on an unremitting campaign against Amerindian 'superstitions', and to achieve this and to teach the Bible they established mission schools where Amerindian children learned to speak, read and write in English and were taught scripture, arithmetic and general knowledge. Literate pupils were encouraged to become evangelists and interpreters for the missions[97].

The missionaries inveighed against Amerindian drunkenness and complained of their indolence and apathy. They sought to encourage hard work and industry so that Amerindians could work for money to meet their need for European goods. But their attitude towards work went beyond this. Work was good in itself. Industrious habits were encouraged by the mission schools. Gardening was part of the curriculum, and Amerindian schoolboys at Bartica mission were apprenticed in Georgetown to trades of their choosing after reaching fourteen years of age. Amerindians from the Moruka and Pomeroon missions provided some workers for the estates in Essequibo county during the nineteenth century, despite Amerindian aversion to estate work because of its recent association with slavery[98].

In spite of these developments Amerindians did not enter the Coastal society in significant numbers. They were antipathetic towards Blackpeople, having developed hostile attitudes towards them during the slavery period[99]. Hostility was mutual, and Amerindians visiting the Coast often were cheated by Blackpeople. Away from the Coast they were exploited by woodcutters, traders, and storekeepers. They were employed as loggers and cheated of their earnings or paid in rum or with Coastal goods at inflated prices, and middlemen employed to recruit workers for the sugar estates recruited Amerindians and cheated them out of their wages[100].

Many Amerindians had also come to distrust White officials. They had been exploited by postholders and other officials and rejected by the government. Their territories had been converted into Crown lands at the bequest of the Governor and they had no rights to their land. As the timber and gold industries developed during the nineteenth century they complained about increasing alienation of their lands. Ordinance number 9 of 1873, which established the Crown Lands Department, assured Amerindians that their traditional claims to their lands would be respected, but made this subject to the discretion of the Governor[101].

Under these circumstances the missions, controlled and operated by expatriate Whitemen who were not government employees, became places where Amerindians not only acquired Christianity, literacy, and 'civilised' habits, but could also find protection from some of the pressures emanating from the Coastal society. British missionaries and churchmen came to be seen as protectors by the Amerindians. For their part they regarded the protection of their flock from undesirable Coastal influences and persons as an important aspect of their role, and the status of mission clergyman as protector of his congregation came to be acknowledged by the colonial administration[102].

While missions were taking responsibility for educating and civilizing Amerindians the legislature of British Guiana was bringing them within the legal system of the colony. Officials and other representatives of Coastal institutions worked through appointed Captains of local communities. Amerindians came to look to Special Magistrates and Superintendents of Rivers and Creeks to deal with conflicts between themselves and non-Amerindians, and with minor problems among themselves. (However, the treatment of Amerindian private delicts such as homicide remained a problem for the authorities until well into the twentieth century[103].)

At the beginning of the twentieth century, the question of estate labour having been resolved, official interest in the Amerindians revived. In 1902 the Amerindians Protection Ordinance established a number of reserves[104], set aside exclusively for Amerindian occupation[105]. In 1910 the Aboriginal Indian Protection Ordinance established 10 reserves and set out regulations to protect Amerindians in their relations with the Coastal society[106]. Amerindian affairs were made the responsibility of the Commissioner of Lands and Mines and administered by the District Officers of his department[107].

In 1939 the West India Royal Commission visited British Guiana and received complaints from Amerindian Captains from the Rupununi that Amerindian lands were being expropriated. They were assured by the Commission that Amerindian interests would be safeguarded before those of any other section of the population. As a result Mr P. Storer Peberdy was appointed Field Officer for Amerindian Affairs and commissioned to examine the position of Amerindians and make recommendations for their development[108].

The Peberdy Report, published in 1948, proposed a change in the policy towards Amerindians. It should aim at their integration into the national society. Peberdy believed many Coastal Amerindians were ready for assimilation, and suggested Coastal Amerindians be given the individual choice of whether or not they wished to remain Amerindians bound by the Aboriginal Protection Ordinance. The report made a number of proposals, the major one being the creation of co-operatives under government direction in areas away from the Coast in order to avoid harmful effects from continuous contact with the Coastal population. Here, in relative seclusion, Amerindians could acquire the qualities necessary to enable them to integrate with the Coastal society. It also proposed changes in the administration of Amerindian affairs, and the establishment of local government institutions in Amerindian communities[109].

Although Peberdy's proposals were modified considerably by the government, the report resulted in a change in Amerindian policy from being solely protectionist to aim at integration of Amerindians into Guyanese society. A Commissioner of the Interior defined this policy as the bringing of Amerindians 'by progressive steps to the

standard of culture which will enable them to take their place with
other groups in the general life of the community...Administration
of their affairs is influenced by two principles – protection and
integration – and a delicate balance between the two has to be
maintained[110]. The Amerindian Lands Commission, established in
1966 to examine the question of ownership of Amerindian reserves,
interpreted the policy as 'the bringing of the Amerindian into the
social, political and economic streams of the society and the provision
of opportunities for his upward mobility[111].' Implementation
concentrated upon projects for economic development, usually
centred on the local community, and the creation of local government
institutions. Policies thus focused on the Amerindian end of the
problem and assumed that if Amerindians could acquire
sophistication and responsibility in local government and develop
some business expertise they would be able to take their place as
equals in the national society. It was taken for granted that the
national society was racially equalitarian, and was prepared to accept
Amerindians as equals – both contentious assumptions.

In 1946 Amerindians became the responsibility of the newly
created office of Commissioner of the Interior, to be administered
through his officers in the three Interior Administrative Districts of
British Guiana. In the Coastal Administrative District different
aspects of Amerindian administration were divided between the
Ministry of the Interior and the Ministry of Local Government. In
1951 the Aboriginal Indian Protection Ordinance was replaced by the
Amerindian Ordinance[112], which reflected the new emphasis on
integration. The Ordinance, with subsequent amendments, was the
official framework within which Amerindian policies were being
pursued when the fieldwork on which this book is based was being
carried out. In addition to protective regulations[113] it provided for the
appointment of captains and the creation of local councils[114].

Through the Aboriginal Indian Protection Ordinance and its
successor, the Amerindian Ordinance, Amerindians were given a
formal status and a position in the national social structure possessed
by no other racial group. They became the only racial group whose
members' interactions with the institutions of the society and with
other racial groups were defined in law. Consequently these
regulations made the Amerindian racial group into a corporate group,
giving its members particular rights and advantages and imposing
upon them certain restrictions as a consequence of their racial
identity. One result of this was to strengthen the Amerindians' sense
of having a common interest against other racial groups in the society.
Another was to strengthen the society's conception of Amerindians as

a backward and inferior group because they were treated officially as an unsophisticated group requiring legal regulation of their relations with other Guyanese.

Although being the only racial group which was differentially incorporated into the society, being incorporated in a position of subordination[115], Amerindians did not form an ethnic group or cultural section as defined by Despres[116]. The group exhibited much cultural and institutional variation. Its major common institutions did not express Amerindian values. They were an aspect of its external relations, imposed through interaction with the Coastal society and controlled by non-Amerindians. On the other hand, with very few exceptions the members of Amerindian communities shared with the wider society cultural patterns regarded throughout Guyana as markers of civilization, and they stressed their cultural similarities with other Guyanese to support their claim to better treatment by the national society.

In contrast to other racial groups Amerindians neither were distributed in significant numbers throughout all socio-economic classes of the population, as were Africans and East Indians, nor predominantly members of the higher social strata, as were Europeans, Portuguese, Chinese, and to a lesser degree Coloured. With extremely few exceptions Amerindians were in the lower socio-economic sector of the population and they rarely had the opportunity or the persistence to become upwardly mobile.

Although the Amerindian Ordinance conveyed upon Amerindians rights no other racial group possessed it also placed in the hands of the government immense legal power over them. It gave the Commissioner of the Interior complete control over the property of Amerindians[117]. It determined who might reside on Amerindian reserves by giving the government the right to determine the residence of non-Amerindians in these areas[118]. It gave the representatives of the government the right to determine the conditions of employment of Amerindians; power to control Amerindian drinking of alcoholic beverages; and control of local government[119]. Land officially designated as Amerindian reserves belonged not to the inhabitants but to the government, which could create and terminate reserves and vary their boundaries as it chose[120]. Section 39 of the Ordinance entitled the Governor in Council to make regulations for the proper administration of reserves; for removing Amerindians from one reserve to another; for the custody, education, and employment of Amerindian children; for maintaining 'discipline and good order' in Amerindian reserves; and for prohibiting 'any rites and customs (considered) injurious to the welfare of Amerindians'. Even the decision as to who constituted an Amerindian ultimately rested with the administration. Section 2 of the Ordinance defined an Amerindian as:

'(a) any Indian of a tribe indigenous to the Colony or to neighbouring countries;

'(b) any descendent of an Amerindian within the meaning of paragraph (a) of this definition to whom, in the opinion of the Commissioner (of the Interior), the provisions of this Ordinance should apply.'

These regulations were formulated with a view to assisting Amerindians in their relations with members of the national society. During the colonial period they appear to have been administered diligently, but in the 1960s, with the prospect of national independence and a government free of restraint by the metropolitan power, fear of loss of their special rights and abuse of these powers was an important factor influencing the behaviour of Amerindians in national politics.

3

Through increasingly intimate contact with the Coastal society, in many cases over a long period of time, Guyana's Amerindians came to acquire many of the values and standards of the Coastal colonial society, including the value attached to Whiteness and deference to metropolitan individuals and institutions. They also came to conform to or idealize many of the society's most prestigious institutions. They became Christians. They learned to wear European clothing. They worked for money and used money as a medium of exchange in many of their economic transactions. They were taught to practice monogamous marriage. They came to speak a creolised European language, generally English[121], as a first or second language. But they learned to do so on the periphery of the society under conditions which maintained their separation from the rest of the society. Consequently the majority of the Coastal population continued to see them as backward and uncivilised.

Although Amerindian relations with the Coastal society changed radically over the colonial period, the nature of the relationship consistently operated to link them to the higher strata of the society, identified with White and higher-status racial groups, in opposition to the lower, which overwhelmingly consisted of Blackpeople and East Indians. Because of the nature of this relationship Amerindians remained insulated from developments on the Coast as the twentieth century progressed. These culminated in a widely supported movement opposed to 'White' domination of the status system and the colonial nature of the power structure. To all this the Amerindian remained a spectator; history, his special position in Guyanese society, and his special relationship with Europeans binding him to 'Whiteness' and causing him to see Europeans as his protection from the Coastal society.

Notes

1 L.A. Despres, (1967); L.A. Despres, (1975).
2 L. Drummond, (1981).
3 R.T. Smith, (1976); R.T. Smith, (1982).
4 M.G. Smith, (1965); M.G. Smith, (1974), pp. 334–7.
5 L.A. Despres, (1970), pp. 263–4
6 M.G. Smith, (1974), p. 336.
7 L.A. Despres, (1967), p. 25.
8 Ibid., pp.13–27.
9 Ibid., pp. 68–120.
10 Ibid., p. 23.
11 Ibid., pp. 121–76.
12 Ibid., p. 175; L.A. Despres, (1970), pp. 263–4.
13 L.A. Despres, (1967), pp. 254, 256.
14 Ibid., p. 260.
15 L.A. Despres, (1970); L.A. Despres, (1975).
16 L.A. Despres, (1975), p. 112.
17 Ibid., p. 110.
18 L.A. Despres, (1967); L.A. Despres, (1970).
19 L.A. Despres, (1975).
20 R.T. Smith, (1976); R.T. Smith, (1982).
21 R.T. Smith, (1976), pp. 205–6.
22 R.T. Smith, (1982), p. 116.
23 Ibid., p. 118.
24 R.T. Smith, (1976), p. 199.
25 Ibid., pp. 198–208, 225; R.T. Smith, (1982), especially p. 116.
26 R.T. Smith, (1976), especially pp. 198–208; R.T. Smith, (1982), especially pp. 98–102, 116–9.
27 R.T. Smith, (1976), p. 205.
28 Ibid.
29 Ibid., p. 206.
30 Ibid., pp. 198–208; R.T. Smith, (1982).
31 R.T. Smith, (1976), p. 206.
32 Ibid., pp. 207–8.
33 R.T. Smith, (1982), p. 116.
34 R.T. Smith, (1962), pp. 134–43; R.T. Smith, (1966); R.T. Smith, (1967).
35 W.G. Runciman, (1972), pp. 10–41.
36 L. Drummond, (1981).
37 Ibid., p. 354.

38 L. Drummond, (1974), p. 19.
39 L. Drummond, (1981), pp. 353, 368.
40 Ibid., p. 360.
41 L. Drummond, (1974); L. Drummond, n.d.
42 L.A. Despres, (1973), p. 128.
43 For data on the traditional societies and cultures of the tribes of the Guianas see A.J. Butt, (1965–6); A.B. Colson, (1969); N. Fock, (1963); J. Gillin, (1963); P. Kirchoff, (1963); P. Kloos, (1971); P. Riviere, (1969); P. Riviere, (1984); I. Rouse, (1963a); I. Rouse, (1963b); W.E. Roth, (1915); W.E. Roth, (1924); W.E. Roth, (1929); J.H. Steward and L.C. Faron, (1959); M.M. Suarez, (1968); M.M. Suarez, (1971).
44 M.N. Menezes, (1977), p. 2.
45 M.N. Menezes, (1977), p. 53.
46 M.N. Menezes, (1979), pp. xvii–xviii, 161.
47 The following brief account of the development of Guyanese society draws heavily on the work of R.T. Smith.
48 M.N. Menezes, (1973), p. 67; J. Rodway, (1891–4), vols 1 and 2; R. Schomburgk, (1922), vol 1, p. 33.
49 M.N. Menezes, (1979), p. xvii, 161.
50 V.T. Daly, (1966), pp. 104–5; R. Schomburgk, (1922), vol 1, p. 54.
51 M.N. Menezes, (1973), pp. 65–6; M.N. Menezes, (1977), pp. 44–7; M.N.Menezes, (1979), p. xviii.
52 W.H. Brett, (1868), p. 6.
53 Ibid., p. 475; R. Schomburgk, (1922), vol 1, p. 52.
54 W.H. Brett, (1868), pp. 143–5; R. Schomburgk, op.cit.
55 Ibid., pp. 251, 283, 315–6.
56 J.H. Bernau, (1847), p. 25.
57 W.H. Brett, (1868), pp. 413–4, 494; J.H. Bernau, (1847), pp. 226, 230; C.Henfrey, (1964), p. 263; R. Schomburgk, (1922), vol 1, p. 54.
58 W.H. Brett, (1868), pp. 117, 478, 481, 472–3; R. Schomburgk, (1922), vol 2, pp. 40, 50, 82, 118, 235.
59 M.N. Menezes, (1973), p. 68; M.N. Menezes, (1979), pp. 49–104.
60 Ibid., p. 161.
61 M.N. Menezes, (1977), pp. 49–72; M.N. Menezes, (1979), pp. 25–50.
62 M.N. Menezes, (1977), pp. 53–85; M.N. Menezes, (1979), pp. 73–104.
63 M.N. Menezes, (1972), pp. 57–61.
64 J.H. Bernau, (1847), p. 74; M.N. Menezes, (1977), p. 260; M.N. Menezes, (1979), p. 273; R. Schomburgk, (1922), vol 1, p. 54.
65 J. Rodway, (1891–4).
66 The Court of Policy sitting with the Financial Representatives (R.T. Smith, (1962), p. 26).
67 M.N. Menezes, (1977), pp. 72, 255; M.N. Menezes, (1979), pp. xx, 29, 54, 274.
68 M.N. Menezes, (1977), pp. 105–27; M.N. Menezes, (1979), pp. xx–xxi, 53–85.
69 M.N. Menezes, (1977), pp. 110, 126; M.N. Menezes, (1979), pp. xx–xxi, 54.
70 E.P. Skinner, (1960), p. 904; R.T. Smith, (1962), pp. 49, 104–5; R.T. Smith, (1982), pp.113–4.
71 R.T. Smith, (1962), pp. 59, 104–5.
72 R.T. Smith, (1976), p. 207.

73 R.T. Smith, (1967), pp. 237–42; R.T. Smith, (1982), pp. 108–11, 113–5, 118–9.
74 Ibid., pp. 113–4.
75 Ibid., p. 95.
76 Ibid., p. 114.
77 R.T. Smith, (1966), p. 52; R.T. Smith, (1967), pp. 237–242; R.T. Smith, (1982), pp. 108–11, 119.
78 R.T. Smith, (1966), p. 52; R.T. Smith, (1967), p. 243; R.T. Smith, (1982), pp. 111–5.
79 R.T. Smith, (1966), p. 52.
80 R.T. Smith, (1967), p. 254.
81 R.T. Smith, (1966); R.T. Smith, (1967).
82 R.T. Smith, (1982), p. 109.
83 R.T. Smith, (1967), p. 234.
84 L. Drummond, (1981).
85 R.T. Smith, (1982), p. 104.
86 R.T. Smith, (1976), p. 207; R.T. Smith, (1982), p. 93.
87 Ibid., p. 102.
88 R.T. Smith, (1967), pp. 245–58.
89 Ibid.; R.T. Smith, (1982), pp. 15, 19.
90 V.T. Daly, (1966), pp. 104–5.
91 See for example comments in J.H. Bernau, (1847), pp. 144–7; W.H. Brett, (1868), pp. 343–403.
92 J.H. Bernau, (1847), pp. 67–73, 76–132, 144–55; W.H. Brett, (1868), pp. 50–4, 56–7, 60–6, 70–91, 100–18, 150, 200–5, 220–1, 255–81, 283–4, 295–312, 321, 425; A.J. Butt, (1954); M.N. Menezes, (1977), pp. 208–53, 255–9, 262–4; M.N. Menezes, (1979), pp. xx, xxii, 215–69, 273–4.
93 M.N. Menezes, (1977), pp. 258–9, 262–4; M.N. Menezes, (1979), pp. xx, xxii, xxviii, 217, 274.
94 Bernau, (1847), p. 29, 115–6; W.H. Brett, (1868), pp. 80–91, 143–5, 223–9, 255–81; 319, 342–3, 412–3, and *passim*; E.D. Rowland (1892); R. Schomburgk, (1922), vol I, p. 54, vol II pp. 40, 50, 82, 115, 118, 155, 235.
95 J.H. Bernau, (1847), p. 200; W.H. Brett, (1868), pp. 83, 178–84, 250–1, 256–9; A.J. Butt, (1954); M. Swann, (1961), pp. 264–6.
96 W.H. Brett, (1868), pp. 76, 406–7, *passim*. In 1967 members of the Unevangelised Fields Mission working among the Waiwai informed me that their first act with respect to new members of the mission settlement was to induce women to wear clothes, and said they would not approve taking photographs of women with exposed breasts.
97 J.H. Bernau, (1847), pp. 144–52, 155; W.H. Brett, (1868), pp. 76, 100, 106, 287, 296–313, 320–36, 351–3, 406–7, and *passim*.
98 J.H. Bernau, (1847), pp. 48, 50, 74, 109, 144–52, 215; W.H. Brett, (1868), pp. 90–1, 323–4, 349, 406, and *passim*; M.N. Menezes, (1977), pp. 190–201.
99 J.H. Bernau, (1847), p. 177; R. Schomburgk, (1922), vol I p. 44, vol II p.58.
100 W.H. Brett, (1868), pp. 166, 254; M.N. Menezes, (1977), pp. 179–207; M.N. Menezes, (1979), pp. 161–211; R. Schomburgk, (1922), vol I p. 52.

101 J.H. Bernau, (1847), p. 165; M.N. Menezes, (1977), pp. 179–207; M.N. Menezes, (1979), pp. 161–211: R. Schomburgk, (1922), vol 1, p. 53.
102 See for example L. Drummond, (1974), p. 297.
103 M.N. Menezes, (1973), pp. 128–53; M.N. Menezes, (1979), pp. 89, 117.
104 I use the term 'reserve' because it adequately describes the aim of the legislation. The terms in the Amerindian Ordinance are Amerindian Villages, Amerindian Areas, and Amerindian Districts (*British Guiana*, (1951), Part I). They were specified areas which non-Amerindians should not enter without official permission. Amerindians were not restricted to living in these areas.
105 *Amerindian Lands Commission*, (1969), p. 10.
106 *British Guiana*, (1910).
107 *Amerindian Lands Commission*, (1969), p. 11.
108 M.N. Menezes, (n.d.).
109 P.S. Perberdy, (1948).
110 *Amerindian Lands Commission*, (1969), pp. 62–3.
111 Ibid., p. 63.
112 *British Guiana*, (1951).
113 For example, regulations intended to safeguard Amerindian property and provide legal representation (Ibid., part III); provide protection for Amerindians in employment (Ibid., part VII); and control the sale of intoxicating beverages to Amerindians (Ibid., part VIII).
114 Ibid., parts IV and V.
115 M.G. Smith, (1974), pp. 333–6, 338–45.
116 L.A. Despres, (1967); L.A. Despres, (1975).
117 *British Guiana*, 1951, section 12.
118 Ibid., sections 5 and 6.
119 Ibid., parts VII, VIII, and V.
120 Ibid., section 3.
121 In the Rupununi Amerindians in their late fifties and over usually speak Portuguese as the second language to their own. (T.McCann, (1969), p. 12.)

CHAPTER 3

The Village as Oreallans
The Indian Right

1

The Corentyne river rises in the Guiana Highlands, which divide the Guianas and Venezuela from Brazil, and meanders northwards 500 miles to the Atlantic Ocean. Its last 100 miles are tidal and contain numerous islands, which are usually long shoals clothed with manicol palms[1]. It forms the border between Guyana to the west and Suriname to the east. The border is the high water mark on the Guyana shore, and the river is part of Suriname and is patrolled by the Suriname police.

In the 1960s West Indian settlement ended at the wide Corentyne estuary. In Guyana the continuous belt of Coastal settlement which stretched east from the city of New Amsterdam, on the right bank of the Berbice river, terminated with the port of Springlands, Skeldon sugar estate, and the large village of Crabwood Creek (Map 1). In Suriname the main settlement on the Corentyne mouth was the town of Nickerie, which was the administrative centre for Suriname's control of the Corentyne river.

During the period in which this study was carried out there were five villages above the Coastal settlements, all on the lower reaches of the river and within 100 miles of the coast. The large Amerindian village of Orealla was on the Guyana shore 56 miles above Crabwood Creek. Above Orealla were three smaller Amerindian villages, each with a resident population of around 100 persons. Sipuruta was eight miles above Orealla on the Guyana shore. A few miles above Sipuruta the Corentyne made a large eastward meander, about twenty miles long but only two miles across at the neck, which was easy to traverse on foot. The village of Wassiabo was on the lower part of the meander, on the Suriname shore about twenty miles above Orealla. Also on the Suriname shore was the village of Apoera, about ten miles above Wassiabo and on the easternmost point of the meander. All four Amerindian villages contained mixed populations of Arawak and Warao Amerindians, the great majority of whom were born on the river or were from neighbouring areas of Guyana and Suriname. There was also a small village of Bush Negroes on the Suriname shore

The Corentyne river

about three miles above Orealla, the westernmost Bush Negro settlement.

There were some isolated homesteads, mainly East Indian, on the Guyana shore above Crabwood Creek. The Suriname shore was low and swampy and had few homesteads. There was a small Suriname police post below Wassiabo, which supplied permissions to Amerindians from the Guyana shore to work on, or collect natural products from, the Suriname shore, and another at Apoera. On the Guyana shore were two small sawmills, 'Deanville' just below Sipuruta and 'Glasgow' just above, owned by East Indians, and there was a forest ranger station at Sipuruta.

No-one lived above Apoera. On the Guyana shore a few miles above the big meander was the deserted Amerindian reserve of Epira. It was abandoned shortly after the First World War as a consequence of a disastrous 'flu epidemic and of conflict between the Amerindians and their Black schoolteacher, and most of the survivors joined Orealla. However Epira remained an Amerindian reserve and non-Amerindians had to obtain official permission to go there or to exploit its resources.

Canoe travel between the four Amerindian villages was relatively easy, and there was frequent and easy communication between the villages and the Coast. Two boats came up-river every two or three

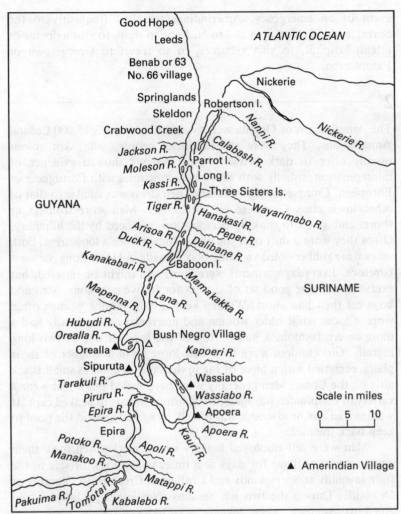

Map 1 The Corentyne River

days to collect sand from a point above Sipuruta, and carried passengers and freight. A motor launch carried the mail to Orealla and Sipuruta every fortnight. The Anglican vicar of Skeldon parish visited Orealla once a month, and a medical dispenser visited Orealla and Sipuruta each month. A Roman Catholic priest from Suriname visited the church and school at Wassiabo every month, and one from Guyana visited the church and school at Sipuruta about once every three months. The police on the Suriname shore, the Assistant District Officer at Orealla, and the forest rangers at Sipuruta all had outboards and would carry persons and messages to the Coast in the event of an emergency. Amerindians travelled frequently to the Springlands-Skeldon area and to Nickerie to shop, to visit a doctor or attend hospital, to visit relatives, or to travel to Georgetown or Paramaribo.

2

The Amerindians of Orealla were typical of Guyana's 15,000 Coastal Amerindians. They were short, stocky people, with skin colour usually olive to dark brown. Many persons showed evidence of miscegenation, usually with Black but sometimes with Portuguese or European, Chinese, or East Indian. Their dress was similar to that of other lower-class Guyanese or Surinamers. Men wore trousers or shorts and a vest to soak up perspiration produced by the humidity. Often they wore a shirt over the vest. Women wore a long dress. Both sexes wore rubber-soled yachting boots, made in Hong Kong, or went barefoot. Everyday garments were worn and might be tattered, but everyone had one good set of clothes for festive occasions. Men and boys cut their hair short. Women kept it long. Young women often wore it loose while older women and married women usually had a more severe fashion, a bun on top of the head or one or two long pigtails. Girl children wore their hair loose or in a number of short plaits, each tied with a piece of rag in the same fashion as small Black girls on the Coast. Men generally went bareheaded but might wear a variety of dilapidated headgear, from brimmed hats to peaked caps. If women had any headwear it was merely a rag tied around the head to keep back the hair.

Men were self-employed loggers whose work often took them away from the village for days at a time, felling logs for sale to the four sawmills at Springlands and Crabwood Creek or to Glasgow or Deanville. During the two wet seasons (November to January and April to August), when logging was more difficult, some men collected balata, the latex of the bulletwood tree[2], to be sold to the balata agents for the Guyana and Suriname shores. Women engaged in domestic tasks and farming, in which they were assisted by men[3].

Like other Coastal Amerindians, Oreallans were river people. Every household had its landing at the riverside where men moored their canoes and women washed the household laundry. The river was the villagers' avenue of communication, linking them with the outside world and the other Amerindian villages of the Corentyne river. Whenever possible they travelled by canoe, as it was quicker and much easier than walking along a path through the savannah or the forest.

At Orealla the river was about a third of a mile wide and made a large westward meander, known locally as 'the bucket'. The village was in the bottom of the bucket where a steep chalk escarpment, about fifty feet high and running north-south, met the river (Map 2).

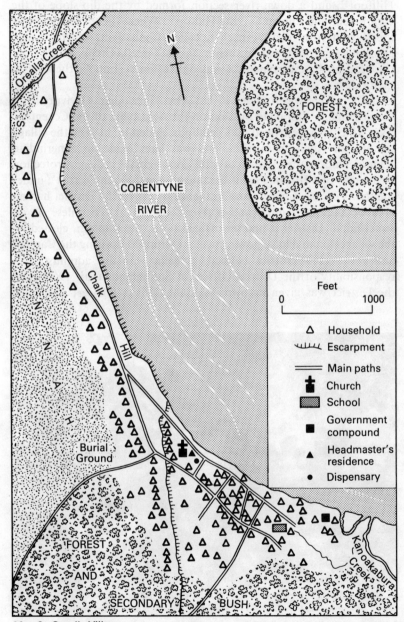

Map 2 Orealla Village

It divided the village's two miles of river frontage into two almost equal parts, and divided the village topograhically into an up-river section below the escarpment, called "the Flatland" or "the Hillfoot", and a down-river section formed by the dip slope of the escarpment and known as "the Hilltop". Where the escarpment met the river it formed a steep cliff, called Chalk Hill, which became gradually lower as it ran downriver until at Orealla Creek, a mile from the head of the escarpment, it was only a few feet above the river at high tide.

The village was founded in 1832[4] by Amerindian survivors from Good Hope, a Moravian mission on the right bank of the Corentyne river which was destroyed by a smallpox epidemic. In 1866 the village became an Anglican mission, and was later made an Amerindian reserve under the terms of the Aboriginal Indian Protection Ordinance of 1910. In 1953 it became an Amerindian District[5], under the terms of the Amerindian Ordinance of 1951. The District had an area of 54 square miles and a river frontage of ten miles. As an Amerindian District it had an official head, the Captain, elected by the villagers, and a local government structure comprising the Captain and an elected District council. Orealla was the administrative responsibility of the District Officer at Springlands until 1962 when the District was given its own Assistant District Officer, who lived

Local government: Orealla Village Captain addressing a meeting

with his family in the ADO's house at the up-river end of the village and served a term of two to three years before being transferred elsewhere.

In June 1967 the Flatland had a population of 462 persons in 66 households. Its clay soil was poorly drained by ditches dug along the main paths. There were two major paths, one running along the riverbank and the other roughly parallel and about one hundred yards inland. These were linked by a number of cross paths, some of which continued inland a short distance.

On the Hilltop the soil was coarse and sandy and less fertile than the Flatland. The ridge carried a similar vegetation to the Flatland, but the dry, quickly draining soil was particularly suited for coconut[6] and awarra palms[7] and there were several groves of coconut. As it progressed southward the escarpment quickly became covered with the rain forest that surrounded the Flatland on its landward side. The forest and occasional savannah which hemmed the village inland and covered the Guyana and Suriname shores were termed 'the Backdam', an analogy with the back dam of a sugar plantation which marks the limit of its cultivated area. Anyone leaving the village and going into the Bush to log, or for any other purpose, was said to be going in the Backdam.

On the dip slope of the escarpment, behind Chalk Hill, was a sandy savannah covered with coarse grass and stunted trees, with islands of gallery forest in wet, low-lying areas. It stretched from Mapenna Creek to the north of the village four to five miles to Tarakuli Creek to its south, reached the cliff edge from Chalk Hill to Orealla Creek, and was about three miles across. Along its eastern, north-eastern, and south-eastern edges, where it was bordered by the forest, the well-drained sandy soil was more fertile and was used for cassava farms. Behind Chalk Hill, on the edge of the savannah, was the village burial ground, marked with wooden crosses and dotted with wild cashew bushes[8]. On the Hilltop settlement was concentrated at the head of the escarpment where the riverside path ran steeply up the scarp and divided to run southward along its edge and northward along the cliff top to Orealla Creek. From this area settlement extended along the path to Orealla Creek. In June 1967 the Hilltop had a resident population of 335 persons in 53 housholds.

At the up-river end of the Flatland, near the riverbank, was the Assistant District Officer's house, a large white two-storey wooden building erected in 1962. The village school was also at the up-river end of the village, inland from the ADO's house, a long concrete building built in 1963 to replace the old school. Also on the Flatland was the village church, by the riverbank near the foot of the

Houses on the Flatland

escarpment. It was a grey building walled and roofed with wooden
shingles. Next to the church was the house of the school headmaster
and the village nurse's small dispensary-cum-residence. Both were
built in Coastal style, with walls, glass windows, and doors, but unlike
typical Coastal houses, and like Amerindian houses, they were
elevated only a few feet and not a fully storey above the ground. The
headmaster's house had a dalibana palm[9] roof, in the fashion of
Amerindian houses, while the dispensary was roofed with shingles.

3

Oreallans defined the model of their village as a residential unit in
terms of corporate rights and responsibilities, summed up in their
concept of the Indian Right, and of common personality and
behaviour. They saw themselves as differing in identity and character
from the inhabitants of the other three Amerindian villages and
expressed this in comment and in their festive songs. At the same time
they defined village membership in terms of rights possessed by all
Amerindians, and shared with no other racial group.

At the 'sport' to celebrate the August holiday in 1965 young men
formed small informal groups, one of which called itself 'the Orealla
Merry Boys', and went from house to house in search of home-made
drinks. As they walked the men played improvised musical instruments
and sang,

'Orealla boys are here again
'All away, all away
'Let us drink this bambolay[10].'

In January 1967 the song composed for the 'Shove Down' festivities, which celebrated the end of the Old Year, was,

'Orealla girls are handsome looking girls
'Wassiabo girls are too
'I'll give you a dollar and we shall meet again
'And I wish you all a Happy New Year,
'New Year, New Year, New Year,
'And I wish you all a Happy New Year.'

It was sung by the people as they walked about the village looking for drinks, and was soon corrupted by young Orealla wags to 'Orealla girls are whorry, whorry girls...'

Oreallans saw themselves as progressive and sociable people, in marked contrast to their stereotype of Sipurutans, who were lazy, dirty, backward drunkards. They thought the people of Wassiabo and Apoera were similar to themselves. They were more backward economically, but in contrast to Sipurutans this was not their fault. They lived farther up-river and progressive ideas took longer to reach them. Informants said the people of Apoera had only recently started selling surplus game and fish among themselves instead of giving it away, whereas Oreallans had been selling each other their surpluses for several years.

The antipathy between Oreallans and Sipurutans was not due to any competition between them. Sipurutans did appear to spend even more time drinking and being intoxicated than other Corentyne river Amerindians and their village was less well kept than Orealla, its paths choked with weeds and bushes. Some Sipurutans were Oreallans who had left the village to avoid the consequences of anti-social actions, such as married persons who were running away together. However, out of Sipuruta's 17 households ten were of men from outside the Corentyne river who said they settled at Sipuruta instead of Orealla because they were Roman Catholics and it was a Catholic mission. Oreallans' dislike of Sipurutans may have been influenced by Amerindian distrust of outsiders. For their part Sipurutans believed Oreallans arrogant and conceited.

To Oreallans, being an Oreallan meant having an automatic right to live on the reserve and exploit its resources and to share in any village resources. In principle, these rights did not extend automatically to other Amerindians. For example, in 1965 the village obtained its own tractor to haul to the river logs cut on the reserve. The villagers were adamant that it was for their use only. Their

District council obtained the loan from the Ministry of Agriculture to make the down payment, and they would have to pay for the tractor. They did not want Sipurutans to use it as Sipuruta was not part of the Orealla Amerindian District[11].

Being an Oreallan also meant being subject to regulations passed by the District council as the organ of local government – such as paying $1.25 to the village fund if you were working on the Suriname shore, to help pay for the village tractor. It also meant helping to weed the village. Amerindians believed use of land established your right to it, and that once you ceased to utilize it you relinquished that right. Consequently people who travelled to Epira to cut logs believed that by doing so they were maintaining Amerindian rights to the reserve. Periodically weeding a plot of land on which you intended to build your house maintained your right to it, and if you allowed someone to build on it and reside there temporarily you continued to weed it to show it was still yours[12]. Conversely, if non-Amerindians used village resources they were thought to be attempting to establish a claim to those resources which could set a precedent resulting in their alienation. Co-operative weeding of the village was not only an instrumental act, it was a claim that the village and the land on which it was situated belonged to the villagers.

Each Orealla household also participated in village drinking festivities. There were four holidays set aside for 'sporting' – village drinking in which people went from house to house in search of

August sport: women searching for drinks

drinks. They were Easter, the first of August, Christmas, and 'Shove Down'. The first three, known as 'the Easter sport', 'the August sport' and 'the Christmas sport', lasted three days. 'Shove Down' lasted the whole of the first week of January. Although these festivities were not organized at the village level each household made alcoholic drinks and invited friends and relatives to partake.

In the Oreallans' model of their village as a residential unit Amerindians born in the village were Oreallans. If they left they remained members with the right to return, and their children were villagers, no matter where born. In June 1967 there were at least 117 persons who qualified for membership but were residing permanently elsewhere, not only on the river but in Nickerie, Paramaribo, Georgetown, Kwakwani (on the Berbice river), the Pomeroon river, and other places. Amerindians who came from elsewhere but had lived in the village for a long time were also regarded as villagers. Thus many Oreallans were members of more than one village.

However, in practice an Amerindian could join any Amerindian village provided he had relatives or friends there or his spouse was from the village. (Since many Amerindians travelled widely in Guyana and Suriname, Amerindians had kin and friends in many villages throughout the two countries.) While this was not part of their conception of village membership few Orealleans would be likely to dispute his claim, and any that did could not take effective action to expel him. As an Amerindian he had the legal right under the Amerindian Ordinance to enter and reside in any Amerindian reserve in Guyana[13].

The only residents whom Oreallans regarded as having no right to live in the District were non-Amerindians living in domestic unions with Amerindian spouses. They usually were accepted as members of the village by only a few close relatives, but their children were villagers within the model of village membership.

The *de facto* extension of village membership to include virtually all Amerindians who chose to reside at Orealla was recognized in the manner in which village membership and its attendant privileges was often referred to as the Indian Right, or simply 'The Right'. This was the term for the collective body of rights and privileges Amerindians had in Guyana as a consequence of their special racial status. It included the legal right to enter any Amerindian reserve, reside there, and exploit its resources without obtaining permission from the representatives of the national government, a right from which non-Amerindians officially were excluded. It also included exemption from some of the obligations incurred by other citizens, such as payment of certain taxes. It included social rights, such as the right to special legal protection in relations with non-Amerindians[14]; and rights to exploit certain natural resources, such as free use of forest products for domestic purposes and the right to open cast mine alluvial deposits within Amerindian reserves, some of which were legally guaranteed while others had become customary rights[15]. Oreallans often talked about village membership in terms of The Right, an idiom which included more than residence within the village and incorporated all Amerindians. Thus non-Amerindians residing at Orealla or working on the reserve were thought to be trying to take away the Indian Right by establishing a precedent to its use by non-Amerindians. By viewing village membership in this way, the main distinction in the Oreallan's model of his community as a residential unit ceased to be between villager and non-villager and became between Amerindian and non-Amerindian.

4

A marked theme in Oreallans' conceptions of their village and their world was the assumption that outsiders or strangers were potentially dangerous. Most Oreallans could not articulate this theme, but it could be deduced from their beliefs and behaviour. I will give two examples.

Case 3:1   David Benjamin (age 44)[16] had a pain in his right forearm. He told me he fell in a creek while he was logging and thought he may have struck his arm against a takooba — a floating log or tree. He decided to go and see Edward Cotton (64), an old man skilled in doctoring, and I accompanied him. David told Edward the story about the takooba, but at the same time they were holding another conversation in a combination of Arawak and Creole English which was intended to prevent me from understanding their discussion. David told Edward that while he was walking along the shore he passed a stranger, a non-Amerindian, sitting on the side of a beached canoe and smoking a cigarette. The man was watching him, and shortly afterwards he began to feel the pain in his arm. He thought the man may have put a bad spell on him. Edward agreed. He blew two long breaths on the bad arm[17] — although he was smoking a cigarette that David gave him he did not blow with cigarette smoke — and then blew into his left hand and passed it lightly over the arm as though he were massaging it. He repeated the procedure twice more, the second time blowing on the arm with three long breaths instead of two, and the third time with four. He then massaged the arm with limacol, a soothing medicant sold in Coastal stores and chemist shops. The next day David's arm was still bad and he went to the village nurse who gave him some tablets and warned him not to drink alcohol while he was taking them.

The second example concerns kanaima, the traditional Night Witch[18] of the Amerindians of the Guianas[19]. Kanaima are evil witches who hide in the Bush and kill people. They eat raw meat and have their own language, kanaima language. They can change themselves into any object, natural or man-made, and can make themselves invisible. They like to change into logs and lie across paths in the Bush, then when women step over them they can look up their skirts and try to see their genitalia. They are sometimes seen as old men walking in the Bush. Although they seem to be walking slowly you can never catch them up, and if you take your eyes off them they vanish. A kanaima may be employed by someone to kill an enemy. He will go to where he is told he can find his intended victim, but should he fail to find him he will kill someone else.

Case 3:2   Ronald McIntosh, who died in the early 'sixties aged 72, was an Amerindian from Mahaicony in Demerara. He lived at Orealla for more than fifty years, where he married and raised a family. One of my informants, a woman in her late fifties, told me he was a bad obeah man[20] and a kanaima. He could change himself into a leaf, a cup, a metal file, anything that took his fancy. He buried a gobi — a hollowed out calabash — containing medicines in his field, so that if anyone entered the field snakes or vicious stinging wasps came from the gobi and chased them away. He had a house on the Suriname shore filled with paddles, bows and arrows, and other artifacts. If anyone stole anything from it they would die, killed by snakes, wasps, or other poisonous creatures.

Old McIntosh would change himself into a takooba — a fallen log — and lie in the path, and when a woman stepped over him he would look up her skirts and laugh. Once when his wife was walking to her farm she saw a takooba which she guessed was her husband and chopped it with her cutlass. A few minutes after she reached the farm he came along with a deep cut in his leg. He did not know she had recognisd him but he vowed never to do it again.

McIntosh went to live at Tarakuli Creek, a few miles south of Orealla. Kanaimas from the Berbice river would come and visit him. They announced their presence by whistling outside his house at night and he would invite them in to drink bamboli. They would ask him where the bad people from the Berbice river lived that they had been hired to kill. One night a kanaima came who had been hired to kill McIntosh himself. Not knowing who he was the kanaima asked him where McIntosh lived. He told the kanaima that the man he wanted lived on the Suriname shore. When he failed to find him the kanaima returned and told McIntosh he was going back to the Berbice river. Finally McIntosh died, full of years, killed, my informant said, by his own wickedness.

At Orealla kanaima were associated particularly with the Berbice river, the next river system to the west, but other places mentioned were Mahaica and Mahaicony in Demerara, and Essequibo county. Some Oreallans believed kanaima were members of particular Amerindian tribes. Macusi and Wapisiana were frequently mentioned. Others believed they were a tribe of their own. They came to Orealla in the dry seasons. They hid in the Bush and made their presence known by whistling in the night and by pelting people with the fruits of kukret[21] and awarra palms. Monkeys throw fruits at people in the Bush; *ipso facto* a monkey which throws a fruit at you is a kanaima that has assumed animal form. Most Oreallans believed in kanaima, and people would abandon logs and go to work elsewhere in the Backdam if subjected to experiences they associated with kanaima.

Informants said the last kanaima murder at Orealla occurred some twenty years before I did my fieldwork. Despite the fact that several Oreallans were born elsewhere I was told there were no longer kanaima at Orealla, and I know of no resident who had been accused of being a kanaima or who was believed to be one. I doubt if anyone would have been accused, if only because of the nature of contemporary religious beliefs. Amerindians were Christians. At Orealla they were Anglicans. Christianity was the field of group ritual and was used to validate status changes, such as birth, marriage and death. It was also an important expression of the civilised state and associated with respectable behaviour. But there was another corpus of beliefs, drawn from many sources – traditional Amerindian beliefs; Creole and East Indian beliefs; and Christian and quasi-Christian beliefs. Oreallans regarded these as morally and intellectually inferior to Christianity and called them 'superstition', but they operated in a different social field. They were used in everyday life, to explain specific events and attain specific ends. This was the field of individual practice and interpretation. Different persons believed in them to different degrees and in different forms. Someone accused of being kanaima would not merely deny it. He would deride his accuser as foolish for behaving in accordance with 'foolish superstition', even though in all probability he believed in kanaima himself, and would be supported by many members of the village. Any would-be accuser knew he would be derided by many villagers and that he would be appealing to beliefs condemned by the church and rejected by the administration, to whom the accused could turn for support.

Other tribes of Amerindians often were believed to be skilled magicians. The more remote the tribe from the Corentyne river and the more primitive its members were thought to be, the more mystically dangerous. The Macusi, Wapisiana, and Waiwai were frequently quoted as dangerous kanaima and powerful sorcerers, as were the primitive Carib.

Non-Amerindians often were magically skilled or dangerous. The best 'doctors', who could cure ailments and possessed powerful medicines, were often non-Oreallans and frequently non-Amerindians. The Djuka (Bush Negroes)[22] were renowned as obeah men, and persons with Black ancestry might be vampires.

Non-Amerindians often were also powerful and dangerous in a non-mystical way. They were representatives of a society that wished to take away the Indian Right, and of its institutions, against which Oreallans ultimately were powerless. All influential persons were non-Amerindian outsiders. Within Orealla they were the representatives of the institutions that helped to create the village, that stabilized its population, and formally linked it to the wider society — the church, whose agent was the Vicar of Skeldon Parish; the school, whose agents were the headmaster and the Vicar of Skeldon Parish; and the administration, whose agent was the Assistant District Officer. On the Coast they included officials such as policemen, magistrates, and representatives of development agencies. All were agents of a Coastal government whose intentions were suspect. Individuals who had important economic relations with Oreallans, who paid them wages or bought their products or upon whom they depended for assistance in their economic activities, were all non-Amerindians from the Coast. Their interests were believed to be opposed to those of Amerindians and Oreallans believed they were exploited by them. They included saw-millers, 'buymen' (saw-millers' buyers), balata agents, tractor owners and drivers, and forest rangers.

Non-Amerindians who entered domestic unions with Oreallans and came to live in the village were viewed with suspicion. They were exploiting the Indian Right, enjoying its privileges while having no right to do so. But what was seen as dangerous about them was that they formed a vanguard which could establish a precedent that other racial groups, of right, could share in Amerindian privileges, which would lead ultimately to loss of The Right.

Notes

1 *Enterpe edulis.*
2 *Manilkara bidentata.*
3 For a detailed account of the Orealla economy see A.D. Sanders, (1972), pp. 122–224.
4 F. Peneux, (n.d.), p. 6. See also M.N. Menezes, (1977), pp. 239–40; M.N. Menezes, (1979), pp. 222–4, 249–50.
5 *British Guiana* (1953a).
6 *Cocos nucifera.*
7 *Astrocaryum tucumoidies.*
8 *Anacardium occidentale.*
9 *Geonoma baculifera.*
10 Bamboli – home-made cassava beer.
11 Sipuruta was not a reserve. It was a mission on land leased to the Catholic Church.
12 House land at Orealla was formally lotted and recorded in 1962 (Ministry of Lands and Mines, Georgetown, maps 10511 and 10542) and it had become possible for people to build on land belonging to someone else. (A.D. Sanders, (1972), pp. 215–9.)
13 *British Guiana*, (1951), part 1, sec 3–4.
14 Ibid., part 3, sec 12–13.
15 *Amerindian Lands Commission*, (1969), pp. 20–1.
16 Figures in brackets after the names of individuals are their ages at the relevent time.
17 Amerindian spells are accompanied by mystical blowing. (A.J. Butt, (1956).)
18 L. Mair, (1969), pp. 38–9.
19 See e.g. J. Gillin, (1963), p. 856.
20 The West Indian term for a person skilled in medicine and magical techniques.
21 *Cenocarpus* sp.
22 Amerindians call all Bush Negroes Djukas. In fact the Djuka are only one Bush Negro tribe, from the Commewijne river in Suriname.

CHAPTER 4 | The Village as Families
Manners and Respect

1

When Oreallans described their village they often said 'We is all families'. By this they implied that all members were kin. The term Families could be interpreted as 'relatives'. Any two persons with a kinship tie were Families to one another. As with the English 'relatives' it could be applied to members of groups and entities of various kinds and sizes, from the relationship between two persons to relationships between all members of the village or between the members of all the Amerindian villages of the Corentyne river. (For example, it might be said of a part of the village in which many residents were particularly closely related, 'They is all Families'.) The entity to which the term was being applied was evident from the conversation, and its use did not imply that persons not included were not Families to those who were, merely that the people referred to were related and that in the context of the conversation the speaker considered this significant.

Most Oreallans were related genealogially and could trace what they believed to be the real genealogical links between themselves. In fact, given the narrow range of exogamic regulations[1] many persons could trace several different genealogical linkages with each other. The significant genealogical relationship often was that which was genealogically closest, but the kinship relationship recognized between two persons often subordinated genealogy to relative age. A simple extendable system of terms of address was used for all relatives beyond a narrow range of close affines and consanguines[2]. Terms were those used to designate certain close kin, and were sex and generation terms. Persons of parents' generation could be addressed as uncle/aunty. Persons of grandparents' generation as grandfather/grandmother. Persons of own generation as cousin. Persons of children's generation as son/daughter or nephew/niece, depending upon genealogical distance, and of grandchildren's generation as grandson/granddaughter. Although the terms were generation terms, their application was influenced by age difference between Alter and Ego. Thus a distant uncle or aunty of same age as Ego was brought down to Ego's generation and became cousin, and his children were sons and daughters or nephews and neices and were cousins to Ego's children. A cousin who was much younger than Ego became his son or daughter or nephew or neice, cousin to his children. Thus more distant kinship was a simple matter of ascription by sex and age. Consequently it was easy to allocate kinship statuses to non-relatives.

Behaviour proper to kinship was summed up in the Orealla concept of Manners and Respect. The proper attitude that people should adopt towards themselves and others was known as Respect. An adult should Respect himself. He or she should behave responsibly. The attitude and behaviour proper to adults was contrasted with the ignorance and lack of awareness of young children. Adults were 'big men' or 'big people', not 'small children' lacking knowledge or awareness of right and wrong. They should not neglect their domestic responsibilities and spend all their time drinking or lazing about or engaging in frivolous or anti-social activities. They should behave with propriety. When they were drinking they should not act foolishly or cause fights. When people did not behave in this way they were said to be 'playing bad' or 'behaving bad'. They were behaving like small children and not big people.

Case 4:1   At a public meeting called by the Orealla Captain to discuss possible future development projects for the village the Captain, addressing the meeting, complained that bad behaviour had become rife in the village. Children were running wild and misbehaving. Parents were ignoring their responsibilities. They must discipline their children and stop them misbehaving, particularly girls, who ended up pregnant. The behaviour of the older children was teaching a bad example to the younger ones. The parents were responsible for this state. Instead of performing their responsibilities they spent much of their time drinking. Drinking was getting out of hand, resulting in fights, neglect of domestic responsibilities, and anti-social and immoral behaviour. People went drinking instead of carrying out their duties, and when they were drunk they complained vociferously to one another that the Captain and District councillors were useless and did nothing to develop the village economically; to curtail bad behaviour; or to protect the Indian Right. It seemed that all the laws were being made in the bamboli jug. The Assistant District Officer (a government official) and myself (a Whiteman) were the two authority symbols present at the meeting. Pointing to us the Captain declared dramatically, 'If we cannot Respect ourselves, how can we Respect this man and this man?'

The concept of Respect thus meant belief in the rightness of proper, respectable behaviour, and determination to act out that belief. Just as people should Respect themselves, so they should Respect one another. The norms of behaviour between persons were called Manners and Respect. Persons who Respected themselves behaved with Manners and Respect, acting responsibly and behaving with propriety. They deferred to the opinions of persons of higher status and behaved respectfully towards them, expressing their subordination by deferential behaviour. Children should show Respect for adults by listening to them and not answering back. Younger persons should Respect older persons. In relations with outsiders, Oreallans should Respect persons occupying important social statuses or with particular expertise, such as priest or schoolteacher. Amerindians and other non-Whites should Repect Whitepeople.

In the kinship domain there should be harmonious relations between adult kinsmen and people should Respect persons ascribed to older generations than themselves, and their older siblings and first cousins. Consequently Ego made a terminological distinction between his 'big brothers and sisters' and his 'small brothers and sisters'. (The terms brother and sister here included first cousins as well as siblings.) Kinsmen should advise relatives ascribed to generations junior to themselves, who should listen to their advice. Manners and Respect were expressed in deference to opinions and use of the appropriate terms of address. Persons of senior generation should be addressed by kinship term; of junior generation by Christian name, nickname, or kin term. Terms used were generally the English terms given above, but for some kinship statuses Arawak or Warao terms could be used as alternatives[3]. Persons of the same generation usually addressed one another by name or nickname. Men of the same generation often addressed each other as *swa:gri*, the Surinamese (*Takkie-takkie*) term for brother-in-law, which they often abbreviated to *swa:g*. Youths and young men often addressed each other as 'frenno', slang for friend. When they reached their early to mid-twenties, the time when they usually entered domestic unions, frenno was replaced by *swa:g*.

At the same time there was a norm of equalitarianism between adult Oreallans which crossed age differences and genealogical relationships. With the exception of a man's authority over his spouse no Oreallan had authority over any other adult[4]. This was expressed in the saying that it was wrong to 'mix in another man's story' – to interfere in another adult's affairs.

Close relatives should co-operate in economic activities, engage in common recreational activities, and demonstrate a high degree of interpersonal solidarity. More complex norms of kinship behaviour applied only to the relationship between spouses and between parent and non-adult child, where each had certain rights over the other and where there was a constant reciprocal exchange of services [5].

2

Whereas the term Families was used to described relationships between individuals, the term Family was used to designate certain small groups and quasi-groups, visualised as consisting of close relatives, whose members interacted constantly and intimately and had common everyday interests. Like Families, the term was flexible and the unit referred to was evident from the conversation.

At Orealla the domestic and residential unit usually consisted of the inhabitants of a house. This was one of the units to which Oreallans applied the term Family. Membership was recruited around a couple in a domestic union, or the remnant of such a union — a widowed or separated individual.

Houses were often substantial open-sided structures with a high gabled roof thatched with leaves of dalibana palm. The inhabitants constituted a household[6], which typically passed through a developmental cycle beginning with a young couple in a domestic union and their children; matured into a joint family — usually a matrilineal joint family; and disintegrated to leave an aged couple or individual when adult children moved out of the household.

A household had a head, usually the husband[7] in the focal domestic union, and the community identified the household as his Family. A woman was head only if she had no husband and had an adult son who would live in the household and provide her with monetary support. The head's authority *qua* head was minimal. He could order adult members to leave his household if he came into disagreement with them. During the growth phase, when the household typically consisted of the head, his wife and their young children, his authority derived not from his position as household head but from his status as husband and father. When his children became adult he ceased to have authority over them as father. A household head was not the manager of a team engaged in productive activities. Such activities were not organised on a household basis. Adult members of both sexes had their own farms which they worked by a system of co-operative labour known as matrimani which was not organized on a household basis, and cash-producing activities were carried out by small, temporary teams of men working together voluntarily. Adult members of the household were expected to give one another economic assistance and to contribute to the food consumed by the household.

Because of this, and because of the existence of a limited degree of authority of its head *qua* head, the household could be said to have a limited degree of corporateness. It was also the major unit of food consumption.

Within a household domestic couples and single adults had their own savings and provisions, but any food which was prepared was eaten by all, and all were expected to contribute their share of food and income to the operation of the household. There was no measured contribution of income, produce, and labour, and the informal nature of this system led to constant complaints about the meanness or laziness of members, particularly by the household head and his wife. These complaints were a constant theme in Orealla domestic relationships and appear to have had a ritual aspect. They were an expression of the way adults saw relationships between parents and adult children and between older and younger generations at least as much as they reflected actual behaviour.

Within joint family households domestic couples and their young children formed functionally differentiated sub-units, the nuclei of future independent households. Each was designated the Family of the man in the status of husband/father. He was responsible for providing it with money for expenses and for non-food items and, with his spouse, responsible for the children's behaviour. A joint family household might contain a single woman and her children by casual liasons or from past domestic unions. They also formed a sub-unit with regard to child discipline, but were supported by the household head, who was usually the woman's father. Adult sons who were not in domestic unions often remained in the household as independent adults.

Houses were usually separated by a secondary growth of planted trees and bushes which included scattered fruit trees such as mango[8], orange[9], avacado pear[10], and pawpaw[11]; palms such as coconut and awarra; bushes such as cotton and peppers; and various canes. The members of neighbouring houses often interacted intensively, visiting and assisting each other continually. Where the rate of interaction was high, and particularly if the houses were spatially separate from others, such a set of households might be referred to as a Family by the community. These Families were not corporate groups. Each was a common field of interaction for all its members, a field that extended beyond the households to include other individuals living in the village. It had no organisation and no head and was not designated by the community as the Family of any particular member, in contrast to the way a household was designated the Family of its head. It was not the basis for co-operative activities. These were organised around individuals and involved persons outside the Family. Members had no obligations towards one another that were specifically the consequence of common Family membership. Nor was membership of Families mutually exclusive. The same household might belong to two, or even three, such Families[12]. Various factors promoted the formation of interacting households, the most common being division of an existing household with a married couple leaving and establishing their own household close to the one they left. Particularly important among the ties between households of a Family were relationships between women, especially between mother and daughter and between sisters. These were often the strongest relationships between the households (in terms of emotional strength of tie; degree of mutual identification between the two parties; and degree of inter-personal interaction) and the ties which brought the interaction between the households into being.

An intimate network of close relatives, dispersed throughout the village, would also be referred to as a Family, especially if its members were believed to have common interests. For example, in 1966 the village Captain's son-in-law was in charge of the village tractor. The people complained that the tractor was only 'working for the Family' – for the Captain's close relatives. They said their logs were ignored while the tractor hauled the logs of the Captain and his relatives. Such usage implied a boundary to the entity concerned, associated with closeness of kin tie, but it was a boundary that was vaguely defined. Orealla village was never referred to as a Family as it was too large for all its members to interact constantly in everyday affairs.

3

At Orealla work groups were recruited on the basis of personal relationships and were temporary groups of voluntary composition and informal structure. Non-cash-producing work was often carried out by a system of co-operative labour called matrimani[13]. An individual requiring labour to carry out a task invited friends to help and rewarded them with a meal, drinks, and cigarettes when it was completed. The reward was regarded as payment for the work performed. But people did not attend matrimanis merely for the material reward. They enjoyed the conviviality of the occasion and the drinking party that followed the work, and close friends and relatives had a degree of obligation to attend one another's matrimanis. If they consistently failed to do so it was taken as an indication that they no longer valued the relationship.

On the Corentyne the institution of matrimani had been adapted for most kinds of non-cash-producing work, and was not restricted to farming and a few other arduous tasks as was the case in some Amerindian areas of Guyana[14]. Matrimanis were particularly common in the dry seasons, which were the seasons for cutting and clearing the Bush to make farms[15], when several might take place in the village on the same day. The number of workers at a matrimani tended to vary between six and twelve, depending upon the task and on the availability of workers. As matrimani activities required little or no direction matrimanis lacked any formal organisation.

A matrimani could be convened by a member of either sex. All that was necessary was cassava to make beer or a small amount of money to buy the ingredients to make 'tonic', a strong home-made wine, and a little money to buy cigarettes. Because all farming tasks could be performed by matrimani women had their own farms and were not dependent on their husbands for farming produce. Attendance at a matrimani was by personal request of the convenor. Persons who were at enmity avoided attending the same matrimani, and it was acceptable to excuse oneself from attending a matrimani because one's enemy would be present. Consequently matrimanis consisted of friends of the convenor who were friendly with each other. Although members of the convenor's household or Family of households were likely to be well represented, matrimanis were not based on these units[16].

The other main type of work group was the party of men logging in the Bush. These usually consisted of from two to six persons working together in order to cut, and sometimes corduroy, paths through the Bush to enable tractors to haul their logs to the river. If they were working crabwood[17] in the dry seasons they might operate as a team to haul their logs manually to creeks and float them down to the Corentyne. Working together had other advantages. If men worked in a party one member could hunt meat to feed them all. Economic reasons were not the only ones why loggers preferred to work in groups. They enjoyed conviviality while engaged in arduous work.

Logging parties were made up of men who wished to work a particular area and between whom amicable relationships existed. Some persons, such as close friends (Matties), worked together frequently, but whether or not they were in the same party depended ultimately on their economic interests at the particular time. Enmity was not the only reason why two persons would not work together. Someone with a reputation for laziness would find difficulty being accepted into a work party, especially one which had elected to work as a 'company' – pooling all logs cut by members with each adult getting an equal share of the price. Individuals might decide not to work together because past experience suggested they had bad luck if they did so. (They might have found few commercially valuable trees or their logs may have been washed away by the river and lost.) Logging parties had a life of from a few days to a few weeks and broke up as members left to work elsewhere. They lacked any positions of leadership or authority as differences of opinion were unlikely, all members being excellent Bush men.

During the wet seasons a few Oreallans would collect ('bleed') balata, the latex of the bulletwood tree, for sale to the agents with the balata concessions for the Guyana and Suriname shores. Usually they worked alone or with a friend and worked close to the village, but occasionally small parties[18] went out for a season under a foreman, a man asked by the agent to recruit workers and paid a price for his balata slightly higher than that for the season. The foreman had no authority and the group lacked any formal structure. Men joined a bleeding gang because they found the season's price attractive and believed they could make more money bleeding balata than logging in the wet Bush. The same factors influenced the composition of a bleeding gang as that of logging parties.

4

At Orealla the division of labour focused women's interests upon household and domestic activities and upon farming, and men's upon work in the Bush in the company of other men. It was complemented by differences in values held by women and by men. In addition to values associated with Manners and Respect, also held by women, men held values of manliness antithetical to some aspects of Manners and Respect, and therefore to those held by women. To men drinking and womanizing were not only enjoyable, they were expressions of manliness, boasted of to other men. When not working in the Bush they spent much of their time drinking and playing cards with their friends.

A consequence of the different interests and values of men and women was the informal pattern of sexual segregation that characterized recreational activities. At parties men and women tended to sit on different sides of the house, where they drank and chatted in single sex groups and mixed only to dance. At the drinking party that followed a matrimani men sat together and drank and played cards while women sat together and drank, chatted, and often engaged in some domestic activity such as making cord from silk grass[19] leaves. Often the men sat outside and the women were in the house or kitchen. In church the few men present sat apart from the women and children, who comprised the great majority of the congregation.

Because of their different interests and values women's closest personal ties were inter-generational while men's were with age peers, and women described their relationships in terms of kinship while men described theirs in terms of friendship. A woman's closest relationships tended to be with her mother, daughters, and sisters. For a man they were with age peers most of whom were outside the household and Family of households. As people aged their network of close ties changed until for the elderly the closest relationship tended to become that between spouses.

The difference in the pattern of relationships was recognized in the way parents contrasted their relations with adult sons with those with adult daughters. They saw the relationship with sons as asymmetrical. Sons were brought up by their parents, but when they grew up they neglected them. Parents complained that sons spent their money drinking with friends and they saw none of it. To make the point more forcibly they would say that sons spent their money on non-Amerindian friends — 'Coolie and Black'. They emphasized what they saw as their rejection by claiming that sons not merely neglected them, they neglected them for non-Amerindians who were working against the Amerindian's interests. This contrasted with their attitude to adult daughters, who constantly worked with, helped, and visited their parents. Oreallans said it was good to have at least one daughter, because when they grow up 'daughters cleave to their parents, but sons cleave to their family (of procreation)'. They recognised that sons acquired responsibilities when they entered domestic unions, but even so elderly parents complained their married sons neglected them while sporting with Coolie and Black.

Among those age peers with whom he had friendly relations a man usually had one he considered his closest friend, whom he addressed and referred to as his 'Mattie', less frequently as his 'buddy' or 'pardner'. Only where a Mattie relationship existed between full or half brothers did they use kinship terms to the exclusion of the term Mattie, otherwise Mattie was used, even by first cousins, who terminologically were 'brothers'. (Because most Oreallans were related a man's Mattie was usually a relative, often a cousin of some kind or a brother-in-law.) The concept of best friend was not institutionalized among women, who did not have Matties. Two women who had a particularly friendly relationship continued to describe it in terms of the relationship. But women used the term Mattie in all the other meanings of the concept, to be analyzed later.

A Mattie relationship was the epitome of male friendship. I assume the term to be derived from the English 'mate'[20]. It was an informal voluntary relationship, a reciprocal relationship that developed out of qualities in the individuals concerned. Two persons became Mattie because they wished to be. Because they liked each other. Matties were of similar age and they saw their relationship as being between equals. The obligations of being Mattie were broad and imprecisely defined. There were no detailed obligations of the kind described, for example, for compadrazgo in Latin America[21], but the relationship demanded constant interaction and mutual assistance. Matties worked together often in the Bush, either as a pair or as members of the same work team. They assisted one another in many ways and attended each other's matrimanis frequently. The obligation on a man to attend his Mattie's matrimanis was greater than that between persons in any other relationship. Matties spent much of their recreation time together. They played cards and drank together in the village shops, and during holidays or when one returned after an absence from the village they were almost under an obligation to sport together.

A Mattie relationship implied friendship, social equality, economic co-operation, and mutual assistance. If either party ceased to behave according to the ideals of Mattie it was taken as an indication, by the other party and by the community at large, that he no longer valued the relationship, which was considered terminated. However, because Matties were close friends their relationship was capable of withstanding the stresses that could destroy less close friendships.

The concept of Mattie was a flexible one. It was applied to persons as members of groups as well as to individuals, but the same fundamental qualities were implied whatever its usage. A man usually had one particularly close friend, who was his Mattie. But on occasion he would use the term as equivalent to friend, addressing any friend as 'Mattie' but without implying that the relationship between them was as intense as that between real Matties. He would do so particularly when he wished to stress that the relationship between them was one of friendship. (Consequently, when a man sought assistance from another he might address him as 'Mattie' to suggest he considered them to be friends, even when he believed they were not.) The term was also used by both sexes to describe the ideal relationship between co-members of groups, such as villages, racial groups, up to mankind in general. When used in this way the term invoked certain ideal qualities of the relations that should pertain between members of these groups, and these qualities were certain of those that characterized the relationship between a man and his Mattie.

5

Because of the compactness and relatively small size of Orealla village its adult members[22] knew each other by sight and name and most had some kind of inter-personal relationship with one another, even if it was determined by a relationship with a brother, sister, or other close relative of either party. Inter-personal relations did not stop with the boundaries of Orealla. They incorporated the villages of Sipuruta, Wassiabo and Apoera. A generous estimate of 1200 residents for the four Amerindian villages of the Corentyne gave an adult population of about 150 for the three smaller villages combined. An Oreallan knew many of these personally and had friends and enemies in the other three villages.

Oreallans' kinship networks included most members of the four villages and could incorporate all. Strangers entering the community could be allotted appropriate kinship statuses, determined by sex and age. If they remained in the community they developed personal relationships with many of its members and interacted as personae and not as kinship statuses. Inter-personal relations were influenced by many factors, were often multiplex and used for many purposes, and had an important affective component. However Oreallans regarded the relationships Amerindians had with other Amerindians as fundamentally different in nature from those with non-Amerindians. Consequently, although relationships between Oreallans and non-Amerindians living in the village superficially might appear similar to those between Amerindians, at root they were qualitatively different.

Notes

1 A.D. Sanders, (1972), p. 82; A.D. Sanders, (1973), p. 444. These two works contain a detailed account of Coastal Amerindian kinship.
2 A.D. Sanders, (1972), pp. 88–105; A.D. Sanders, (1973), pp. 442–4.
3 A.D. Sanders, (1972), op.cit.; A.D. Sanders, (1973), op.cit.
4 The situation of the village Captain will be dealt with later.
5 A.D. Sanders, (1972), pp. 225–310, 359–387; A.D. Sanders, (1973), pp. 449–60.
6 For a detailed examination of the household see A.D. Sanders, (1972), pp. 311–87; A.D. Sanders, (1973), pp. 454–70.
7 Coastal Amerindians began domestic unions as consensual unions which they termed 'keeping' as distinct from Christian, legal, 'marriage' – as did lower-class Black Guyanese (A.D. Sanders, (1972), pp. 225–310; A.D. Sanders, (1973), pp. 449–54). Oreallans designated both man and woman in a consensual union as a 'keeper'. As both unions were sociologically marriage (A.D. Sanders, (1972), pp. 295–8; A.D. Sanders, (1973), pp. 449–50), and in order to make for clarity of writing, I will designate spouses in either type of union 'husband' and 'wife' throughout, drawing attention to the type of union in any instance only where this is pertinent.
8 *Mangifera indica.*
9 *Citrus guianensis.*

10 *Persea americana.*
11 *Carica papaya.*
12 For a detailed account of such Families see A.D. Sanders, (1972), pp. 388–409; A.D. Sanders, (1973), pp. 471–5.
13 A detailed account of matrimani is given in A.D. Sanders, (1972), pp. 177–92.
14 For example, Santa Rosa, Moruka river.
15 A.D. Sanders, (1972), pp. 122–224.
16 Ibid., pp. 184–7.
17 *Carapa guianensis.*
18 The only party I observed consisted of seven men. (A.D. Sanders, (1972), pp. 145–6.)
19 *Bromelia* sp.
20 The term was widely used among lower-class Guyanese and Jayawardena, writing about East Indian sugar estate workers, also assumes its derivation from the English 'mate'. (C. Jayawardena, (1963), p. 48.)
21 For example, G.M.Foster, (1961); G.M.Foster, (1963).
22 In June 1967 there were 341 residents of 20 years and over. (A.D. Sanders, (1972), pp. 39–43).

CHAPTER 5 | The Village as Nations
Mattie

When lower-class Guyanese used the coloquial term 'Nation' they meant the 'races' from which they saw themselves as being descended — African, East Indian, European, Portuguese, Chinese and Amerindian. Amerindians also used the term in this sense. When discussing relations between themselves and non-Amerindians they said their Nation was 'Buck' (Amerindian), but among themselves they also used the term to designate the tribes within the Amerindian category.

The overwhelming majority of Amerindians living on the Corentyne river belonged to one or other of two tribes, Arawak and Warao. All four Amerindian villages had mixed Arawak and Warao populations. There were a few Amerindians from other tribes, mostly Caribs, usually from Suriname. In June 1967 there was only one Carib living at Orealla, a man from Suriname, although several other residents claimed some Carib ancestry.

The Arawak are a tribe native to the coastal areas of the Guianas, including the Corentyne river[1]. The Warao on the other hand are native to the Orinoco Delta and the region between the Orinoco and the Pomeroon river in western Guyana. During the colonial period in Venezuela some migrated eastward along the coast and settled on the Corentyne. Oreallans said the Waraos came from Moruka or the North West District, in western Guyana, in large canoes that held 50 persons[2]. Amerindians' depth of genealogical remembrance was very shallow. Often they knew little of their great grandparents[3]. They also had a poor conception of historical time. Something that happened a considerable time ago often was said to have happened in one's great grandparents' time, or even when one's grandparents were young. Waraos at Orealla usually believed their grandparents or great grandparents were born on the Corentyne shortly after the Warao arrived there. One old man in his seventies said his grandparents came from the north-west with the other Waraos and his parents were born at Orealla. In fact the migration took place in the eighteenth century, when the Waraos were resisting Spanish and English attempts to pacify them and confine them to permanent settlements[4].

Oreallans said the Carib (whom they called Caribees) came from

67

Suriname or the North West District to fight and take their land. In fact
they were native to the Corentyne river[5]. There were places on the river
that Oreallans associated with the wars between the Carib and the
Arawak. One was Baboon Island below Oreala. There were various
accounts of how it got its name. One was that when Caribs raided the
island the Arawaks tried to escape by climbing trees. The Caribs shot
them out of the trees and boasted that it was just like shooting
baboons[6]. Another was that Caribs kept Arawak captives in cages on
the island, fattening them until they were ready to eat – 'just like they
were baboons'. The Arawak claimed they finally defeated the Carib in
a battle at Second Hill, a few miles above Sipuruta.

At Orealla the proportion of the population who were Arawaks
and the proportion who were Waraos was in the ratio of 3:2. Tribal
distribution was not random. Arawaks were associated with the
Flatland and Waraos with the Hilltop, and Oreallans had a model of
their village in which Waraos lived up the hill and Arawaks down the
hill. This was supported by beliefs that tribal membership was
transmitted matrilineally and that domestic unions began with a period
of uxorilocal residence. In inter-tribal domestic unions Arawak men
were thought of as going uphill and producing Warao children while
Warao men were doing the opposite. So strong were Oreallans'
associations of the topographical division of the village with tribal
identity that they often said that all the people on the Flatland were
Arawaks and all the people on the Hilltop were Waraos. Often when
they talked of 'Uphill people' and 'Downhill people' they were using
the terms to mean Waraos and Arawaks respectively.

In fact the majority of Oreallans who classified themselves as
Arawaks did live on the Flatland and the majority of persons who
classified themselves as Waraos did live on the Hilltop, the actual
situation being that the Hilltop was predominantly Warao while the
Flatland was more mixed. It appeared that there had always been some
association of the two areas of the village with the two tribes, but
informants claimed it had strengthened in recent years and that in the
past tribal distribution was more random. In the 1960s many older
Oreallans residing in the 'correct' half of the village in fact were living
in the opposite half to that in which they had been born and brought
up. For example, when house land was officially lotted at Orealla in
1962 several Warao men living on the Hilltop with Warao wives
claimed, and received, lots on the Flatland at the places where they
were born or where they had lived during their youth. Why there
developed a greater *de facto* association of tribal distribution with
topographical area I am unable to say. It appeared fortuitous. One
influence could have been a recent increase in the size of the Warao

community, as old persons were agreed that in their youth there were fewer Waraos and that only in the last generations had their numbers increased. Any contemporary movement of households between the two parts of the village tended to be down the hill, households moving to make the task of carrying water easier. Water for drinking and washing crockery had to be carried from the river, and it was an arduous task carrying buckets of water to the Hilltop. The advantages of living uphill were the lighter soils, which required little drainage, and proximity to cassava fields, but these appeared to offer little attraction to downhill people.

Both Arawaks and Waraos held uncomplimentary stereotypes of one another. Historically Waraos were regarded as the bottom of the tribal pile, both by other Amerindian tribes and by missionaries and the White representatives of the metropolitan power, who considered them the most backward and primitive tribe of the Guianas and stressed their 'filthy' personal habits[7]. On the other hand nineteenth century Whites regarded the Arawak as the most intelligent and progressive Amerindian tribe and admired the Carib for their martial ability[8]. Today many Arawaks look down on Caribs and Waraos as backward peoples.

At Orealla the Arawak conception of Waraos was the most elaborate of the two stereotypes. Waraos were lazy, conservative, stupid, and did not know how to behave properly. They did not have 'sense' and they lacked Manners and Respect. When people from down the hill heard I had been involved in an argument with friends uphill they warned me to be careful. The Warao were violent people who would fight me, 'because that is how the Warao does stay', whereas the Arawak 'walk with Manners and Respect'. Arawaks were progressive and sociable and knew how to behave. But Waraos, probably because they were regarded as more primitive, were believed to have greater magical ability, which they could use for good or bad. They could cast particularly strong spells because they knew a more powerful way of mystical blowing, they could blow *hoa*, and people living downhill claimed Waraos threw jumbie arrows, causing illness by mystically throwing objects into a victim's body.

Warao stereotypes appeared to take the form of a defensive response to the Arawak stereotype of themselves. They regarded Arawaks as arrogant and conceited, with 'ideas above their station', but did not consider themselves morally or culturally superior. They claimed both tribes behaved in the same way. They complained that Arawaks said they were dirty and that this was unjustified, the habits of both tribes were the same, and said both Arawaks and Waraos threw jumbie arrows.

However Arawaks and Waraos tended to regard the supposed differences between themselves as learned rather than innate. Arawaks did not see Warao backwardness as evidence of any innate inferiority but rather of bad upbringing, and although they thought Waraos stupid they did not consider this an inherent quality. Waraos could 'grow sense' through learning the ways of Arawaks. Waraos did not consider Arawak conceit to be an inherent consequence of Arawakness. It was due to being raised an Arawak, among Arawaks.

In fact at Orealla there were few differences between the two tribes. The main, and most obvious difference was language. Each tribe had its native language, but with the exception of old persons few people knew their language, and speakers of one language usually did not understand the other[9]. Everyday language was the local varient of Creole English. Overwhelmingly both groups had the same culture and patterns of behaviour, although Waraos often did seem more reticent and more culturally conservative than Arawaks. For example, a greater proportion of Waraos could speak their native language than could Arawaks.

The norm of tribal affiliation was for a child to take that of its mother. In fact tribal membership was influenced by residence during childhood[10]. At Orealla children of Warao mothers and Arawak fathers who were raised on the Flatland among Arawaks tended to become Arawaks. This was not a new process. The village Captain (aged 47 in June 1967) and his older brother were Arawaks with a Warao mother, who was living in the Captain's household. Her siblings had lived in the village and were also Waraos. Another example was Nathan Williams, an old Arawak man in his sixties, whose deceased mother was a Warao. His full sister, living up the hill, was a Warao. She was brought up separate from Nathan, in the household of her mother's second husband, a Warao. As informants both the Captain and Nathan were contemptuous of Waraos, and both insisted that Amerindians always took their Nation from their mother. When I learned — from Waraos — of their parentage and challenged them with it they were embarrassed and admitted that by the norm they should be Waraos, but said they 'cleaved to their daddy's Nation' because they were brought up among his relatives and learned to speak his language. Oreallans regarded them as Arawaks, but some Waraos remembered their parentage and complained that really they were Waraos who had learned arrogant Arawak attitudes.

The less derogatory stereotype of Arawaks held by Waraos may explain why there appeared to be less tendency for children of Arawak mothers who were raised on the Hilltop to become Waraos than there was for children of Warao mothers who were raised on the Flatland to become Arawaks. Although disliking Arawaks in stereotype, Waraos did not consider them inferior. On the other hand Warao women living downhill with Arawak husbands sometimes adopted the conception of Waraos held by their Arawak relatives, which no doubt made their children's tribal transition easier. (One day I was with an Arawak man who kept acting rather stupidly and throwing stones at mangoes. His Warao wife suddenly shouted at him in exasperation, 'You want make me shame, acting like a Warao?')

At Orealla the two tribes did not form groups in any sociological sense. Neither had any organisation; acted as a group; or had interests that set it apart from the other. Although Oreallans made derogatory comments about the other tribe, tribal affiliation had no influence on inter-personal relations. Members of both tribes mixed freely and attended the same school as children. Men made friends at random and mating and marriage were random. Consequently everyone had friends and close relatives from the other Nation. First cousins ('brothers' and 'sisters') could belong to different tribes, even when their fathers were full or paternal half brothers and consequently they had the same 'title' (surname). A man could have children of both tribal affiliations. Because of the belief in matrilineal transmission of tribal affiliation this was much less likely for a woman, but it did happen, as in the case of Nathan Williams and his sister.

There was some opposition between the downhill and the uphill sections of the village. As both the Flatland and the Hilltop contained Arawaks and Waraos members of both tribes were involved on each side of this opposition, but because of the association of Warao with the Hilltop and Arawak with the Hillfoot it tended to be articulated in tribal terms and thought of in those terms. Uphill people complained that village affairs were managed to the advantage of the downhill people. They said downhill people got excessive use of the village tractor to pull their logs from the Backdam, and that it was easier for them to borrow the tractor battery to provide music[11] at birthday parties. They blamed this on the fact that the village Captain was an Arawak and said he favoured his own people, 'his Mattie Arawaks'. In 1965 the Ministry of Local Government had a water tank erected at Orealla and pipes and taps laid down so that the people would have a supply of clean water at the end of the big dry season, around the month of October, when the Corentyne was particularly muddy. The tank was built downhill and all the pipes were on the Flatland. Uphill people complained that the system had been built to the advantage of the people down the hill. (In fact it never worked as far as I have knowledge.)

During the Shove Down festivities Hilltop: Hillfoot opposition was expressed by a tug of war between downhill and uphill people and a canoe race between two canoes, one manned by men from uphill and the other by downhill men. This did not take the form of competition between Arawaks and Waraos. Arawaks living uphill and Waraos living downhill joined or supported the teams representing the section of the village in which they resided.

At Orealla tribal boundaries[12] were revealed mainly by insulting references to tribal identity made during arguments, but tribal membership was unimportant as an influence on interaction between villagers, and between Oreallans and the members of other Corentyne Amerindian villages. As this was so, why did tribal stereotypes remain? Historically Arawaks and Waraos had been culturally distinct peoples with their own languages, and knowledge of this helped maintain the idea of being different peoples. The idea of two distinct Nations gave Oreallans a model of their community which was reinforced by the association of the topographical division of the community with the two tribes. At Orealla, membership and stereotyping were important at the level of classification rather than of interaction, helping to introduce order into the Oreallans's perception of his world.

However, because tribal identity was not important in relations between Amerindians on the Corentyne river it did not follow that it would not be important in relations with other Amerindians from Suriname or Guyana, including other Arawaks and Waraos. Interaction between Orealla Arawaks and members of more conservative Warao groups such as those from north-western Guyana would have been more strongly influenced by tribal membership and stereotype, as would relationships between Orealla Arawaks and Waraos and the more primitive Carib groups of the Maroni river in Suriname[13] and the Barama river in Guyana[14]. Knowledge of Amerindian groups that differed culturally from Oreallans, with some of whom Oreallans could identify themselves or identify the other tribe, helped keep alive the idea of tribal differences at Orealla.

Oreallans' conception of tribes was qualitatively different from their conception of races. Although they called both by the same term, Nation, they were not perceived in the same way. Membership of both was by ancestry, but the qualities attributed to members of racial groups were perceived literally in racial terms, as hereditary, transmitted by 'blood'. Members of different Amerindian tribes might be thought to behave in different ways, but this was attributed usually to differences in learning. If we take those tribes believed by Oreallans to differ most markedly from themselves, such as the Waiwai of the far south of Guyana, they were thought to be backward and primitive people, but nonetheless to be Amerindians with Amerindian qualities.

They wore aprons, were pagans[15], and were ignorant of the use of money. These were derogatory characteristics. But the attitude towards the tribe was not one of derision; it was ambivalent. For in remaining backward they had retained powerful magical practices, and Oreallans admiringly recounted tales they had heard of Waiwai ability as sorcerers. This ability gave them a certain power which was to be feared. They had also retained their traditional language. These attributes were viewed as retentions of a kind of original Amerindianness, part of a common ancestry of all Amerindians, the loss of which had come to be regretted by Oreallans despite the fact that in the process of its loss they had become civilized, and consequently socially and morally superior.

The concept Oreallans used to describe the relationship that should pertain between fellow tribesmen was that of Mattie. Mattie implied equivalence, co-operation, and mutual assistance, and it was also the concept they applied to themselves as members of a common racial group. It will be examined in detail in the following chapter. This is not merely for convenience. Oreallans applied the concept to themselves as Amerindians much more strongly than they did to themselves as members of one or other of the two tribes. Tribal membership was relatively unimportant at Orealla. For Oreallans and for other Corentyne river Amerindians it was eclipsed by the main differentiation in their world, that between Amerindian and non-Amerindian.

Notes

1 J. Gillin, (1963), p. 802.
2 P. Kirchoff, (1963), p. 873.
3 A.D. Sanders, (1972), p. 83; A.D. Sanders, (1973), p. 442.
4 P. Kirchoff, op.cit., pp. 869–70.
5 Gillin, op.cit., p. 806.
6 Howler monkey (Alouatta sp.)
7 M.N. Menezes, (1977), pp. 25, 234; M.N. Menezes, (1979), p. 15; E. Im Thurn, (1967), p. 168.
8 M.N. Menezes, (1977), pp. 24, 184, 188, 239; M.N. Menezes, (1979), pp. 15, 250: E. Im Thurn, op.cit.
9 The exceptions were lewd songs in Arawak and Warao, which were learned and understood by everyone.
10 See L. Drummond, (1974), p. 245; L. Drummond, (n.d.).
11 The tractor battery was used to power a radiogram and amplifiers ('juke box').
12 i.e. the mode of interaction between members of different ethnic groups (F. Barth, (1969)).
13 P. Kloos, (1971).

14 J. Gillin, (1936).
15 In the Waiwai case this assumption was incorrect. They had been
    converted by the Unevangelised Fields Mission and lived in mission
    villages.

CHAPTER 6 | The Village as Bucks
Mattie

1

In Guyana Amerindians are called colloquially 'Buckpeople' or 'Bucks'. The term is derived from the Dutch *bokken*, a word that combined the qualities of being uncivilised and uncouth with wildness and fleetness of foot[1]. As applied initially to the aboriginal inhabitants of the Guianas by the Dutch it implied a combination of admired and despised qualities. As used today in Guyana it is derogatory term.

At the time of fieldwork the stereotype of Amerindians held by other Guyanese and Surinamers consisted of a number of elements considered inter-related in a racial manner, inherent in the nature of the Amerindian. The stereotype was compounded of physical, psychological, and cultural elements. The physical components were taken from the full-blooded Amerindian. In personality the Amerindian was believed to be shy, diffident, naïve and socially backward. Consequently he possessed an inferior, unsophisticated, non-European culture and followed a simple style of life. Cultural inferiority and social naïvety were used to justify ranking Amerindians lowest in the scales of racial ranking adopted by other Guyanese and Surinamers.

Attitudes towards Amerindians differed between socio-economic groups. Lower class and rural groups, mainly African and East Indian, regarded them with contempt and their relations with Amerindians often were overtly exploitative. Urbanized elites, who tended to be associated particularly with Europeans and other light-skinned groups, assumed a paternalistic attitude. They considered Amerindians simple people in need of protection against exploitation by individuals and groups from the more sophisticated Coastal society, at least until they could be advanced to a state where they would be able to fend for themselves. This was the attitude held by the colonial administration of British Guiana during the latter part of the colonial period, which resulted in the formulation of special Guyanese laws to mediate relations between Amerindians and the rest of the society.

The physical stereotype Amerindians held of themselves was also that of the full-blooded Amerindian. They strenuously rejected the

Coastal conception of themselves as uncivilized, claiming to be as civilized as other lower class Guyanese and Surinamers – which to them meant Blackpeople and East Indians. To Oreallans, as to other Guyanese, being civilized particularly meant possessing values and behaving in ways they considered 'English' or 'White'[2]. They stressed three factors as indices of their civilized condition. They wore European clothes; they used money; and they were Christians. Old men said their grandfathers had worn 'laps' (aprons or loin cloths) but that they themselves wore civilized clothes. In saying this they were not simply claiming the right to be regarded as civilized. They were saying they had civilized needs and required employment and other forms of assistance to attain the living standards these entailed.

The most important element of the Amerindian's stereotype of his group was the way he saw its relationship with other groups in the society. Although Guyanese Amerindians had special rights and privileges they saw themselves not as a privileged group but as one that was cheated and exploited by other racial groups and by governments they believed represented the interests of those groups. In Guyana, Dr Jagan's People's Progressive Party (PPP) government of the late fifties and early sixties was thought to represent the interests of its majority East Indian supporters, and Mr Burnham's succeeding Peoples' National Congress (PNC)-dominated government the interests of its majority African supporters. Similarly Mr Pengel's Nationale Partij Suriname (NPS) government in Suriname was believed to represent African interests. Amerindians believed that in Guyana only the existence of the Indian Right prevented even greater exploitation. They believed that through their governments the Black and East Indian communities were trying to take away The Right. If they succeeded Amerindians would lose not only their privileges but also their only safeguard against total exploitation.

Oreallans viewed the densely populated Atlantic coast as an area inhabited by non-Amerindians who had high living standards and amenities unavailable to Amerindians, such as roads, electricity, and piped water. They lived in fine houses and owned cars, radios, and other luxury items and had jobs that were better paid and less arduous than the work available to Amerindians. They believed Guyana's Amerindians lacked such amenities and standards because successive governments had ignored them, choosing to use resources to reward their own racial supporters. This was the Orealla myth of the Coast, but Oreallans visited the Coast frequently, many had worked there, and some had relatives there. They were aware of the high rate of unemployment and knew that many villages lacked amenities. Indeed they said that in Guyana conditions on the Coast had deteriorated since

Independence, with rising prices and increasing unemployment. They blamed this on the 'Black' government. The two views of the Coast, with their different emphases, could co-exist because both were partially true. More facilities were available to Coastal people, but at the same time many Coastal Guyanese were poor and getting poorer. They could also co-exist because together they supported Oreallans' perception of themselves as a deprived group, deliberately discriminated against, while stressing the incompetence and corruption of Black and East Indian governments.

2

Those racial groups with whose members Oreallans had most frequent contact were the African and East Indian ones. In Guyana and Suriname the majority of persons from the Coast working in the Bush are of African ancestry. After emancipation some Africans turned to Bush occupations such as logging and prospecting, in order to earn a living or in the hope of becoming wealthy[3]. Consequently there is a tradition of lower class persons of African ancestry going into the Bush, although it has never involved more than a minority of the African and Coloured populations. However, as the Corentyne Coast of Guyana has a predominantly East Indian population there were also East Indians working on the Corentyne river. Businessmen such as sawmillers, boat owners, and tractor owners, who operated enterprises that affected the lives of Amerindians, were East Indians. Most of their employees working in the Bush – buymen, tractor drivers, boatmen – were also East Indians.

Oreallans held derogatory stereotypes of East Indians and Africans. But although the overall stereotypes were disparaging they contained elements that Oreallans admired or of which they were envious. The East Indian stereotype was defined in terms of behaviour. 'Coolies' were crafty, dishonest, two-faced, mean and grasping. They 'Advantaged' (exploited) Amerindians. On the other hand Cooliepeople were admired because of their enterprise and because they were believed to support one another against members of other racial groups.

Like Coolies, Blackpeople Advantaged Amerindians. Now that Suriname and Guyana had Black governments it had become increasingly possible for them to do so. People quoted the Bible as saying that just before the end of the world 'the Ethiopian shall reign'[4]. They said that time had come, as Blackpeople had achieved power in Guyana and Suriname.

The Amerindian stereotype of the Blackman focused not only on his behaviour but also on his unCaucasoid physical characteristics. These were regarded as undesirable and unhuman. In Amerindian racist ideology Africans were thought of with contempt[5]. The way Oreallans talked about the East Indian racial group showed that they thought of its members as morally inferior to themselves. The Black group was conceived as naturally inferior as well. Insulting terms for Blackpeople were animal terms. They were called apes and alligators. They were thought to behave in ways considered unhuman. They were mentally inferior but crafty and quick to learn, like monkeys. But there were also admirable qualities. Blackpeople were strong and hard workers. Orealla men believed Black men could seduce any girl. Black men were thought to have big sexual organs and both sexes were believed to be natural sexual athletes — again animal qualities. These characteristics aroused admiration and envy.

Oreallans' racist stereotypes had been influenced by attitudes within the wider society and by contemporary experiences, as well as by the history of Amerindian relations with the Coast. They were the stereotypes of Africans and East Indians traditionally held by the European group. This group had a profound influence on the historical development of racist attitudes throughout the society, and had more influence than any other racial group on the development of Amerindian attitudes. They were also the stereotypes many Africans and East Indians held of each other, and the developing African: East Indian opposition in Suriname and the pre-independence racial conflict in Guyana must have served to reinforce Amerindian racial stereotypes.

Oreallans told jokes and stories about Africans and East Indians which expressed and reinforced their stereotypes. Often they were about individuals known to the teller and his audience. The teller might claim to have witnessed the events described or to have been told of them by someone who did. Following are some examples. The first concerns Coolie meanness.

Case 6:1   'Cooliepeople are very mean. Recently a Coolieman died at Skeldon. The police watchman looked after the body all night and had it taken to Skeldon hospital next morning. Doctor Rambihar made an examination and found the man had died of starvation, but when he examined his clothing he discovered $200 in the pockets. The Coolieman was so mean that rather than spend his money he had starved himself to death! When the watchman saw the money he wanted the doctor to divide it between them but Rambihar said no. He said the watchman had had his chance to find it during the night so he kept it all for himself. I don't think the Coolieman had any relatives, otherwise Rambihar would probably have given them the money.'

The second story is an example of Coolie dishonesty.

Case 6:2   Moti was a Coolieman who drove a tractor belonging to an East Indian from Crabwood Creek. He worked in the Bush around Orealla. Moti was considered a 'scamp'[6] by Oreallans. He was a braggart and a liar and they treated him with contempt. With typical Amerindian humour they nicknamed him 'Moti Capone' after the notorious American gangster Al Capone. Usually they referred to him simply as 'Capone'.

One evening Capone was sitting talking around a fire with some Orealla men. When he left they started telling stories about his dishonesty. One man said he was a confidence trickster. Once he went to a hotel in Skeldon. He was smartly dressed and flashed a thick wad of dollar bills when booking in. Because he had money the hotel owner did not ask him to pay in advance. Capone stayed at the hotel for several days and left without paying his bill. In fact he had no money. He had tricked the owner into believing he had a roll of bills by wrapping a single dollar around a thick wad of paper.

Stories about Blackpeople often emphasized what were believed to be their unnatural behaviour or physical characteristics. Two examples are given below.

Case 6:3   Some Orealla men were discussing a Blackman from Suriname who developed a mysterious ailment. His belly started to swell and as his condition progressively worsened he became alarmed and went to a doctor. The doctor examined him and was amazed to discover that he was pregnant. His questions elicited the information that the patient frequently had intercourse with his wife in the position of the dominant male, with the man underneath instead of on top. The doctor said this must have caused him to become pregnant.

Everyone agreed with the doctor's explanation and there the matter would have ended had I not asked what happened to the Blackman. The storyteller was surprised at my naivety and replied that obviously he had died. The baby killed him. He was a man and had no vagina; how could he give birth to the child he was carrying? Someone said his death was deserved. It was unnatural and immoral to copulate with the woman on top. When I ventured the opinion that I saw nothing wrong with this position several men asked me contemptuously, 'What? Would you let your wife ride you?'

Case 6:4   Some young men were drinking together and the conversation got around to the hardness of the Blackman's head. It was claimed that Blackmen have unnaturally thick skulls and hard heads.

Teacher Will, an Orealla man who was a trained teacher and taught at the village school, told an amusing story about when he was a student at the Teacher Training College in Georgetown. He lived in the College residences and one night he got into an argument with a Black fellow student. The man was very stubborn and Will lost his temper and struck him hard on the head with a tin of Ovaltine. The Blackman was unhurt and did not even feel the blow, although its force bent the tin right out of shape. Will said the incident did not affect the man's disposition. He remained as stubborn as ever!

Oreallans stressed physical and psychological (personality) characteristics in their stereotypes of Africans and East Indians. This does not mean that they did not believe there were other differences between themselves and Black and Coolie people. They recognized cultural and organizational differences between Amerindians and non-Amerindian groups, and between the African and East Indian groups.

The cultural features Oreallans thought characteristic of the Amerindian racial group were Amerindian languages; beliefs such as kanaima and mystical techniques such as ritual blowing; and certain kinds of mystical knowledge the most important of which was a body of traditional knowledge known as piai, which Oreallans described as 'Amerindian science'. At Orealla, as on the Corentyne river generally, Amerindians had lost much of their languages and their knowledge of

Mixed (Arawak/Black) Amerindian family

piai, and there was no longer a piaiman on the river. These were matters of regret. They were valued as attributes of Amerindianness. While this appeared the main reason for regretting the loss or degeneration of Amerindian languages, the passing of piai was regretted because it was believed to have given Amerindians some control over the world in which they lived. With piai they had not been totally powerless. However, Oreallans believed many other Amerindian communities had retained these institutions. (In fact they believed they continued in some communities where they had also been lost or drastically modified. Oreallans believed mistakenly that these communities had undergone less cultural change than Corentyne communities[7].) Because all Amerindians shared some common cultural ancestry and a common history of relations with Coastal populations Oreallans saw themselves as sharing in this cultural distinctiveness even though they had lost, or appeared to be losing, much of the Amerindian institutions.

Members of the East Indian group in particular were regarded by Oreallans as possessing some distinctive cultural characteristics, especially in the field of religion but also in the fields of marriage, family life, and community structure[8]. Lower class Africans were perceived as being culturally similar to Oreallans in many respects, for example in religion, marriage, and in beliefs and values in general[9]. Blackpeople had more sophisticated forms of organization, such as complex political, recreational, and educational organizations, because they had much greater opportunities for social and economic development.

However these characteristics were a less important part of Oreallans' stereotypes of the Black and East Indian racial groups than the physical and personality ones. There was no evidence that Oreallans regarded them in a derogatory manner. When interacting with members of other groups they did not disparage their beliefs or cultural practices, in contrast to attitudes often adopted by Blackpeople and East Indians towards Oreallans. More significantly, when Oreallans discussed these perceived cultural differences among themselves they were not the subject of derogatory comment. When Oreallans compared themselves culturally with Blackpeople and East Indians they stressed similarities, not differences. They wanted to show that they were as civilized as Black and Coolie people, so they stressed common characteristics used by Africans and East Indians as symbols of civilized status.

It is interesting that Oreallans did not appear to regard East Indian belief and ritual as inferior to Christianity despite the fact that they equated Christianity with Europeans, and therefore with civilization, and even though members of other racial groups might do so[10]. Attitudes towards Hinduism and Islam may have been influenced by the Oreallan's pragmatic approach to mystical beliefs. In everyday activities magico-religious elements of different origin were synthesized and utilized, and all were potentially powerful. They were probably influenced also by the fact that in Guyana and Suriname East Indian religions are officially granted a status equivalent to that of Christianity, and that members of all racial groups regard Hinduism and Islam as morally superior to the kinds of animistic beliefs popularly thought to have constituted traditional Amerindian religions.

The characteristics singled out in the Oreallan's stereotype of the Blackman and the Coolieman were viewed as innate, hereditary characteristics of Blackness and Coolieness. This contrasted with their stereotypes of each other as Arawaks and Waraos. The derogatory characteristics stressed when comparing themselves usually were regarded as a consequence of upbringing. In contrast those characteristics which made the Blackman and Coolieman Advantage Amerindians had an immutable quality that strengthend the Oreallan's fear of being subordinated to governments dominated by these groups.

3

Oreallans perceived the relations of Amerindians with East Indians and Africans in terms of Advantage. Advantage meant to take advantage of; cheat; exploit; use a position of strength to another's disadvantage. Its root was the misuse of power by the stronger to exploit the weaker. Although Oreallans did not articulate the assumption, their behaviour suggested that they regarded any type of power as likely to be abused, to be used for the benefit of the holder and the detriment of those over whom he had some control. The village Captain was believed to use his position to benefit himself and his Family. Amerindian shopkeepers were believed to cheat their customers. However the main area in which power differences existed was not between Amerindians but between Amerindians and outsiders. Relations between Amerindians and outsiders were perceived as relations of inequality. The outsider or the group to which he belonged was seen as having greater access to power than had Amerindians. There was therefore much greater scope for Advantage in relations between outsiders and Amerindians than there was in relations between Amerindians themselves.

Oreallans believed that because the East Indian and African racial groups were politically and economically more powerful than the Amerindian racial group their members were able to exploit Amerindians. That was why Amerindians were poor. They were a weak group, powerless to prevent their exploitation by other groups. Their poorness and exploitation were constant themes in Amerindian conversation.

Their interpretation of relations with Coolies and Blackpeople as Advantage extended to the policies of governments believed to represent the interests of these groups, and to the actions of agencies of those governments. Oreallans complained that the Guyana government intended to take away Amerindian lands and make Amerindians pay taxes on home-made alcoholic beverages, dogs, canoes, income – and anything else the Oreallan's fertile imagination could conceive. Amerindian policies advocated by the government and local policies initiated by administrative officers were viewed with suspicion as having the hidden aim of taking away the Indian Right. With typical hyperbole Oreallans complained that the government was trying to put them into slavery. They said Amerindians had always been a free people, an invidious comparison with the members of the government trying to take away their rights.

Interactions with East Indians and Africans were coloured by belief in Advantage. Any interaction an Oreallan believed had operated to his detriment he tended to interpret as a deliberate act of exploitation. Oreallans claimed East Indian tractor drivers overcharged them for hauling their logs to the river. Logs cut on the Guyana shore of the river were girthed by the buyman one foot from the narrowest end of the log. This contrasted with the Suriname practice, where the girth was taken in the middle of the log. The Guyanese procedure was a traditional one, but Oreallans believed the buyman was Advantaging them. Oreallans working in Suriname were paid in guilders. During the period of fieldwork the official rate of exchange was 80 Guyanese cents to the guilder. Many Oreallans believed they were being cheated by their Dutch or Surinamese employers and that a guilder was really worth a dollar. Lawyers were said to exploit the Amerindian's lack of legal knowledge. Agents of government were believed to Advantage Amerindians by favouring their own Nations at the expense of Amerindians and by demanding bribes.

Case 6:5   Log prices on the Corentyne river were set by individual loggers bargaining prices per cubic foot for different species of timber with buymen for the sawmills at Crabwood Creek and Springlands. The first prices agreed tended to become stabilized as prices for the season.

In 1967 the Assistant District Officer for Oreallan negotiated a substantially higher price for kabukalli[11] wood than the loggers had previously obtained. The buymen paid the money to the ADO who paid out the amounts owed to each individual, having records from logger and buyman. The ADO received the money periodically, in substantial sums. Although Oreallans received more for their timber the arrangement also had disadvantages for the loggers. Sometimes they had to wait several weeks for their money. Previously, when they were paid directly by the buymen, they received their money quicker. They preferred this because they had expenses to meet and had to pay their credit at the village shop. Also the buyman had paid them to load the logs onto his boat. With the price increase buymen no longer paid for the loading.

The Oreallans complained bitterly, but they did not regard these developments as unforseen consequences of a policy introduced by the ADO to get them more money. They believed he was Advantaging them for his own benefit and for the benefit of his fellow Coolies. It was argued that he must have reached some deal with the buymen to their mutual advantage, and he had done so because they were all Coolies. People believed he had negotiated an even higher price and was keeping the rest for himself. He was 'robbing the people' and putting their money into his own pocket. Loggers complained to one another that when they collected their money from the ADO's office it regularly came to less than it should.

At the same time the haulage fee for the village tractor was raised three cents by the District council at the ADO's suggestion, in order to pay off the hire purchase debt on the tractor. The people said the ADO persuaded the council to do this because the tractor was undercutting those owned by East Indians. The tractor owners had asked him to raise the price and he had done so to help his 'Mattie Coolies' (fellow East Indians).

Claims of Advantage were not made only against East Indians and Africans. Any person in a position of political or economic power could be thought by Oreallans to be Advantaging them. The Chinese shopkeeper at Skeldon who sold goods to Amerindian shopkeepers at Orealla was said to overcharge them. A Portuguese who built a hotel at Springlands was said to have cut the timber at Sipuruta employing non-Amerindian loggers. The concept of Advantage could be applied to all outsiders, that is to all non-Amerindians, and not just East Indians and Africans. But while it was applied to individuals from other 'races' it was less likely to be applied to their racial group. Their group might not be thought to be seeking to Advantage Amerindians even though individuals within it might do so.

There was ample evidence to justify Oreallans' beliefs that people tried to Advantage them. Officials often treated them disdainfully. Governments placed their problems low on their list of priorities, no matter how much they solicited their support at election time. Canvassing political parties made extravagant promises they could not hope to keep. People attempted to cheat them, often in the belief that they were simple people who could easily be fooled. A subcontractor who had engaged Oreallans as drughers[12] to carry gasoline drums over falls up-river said he could not pay them as he had not been paid himself, when in fact he received their money days before. A police inspector would not issue an Oreallan with a firearms license unless first given a bribe. An Oreallan trying to claim on a life insurance he took out on his father was taken for a ride by the lawyer he engaged to act on his behalf. An Oreallan worked for a Coolieman. The man owed him $300 and he twice went to Springlands for his money but received only $15 and $20. Then the man said he had lost the record book. The Amerindian could do nothing. He could not prove he was owed the money. But he said he would get his own back. The next time the man wanted workers he would volunteer and draw his advance rations from him, but he would not work. The Captain engaged a builder to build a house in the Coastal style, on stilts and with glass windows and a corrugated iron roof. He made regular payments to the builder to pay off his debt, but the builder was told by an East Indian friend of the Captain that he had lost the receipts. The builder sued the Captain, claiming to have been paid nothing. The Captain had given his receipts to the East Indian ADO for safekeeping and he defended the Captain and exposed the plaintiff, a fact which would be ignored when the Captain talked about his experience as an example of Coolie duplicity. Another East Indian ADO discovered that the East Indian agent with the balata concession for the Guyana shore was cheating the Amerindian balata bleeders. The company that owned the concession was paying 55 cents per pound for the big wet season. The agent told the bleeders the price was 40 cents per pound and kept the rest. The Coolie ADO exposed the Coolie agent and arranged to deal directly with the company on behalf of the Amerindians, another fact that would be ignored when Oreallans vilified him for robbing the people over the price of kabukalli logs. Numerous examples like these supported Oreallans' conceptions of Amerindians as an exploited people, and influenced their relations with outside individuals and authorities.

However, contrary to one of their most professed self-images Oreallans were by no means merely innocent recipients of Advantage. Because they suspected the intentions of outsiders they might act to defraud them, doubtless often cheating innocent individuals. They might take advances in money and rations from persons who wished to employ them and then not work, or work half-heartedly. They might overcharge outsiders for services, such as doctoring ailments, or cheat them over purchases. Outsiders who employed Oreallans or worked with them often criticized them as unreliable. They did not do things they promised to do. They did not turn up on the day or at the time agreed upon. They worked for a few days and then stopped without informing you. In part this was due to Amerindian attitudes towards time, which were no different from those of many other Guyanese and Surinamers, but it was also a consequence of their perceptions of other racial groups and their belief that outsiders Advantage Amerindians.

To cheat an outsider, particularly an African or East Indian, could become a source of village amusement. The potential exploiter had been exploited. I remember sitting one Sunday morning in the house of a friend, when an East Indian came along the path carrying a parakeet. The Amerindians hailed him and politely asked him why he was carrying the bird. He replied he had come to Orealla to buy a parrot which he could train to talk. He had been up the hill and a Warao had sold him a parrot for five dollars, assuring him it would be a good talker. Gravely my friends informed him he had been cheated. The bird was a 'false parrot', a parakeet, and not a parrot at all, and could not be trained to talk. They kept asking the same questions over and over again, and the East Indian could not tell whether they could not understand what he was saying or whether they thought he was stupid. 'Eh-eh! It a parrot you say?' 'Eh-eh! It how much you pay for he?' 'Eh-eh! And you want for teach he to talk?' When the angry East Indian stormed off in search of the Warao, whom he never found, they howled with laughter and one said to me, 'Chief. Cooliepeople come here and them buy a good parrot for nothing. Now this one man come here and he pay five dollars and he buy nothing. He pay for all!'

4

The Oreallans' stereotype of Bush Negroes was more ambivalent than their stereotype of Coastal Africans. 'Djukas' were despised as uncivilized, in contrast to Oreallans, and because they were Negroes and therefore racially inferior. Oreallans said Coastal people called Djukas 'black Amerindians'. They derided this, saying they had never seen Amerindians that colour — which was not true as there were mixed Amerindians who were phenotypically African. At the same time they respected Djukas because, like themselves, they were superb Bush and river men, and feared them as obeahmen. Oreallans had little contact with Bush Negroes, despite the proximity of the small village on the Suriname shore whose members sometimes came to Orealla to shop. Orealla men and Bush Negro men sometimes were employed to work together as drughers. When Oreallans interacted with Djukas they appeared to treat each other with mutual respect, which often contrasted with Oreallans' interactions with Coastal Africans.

5

In contrast to their stereotypes of Africans and East Indians, the dominant element of the Oreatla stereotype of Whitepeople was its large complimentary component. This part of the stereotype was that which the European racial group developed of itself and which, to varying degrees, was impressed upon or developed by the non-European populations of colonial West Indian societies[13]. Whitepeople were naturally superior people with greater intelligence and ability than other Nations. Caucasoid physical characteristics were admired, setting as they did the traditional standards of beauty in West Indian societies. In contrast to the stereotypes held of East Indians and Africans, cultural factors were important in the stereotype of the Whiteman, but in a general way rather than by singling out specific features. Whitepeople were culturally sophisticated and culturally superior to other people, and this was due to the innate qualities of Whiteness. Oreallans thought of England as paradise on Earth. They were shocked when I told them there are beggars in England, and even more shocked when I said they are Whitepeople, as they were when I confirmed there are Blackpeople living in England.

Whitepeople were believed to be the only Nation concerned about Amerindian interests and welfare. They were the traditional guardians of the Indian Right, and their disengagement from Guyana was placing Amerindians in a precarious predicament. Amerindian concern is summed up in the following (Anglicized) comments by an Oreallan.

Case 6:6 'Things are getting very bad now the Whitepeople have gone. The government is punishing[14] the Amerindian very hard. Other races are pressing the Amerindian down. The Bible says just before the end of the world the Ethiopian shall reign and now that time has come. If you go into any office now you will find it is not a Whiteman anymore, it is pure alligator[15]. The African and the East Indian are ruling. Where have all the Whitepeople gone? Now everyone is trying to punish the Amerindian who is the poorest class of people in Guyana, but who were the first people here, the people who Columbus met when he came from the east.'

There were also negative qualities in the stereotype of the Whiteman, but these were less developed than the positive ones. They had a more idiosyncratic character as the degree to which they were held varied considerably between individuals, and consequently the stereotype had a more ambivalent, contradictionary, and varied character than that of the Coolie or Blackman.

Whitepeople were naturally enterprising; would attempt things other people were afraid of or would not think of; and were always prepared to try something new. That was why they were so advanced beyond other Nations. They were naturally strong. But Whitepeople might also be thought of as soft and unable to endure physical hardship, pampered by easy living. You could rely on Whitepeople. They did what they said they would do and they kept their word. But they might also be thought to be naïve, because they had little contact with the real world, with ordinary people. Consequently they were not only dominant, they could be tricked and taken for a ride. Two stories told me by Oreallans illustrate these beliefs.

Case 6:7   Paris Simmons (44) was once employed by a White American working in the Bush. One day the American shot a camoodi[16] and they pegged it out and skinned it. As he looked at the skinned body of the giant serpent the American said, 'God damn Simmons! I'm going to eat the bitch! See what it tastes like! I never ate snake before.' He built a small fire and cut some meat and roasted it. When it was cooked he ate it and pronounced it good. He offered some to Paris who refused, but he admired the American because he had wanted to do something unusual and had done it. That was typical of a Whiteman.

Case 6:8   Just below Orealla there used to be a sawmill owned by a Belgian or Frenchman. It made railway sleepers. Those were good times because the miller paid your money on the spot and allowed you plenty of credit for rations. The Whiteman sold the mill to a Guyanese, who then sold it to an Englishman. The Englishman allowed Oreallans excessive credit, which many had no intention of repaying. He went bankrupt and blamed the Amerindians, saying they would not work and did not repay their debts. He left the river saying that 'Buckpeople are scamps and not quiet people.'

Oreallans might have more markedly hostile elements in their stereotypes of Europeans. They might say that the Whiteman is an exploiter. That he is 'a thief and a robber'. That you should beware of a Whiteman if he comes to you with gifts because he has come to steal your land. He is not to be trusted[17]. Individuals sometimes mentioned the situation of Amerindians in the United States as an example. Whitepeople killed millions of them and took away all their land. However these hostile elements were less developed than in the stereotypes held of the Blackman and Coolie, and less marked than in the stereotype of Whitepeople held by Coastal people.

Providing the phenotypic characteristics were the appropriate ones, when allocating persons to the category 'White' Oreallans could be influenced by factors such as wealth, social standing, and relations with the Amerindian population. Mr Peter D'Aguiar, founder and first leader of the small United Force (UF) political party, the minor party in the PNC-dominated coalition government in Guyana from 1964 to 1968 and which received the electoral support of the majority of Guyana's Amerindians, was often allocated by implication to the White category and not the Portuguese. In the same conversation people would praise Mr D'Aguiar for fighting for Amerindians and would say 'Only the Whitepeople are fighting for the Amerindian.' This was because he was a public figure whose party Oreallans believed championed Amerindian rights against Advantage by other groups, and of course he was biologically White. Non-Amerindian Guyanese would not make this identification, however implicitly. The fact that he was well-known constantly reminded them that he was also Portuguese. (If asked specifically about this point Oreallans would also say he was Portuguese, but we are talking about tacit identification.)

When Oreallans said 'Whiteman' the term usually was synonymous with 'Englishman'. However they recognized the existence of other White nationalities, who might be thought to have their own characteristics. It is not that they thought other Europeans were not 'White'; merely that usually there was no need to differentiate between types of European.

Living on the border between Guyana and Suriname an obvious distinction was between 'English' and 'Dutch'. Residents of the Corentyne river called the Guyana shore of the river 'the English Shore' and the Suriname shore 'the Dutch Shore'. Besides Englishman, Dutchman, and American, with each of whom many Oreallans had had some personal contact, European types mentioned included German and Russian. The German was a bad kind of Whiteman who was jealous of the Englishman and wanted to conquer him. He was unable to do so because of the Englishman's natural superiority. The Russian was also a bad Whiteman, the enemy of the Englishman, a stereotype resulting from the intrusion of Cold War rhetoric into Guyanese politics, including the emergence of the United Force as a political party committed to oppose 'communism'.

Residents of the Corentyne river categorized one another in racial terms, into different Nations, but in interactions between residents of the two shores they also differentiated each other as 'English' and 'Dutch'. An Oreallan called any native of Suriname a 'Dutchman', whatever his Nation, and in this context Dutchman and Englishman referred to place of birth and national allegience and not to subcategories within the category 'White'. In their relations with non-Amerindians Corentyne river Amerindians usually accorded this designation less importance than racial group. The main exceptions were agents of the Suriname government, such as policemen and forest rangers. They were more commonly perceived as 'Dutchmen' than as Blackpeople or members of any other Nation because their official roles influenced the lives of Amerindians. At the time of fieldwork the party in power in Suriname was the Nationale Partij Suriname. Oreallans identified it as a 'Black' government. Despite this they praised it because, in contrast to their own, they believed it to be concerned about Amerindian welfare. As evidence they cited the building of the Afobaka dam on the Suriname river and the West Suriname Project, work on which had just begun in the area of the Dutch Shore around Matope creek, higher up the Corentyne river. Oreallans were employed on both these projects and believed their purpose was to provide work for Amerindians. (However Suriname's Amerindians made the same kinds of criticisms of their government as Oreallans did of theirs. In particular, they claimed it neglected them in favour of the larger and electorally more important Bush Negro population[18].)

Oreallans did not extend to officials of the Suriname state the admiration they gave its government. Nor was their admiration of its government unequivocal. The following example illustrates Oreallans' identification of state and government with race, and the way they could shift from one idiom to the other in describing their relationships with non-Amerindians.

Case 6:9   In 1967 the 'Dutch police' were carrying out their duties on the Corentyne river with particular heavy-handedness. On the river it was believed this was part of the Suriname government's campaign over Suriname's claim to 6,000 square miles of territory at the headwaters of the Corentyne river. One morning a police launch stopped the mail boat as it left Oreala. It was returning the priest to Skeldon after his monthly visit to the mission, and was crowded with Amerindians travelling down to Springlands, several of whom had been summonsed to Springlands' magistrate's court to face various criminal charges. The police asked the boat's captain for his certificate, examined it, and informed him it was out of order, despite his protest that he had just renewed it in Nickerie. He was told to disembark all the passengers except the priest, whom he would be allowed to carry to Springlands. The priest went aboard the launch, talked with the police for several minutes, and persuaded them to let two boys accompany him. He said they were his assistants, but in fact they were going to court. All other passengers had to disembark. As they streamed back into the village from the riverside the Oreallans angrily cursed the police. They shouted by what right could the Dutch order them off the river? It was not the Dutch who made the river. God made the river. Dutchman was getting as bad as German. But they had better look out or 'Englishman go bust their arse because Blackman not got mind like Whiteman.'

6

Oreallans of course had stereotypes of themselves as Amerindians. Among these was one they described as 'Poor Buck', or 'Stupid Buck', or by some similar name. Poor Buck was ignorant, unsophisticated, and stupid, and blithely revealed his ignorance and stupidity. Poor Buck was the subject of jokes told by Oreallans against themselves as Amerindians, and the following are typical examples. The informant who told me the first story believed it to be true. The second was merely an amusing story.

Case 6:10 A Buckman, a village Captain, was dining with the English Governor of British Guiana at his residence in Georgetown (a most unlikely situation!) They were eating chicken. The ignorant Buckman kept picking up bits of chicken from off his plate, stripping the bones with his teeth and fingers, and throwing the cleaned bones over the Governor's head out through an open window. The Governor assumed this to be the Amerindian way of eating and rather than embarrass the Buckman by correcting his table manners he decided to do the same. As they sat throwing chicken bones out of the window the Governor said, 'Captain, I am sorry to have to tell you that our friend Mr so-and-so is dead.' Exclaimed the Buckman, pausing from his chicken bone, 'True Your Excellency? Oh raas!'[19].

Case 6:11 A Buckman was working in the Bush for a Whiteman. One day he went into the forest to relieve himself and when he came back the Whiteman asked how he cleaned himself after defaecating. The Buckman told him he used a piece of stick. The Whiteman said this was unsanitary and gave him a toilet roll and explained how to use it. To demonstrate he tore off a piece of toilet paper and held it in his hand with first and fourth fingers in front of the paper and second and third behind, so presenting the paper as a wiping surface. When the Buckman next went into the Bush he took the toilet roll. But 'Stupid Buck' put his fingers in the reverse position so that the paper was behind his hand, and consequently he wiped his anus with his fingers.

When he finished he looked at his excreta-covered fingers and said disgustedly, 'Eh-eh! Well look how the Whiteman dirty! He wipe he arse with he hand!'

At Orealla Amerindian identity was not built upon self-esteem based upon any strong sense of the worthiness of the Amerindian Nation's ways and values, or manifested in strong attachment to these values. It was defined largely by comparison with the characteristics of other Nations, particularly with what were believed to be the negative racial qualities of Black and Coolie people and the positive racial qualities of Whitepeople, and by the common relationship of Amerindians to the wider society. In this sense Oreallans can be said to have lacked a strong positive racial identity[20] , and this appeared true of all Coastal Amerindian communities with which I was familiar[21]. (It may not have been true of those communities that had retained their language and a more distinctive culture, and was even less likely of Interior Amerindians.)

At Orealla there was a frequently repeated story that when Columbus first landed in the New World he saw a frightened Amerindian running away, leaping through the Bush, and exclaimed in admiration, 'See him running like a buck!' This was the origin of the term Buck, which initially was a compliment. Other races had since turned it into a derogatory term. In taking its origin back to the very beginning of the modern history of the Americas Oreallans were stressing the Amerindians' status as the original inhabitants of the Guianas. In political arguments they often said, 'When Columbus first come here from the east who he meet? Not Blackman, not Coolie, but we the Amerindian.' Now the Blackman and Coolie were trying to take away the Amerindian's land and keep him down. They believed this status gave them a particular right to, at least, social and political equality with Blackpeople and East Indians. It may be that the frequent Orealla complaint that their young people no longer knew their own languages, and stories about the origin of the word Buck, represented attempts to create a more positive self-image.

7

The type of behaviour Oreallans believed should pertain between Amerindians as members of the same Nation, as Buckpeople, was summed up by the concept Mattie. The qualities of Mattie and its application were not articulated in any precise way by Oreallans. I deduce them from their general behaviour and statements.

Mattie was a flexible concept applied on the basis of one or other of two principles, close friendship or common group membership. In chapter four I discussed the concept as applied to a man and his closest friend. This was an informal, voluntary relationship which developed out of the qualities they brought to their interactions, and its obligations were broad and imprecisely defined. It implied friendship, equivalence, co-operation, and mutual assistance. Oreallans of either sex also applied the term to fellow members of the various kinds of groupings to which they belonged. They also used it to describe the relationship between people who shared membership of the same grouping. Mattie was applied to groups of any type and size, from communities, tribes, regions and racial groups up to everybody, Mankind. Mattie was the idiom of belonging. It symbolized group membership.

People used the term Mattie when they wished to stress common membership of a group. For example, one Oreallan might address another as his 'Orealla Mattie'. Often he did so when both were away from the village among non-Oreallans. They might be working on the Coast, where most of the people they saw were not only non-Oreallans, they were non-Amerindians. In this situation Amerindians from different communities often would use the term Mattie for each other, and would use terms such as 'Mattie Buckman', meaning 'fellow Amerindian'. What was implied was that common membership of a group carried shared moral responsibilities, which included providing mutual help and assistance.

When people used the term Mattie in this way they invoked a relationship which had qualities fundamental to that between close friends. By this I do not mean to imply that Mattie in this sense was derived from Mattie in the sense of personal friendship, or that persons appealing to Mattie were necessarily friends. Indeed, Mattie was often invoked between persons whose personal relationship was hostile. I merely state that the concept of Mattie, however used, had a core of common qualities.

Oreallans always expressed the concept in personalized terms, whichever sense of Mattie was being used. They used phrases such as 'Mattie Buckman' ('fellow Amerindian'); 'Mattie Coolie' ('fellow man who is also an East Indian'); 'Na tief Mattie wife' ('It is wrong to steal the wife of your fellow man.'). They did not talk of Mattie in terms of a code or set of rules, as they did when talking of Manners and Respect or as an Englishman does when he talks of 'The Law'. Mattie was conceived of as a type of person, and when it was appealed to it was an appeal to a type of person rather than a code as was the case with Manners and Respect[22]. In its ultimate sense Mattie was an idealized person, Humanity.

Mattie was a person with particular qualities from which derived certain responsibilities and obligations. Mattie implied equality, but it was the equivalence of being your fellow, not equality of status or relative social standing. As your fellow one had the right to be treated decently and considerately. Mattie was common identity. Mattie meant 'fellow persons', 'people like us', people as 'members one of another'.

Whatever the level of grouping appealed to, Mattie in this sense was based upon the idea of a common quality people possessed as a result of their identity as members of the group. Shared identity was a bond entitling members to consideration and assistance from one another. This bond was a consequence of their common nature. The obligations it entailed were broad, vague, and rooted in the homogeneousness of being. They were not differentiated rights and obligations rooted in different statuses and differential rights to respect. As with Mattie as a relationship betwen two friends, Mattie as group membership was rooted in a quality perceived as inherent in the individuals themselves, but in this case stemming from common identity. Although group membership was often an ascribed status, Mattie in this sense to some extent appeared to partake of the voluntariness of Mattie as friendship; when invoked it appeared to be in the nature of an appeal to the ultimate ideal, rather than a demand for a specified obligation which everyone recognized as your right.

Assistance was not the only obligation involved in Mattie. The other was the responsibility not to behave anti-socially towards Mattie, to behave ethically. People made statements such as 'Na tief from Mattie' ('It is wrong to steal from Mattie'); 'Na fight Mattie' ('It is wrong to fight Mattie'); 'Na tief Mattie wife' ('It is wrong to steal the wife of Mattie'). All were anti-social acts. Mattie was the ultimate validation of ethical behaviour. The social equality of Mattie as a relationship between close friends had its counterpart in the wider application of the term in a general moral equality which carried common responsibilities. There was a sense in which all members of the group were of equal moral worth. However, although Mattie was concerned with the moral value of the being, it did not imply that all of the group's members were of equal social standing or behaved equally morally. Depending on the way individuals behaved some were more worthy of esteem and emulation than others.

When members of different racial groups addressed each other as 'Mattie' usually they were suggesting common membership of some more inclusive grouping which carried obligations transcending the obvious differences between them. Mattie was the idiom of incorporation into the wider humanity that overrode group differences.

When persons from different racial groups used the term in this way they frequently combined it with some term denoting their membership of different groups, of the same order, within the greater unity — as when an East Indian would address an Amerindian as 'Mattie Buckman' and be addressed in return as 'Mattie Coolie'. The implication was of a wider unity overriding the obvious particularisms within it. The Buckman and Coolieman might be implying they were Guyanese, or Surinamers, or members of Mankind.

Case 6:12 An East Indian tractor driver working at Orealla was asked by a Warao if he would use his tractor to haul some firewood from the Backdam. (Oreallans had to fetch firewood from the Backdam as there was none near the village, and this was often an arduous task). The East Indian hauled a large log from the savannah into the Amerindian's yard and told him he had done it for his 'Mattie Warao'. As human beings they had a common tie which made the fact that he was a Coolie and the other an Amerindian irrelevant.

The quality involved in Mattie is V.W. Turner's communitas, which he opposes to structure and defines as 'Undifferentiated, equalitarian, direct, extant, non-rational, I-Thou (in Fuerbach's and Berber's sense) relationships. (It) is spontaneous, immediate, concrete — it is not shaped by norms, it is not institutionalized, it is not abstract[23].' Persons are of equal value, with innate responsibilities of the same kind towards one another which derive from their common identity.

Consequently Advantage was incompatable with Mattie. Advantage was rooted in inequality. It was to use one's position of strength to take advantage of, to exploit, another for one's personal gain. As such it contravened the responsibility people had to respect and assist one another through shared ties of Mattie.

Common group membership implied communitas, which was expressed in Mattie. Since an individual belonged to different kinds and levels of grouping, to each of which he could invoke the concept of Mattie, in any situation it could be implied that communitas had boundaries, set by the boundaries of the grouping membership of which it was being invoked. Ultimately however all persons should be Mattie, because all belonged to one common entity — Mankind.

But because of the antithesis between Mattie and Advantage, for Oreallans implicitly Mattie ended with Buck. They saw themselves as members of a racial group systematically Advantaged by other Nations. Often when Oreallans made general statements regarding Mattie, implicitly it appeared that their referent was the community, and therefore, by implication, Amerindians as opposed to other Nations. General statements to the effect that people should behave in such-and-such a way towards Mattie often were immediately qualified by other statements meaning 'just as other Nations do'. People of other Nations behaved according to Mattie with respect to members of their own Nation and Amerindians should do likewise. In their view of the wider society Oreallans believed that in practice Mattie ended with Nation. They believed members of other Nations acted towards their fellows in conformity with Mattie, but were much less likely to act according to Mattie in relations with non-members. Mattie as Nation took precedence over the wider moral responsibilities inherent in Mattie as humanity, and over the formal obligations and responsibilities of political or administrative office. In Case 6:5 the ADO was accused of raising the tractor price and instituting new arrangements for log payments in order to help his 'Mattie Coolies'. The people believed that because he was a Coolie he felt a closer tie to his fellow Coolies than to his Amerindian charges. When a non-Amerindian appealed to Mattie in his relations with Amerindians they believed it was likely to be a false appeal. It was really made because he wanted something from you, and it was probably done to cloak Advantage.

The association of Mattie with Nation was consistent with other Orealla attitudes and implicit beliefs — that community and kinship ended with Amerindians, and that non-Amerindians Advantaged Buckpeople. It was consistent with what Amerindians saw as the main opposition in their world — that between Amerindian and non-Amerindian. Because some form of equivalence was fundamental to the concept of Mattie the term readily could be equated with 'people like us' or 'poor people'. Given the Oreallan's view of his world, that meant 'Buckpeople'. This view was strengthened by the colonial premise that West Indian society consisted of different kinds of people, with different innate qualities.

Mattie was associated with Buckpeople as a group. They were a group whose members were socially equal in their relationship to the wider society, a social equality defined by low racial status; perceived Advantage; and what was seen as material, social, and political deprivation. Altlhough recognizing themselves as socially equal in this way, Oreallans did not see themselves as all social equals in their interactions among themselves. They were socially equal at the level of Buck but not as individuals within that category. When they talked about themselves as Bucks they were all equal. When they talked about themselves as villagers or persons they were not. Their concept of being 'poor' illustrates this. When talking about themselves as Amerindians Oreallans stressed that they were poor. Indeed, they could be said to wallow in the description. They were poor because they were Advantaged by other Nations who had access to power denied the Buckman. But if one villager called another 'poor' it was an insult – an Eyepass. He was telling him he did not maintain his family properly. That he was lazy and drank away his income. In this context being poor was blamed on the accused. He was personally responsible for his condition. This accusation was possible because Oreallans recognized the existence of different living standards and levels of income within the village and regarded them as socially important. (Typically, a 'poor' person lived in a small house with a dirt floor. It lacked a separate kitchen, might have no sleeping room and be walled almost all around with manicol, and often was overcrowded.)

Oreallans believed members of other Nations behaved according to Mattie in relations with fellow members. The Chinese had their Chinese Society through which they helped one another. The Black government rewarded its racial supporters with jobs and political office. The ADO acted in the interests of his Mattie Coolies. Amerindians did not help one another. They were always pulling against one another instead of acting together to defend their rights. Oreallans believed Amerindians were the only Nation that acted in this way.

Amerindians saw themselves as a group that was powerless to prevent exploitation by other Nations. This was because they were a small, poor group. But it was also a consequence of their attitudes and behaviour. They were envious and suspicious of one another and would not act together for any common good. They did not act according to Mattie and that was an important reason why other Nations were able to Advantage them.

Case 6:13   One Sunday afternoon in June, in the big wet season, a boatload of East Indians came to Orealla. They were from the Springlands–Skeldon–Crabwood Creek area, and were on a Sunday afternoon excursion and had come to Orealla to see what an Amerindian village was like. A few were agents for Dr Jagan's People's Progressive Party who had come to canvass at Orealla. After about two hours, when it had begun to rain, the boat prepared to leave. A few Amerindians went aboard with the East Indians to get a passage down to Springlands, but since the boat docked the tide had gone down and it had grounded.

One of the Amerindians who had gone on board, Aaron Klaverweide (40), was drunk and got into a fight with some East Indians. Aaron's son went to help his father and both were thrown out of the boat. Another Oreallan, Joseph Simmons (47), got hold of

Aaron and tried to drag him away, with Aaron struggling violently and shouting drunkenly that he was going to bust the Cooliepeoples' raas. I came to Joseph's aid and together we dragged Aaron away. A crowd had gathered to watch the boat sail and many of the Amerindians and some of the East Indians were drunk. Threats were exchanged between them and there seemed the likelihood of a general mêlée. The ADO tried to calm the situation, but at this juncture a sand boat came in to dock at Orealla and it pulled the excursion boat into deeper water. Meanwhile the other Amerindians on board had also been thrown off.

As the boat left Joseph told me to 'see how Orealla people stay' (how they behave). Aaron could have got murdered on the boat but nobody went to his aid. I must confess that it seemed to me that many Oreallans were only too eager to assist Aaron. There were a lot of Amerindians present and many were drunk and in an aggressive mood. Nonetheless Joseph interpreted the situation as a typical failure of Amerindians to help one another when threatened by outsiders.

The perceived failure of Amerindians to act together was often spoken of by Amerindians as though it were a natural Amerindian characteristic. When faced with examples of failure to co-operate or help one another they adopted a fatalistic attitude and said simply 'that is we way' or 'that's Amerindians', or some other comment implying its inevitability. This being so, they saw the Amerindians' future position in Guyana as a particularly desperate one because they would be unable to attempt any initiative against Advantage. Similarly, conformity of other Nations with Mattie tended to be regarded by Amerindians as natural to them as Nations. There was a large measure of belief among Oreallans that it was natural for different Nations to try to Advantage each other, and this helped explain racial conflict in Guyana and Suriname. This made the Amerindians' position even more desperate. Not only were Amerindians unable to defend themselves; it was natural for other groups to try to Advantage them.

Admiration was commonly expressed for other Nations because their members supported each other against similar groups. To some degree this form of Advantage was not only natural, it was laudable. What was specifically wrong about it from the Amerindians' point of view was that whereas other groups were powerful enough to protect their members' interests Amerindians were not. And what was especially wrong was that Amerindians were administered by officials from the Black and Coolie groups, who were bound by Mattie to these groups whose interests were antithetical to those of Amerindians. They could not be trusted, because when their duties conflicted with the obligations of Mattie it was natural for the latter to win.

I think this interpretation of Mattie helps explain why Oreallans identified their interests with Whitepeople and were afraid of the future because Whitepeople were disengaging from Guyana. Whitepeople were superior people. They had everything. Consequently there was no need for them to Advantage Amerindians. There was nothing Amerindians had they could possibly want. But when they left they handed over to groups who did Advantage Amerindians, and Amerindians were powerless against them.

Jayawardena discussing the concept of *mati* (Mattie) among Guyanese East Indian plantation workers defines this concept as 'a relationship between persons of relatively equal social status which should be characterized by amity, respect, and consideration for the prestige of each[24].' In a later article he reinterprets the concept to mean an equality based upon recognition of the personal worth and right to self respect of one's fellow[25]. It is an equality of men perceived as deriving from their basic human worth[26]. This is what was involved in the concept I term Mattie in accordance with the Orealla pronunciation (and probably the plantation one also). It was a flexible concept with many refractions, as Jayawardena also records for sugar workers[27]. As used by Oreallans I believe I can designate at least four significant levels of refraction or extension of the concept — a constantly activated relationship of intimate friendship between two men; the totality of an individual's friendship relations; the relation between people of the same kind in opposition to persons of a different kind; and the relation between people as members of Humanity. The relationship involved in the latter two refractions was that which Turner terms communitas. At its widest *de facto* appeal, at the level of Buck, the appeal was buttressed by common social deprivation and common status as members of an Advantaged group with low racial status.

In Jayawardena's analysis the concept of *mati* leads to the development of egalitarian norms[28], which are also known as *mati*. By 'egalitarian norms' Jayawardena means the recognition of an ideal of equality of social standing among all members of the community; the belief that all members of the community are equal in status and prestige[29]. At Orealla Mattie was not conceived in terms of abstract beliefs or rules, but as an idealized person.

Oreallans believed that all villagers were socially equal as Bucks in their relations with the national society. They saw themselves as members of a racially defined category which imparted a common status to its members. This was defined in terms of the relationship between the group and the rest of the national society. Its members were despised and Advantaged. There was also an equality at all levels of social grouping up to that of Mankind, the moral equality of Mattie. But in the context of social status and reputation within the community, and by extension within the category Buck, one cannot talk meaningfully about egalitarian norms in the sense in which the term is used by Jayawardena. Here there was open recognition that as members of the community persons could be of different social and moral standing. (At the same time Oreallans believed that no adult member of the community should have authority over any other, except for that of husband over wife — which in practice was rejected by the wife. Adults were responsible for their own actions. But this should not be confused with equality of social standing.)

Discussing East Indian plantation workers, Jayawardena hypothesizes that *mati* developed as a basis for common political action among the members of a socially deprived group of social equals in a complex, stratified society, who lacked formal institutions to achieve this end[30]. At Orealla, at the *de facto* highest level of Mattie a common deprived status reinforced the concept of Mattie, but Mattie nonetheless did not operate to promote common action despite the Amerindian belief that it ought to do so.

8

In interactions between Amerindians and non-Amerindians there were a number of symbols indicating membership of the Buck category. The most obvious of these was phenotype. Most Amerindians belonged to a particular physical type. However, many Amerindians with mixed racial ancestry diverged from this type and some possessed phenotypes identified with other Nations, although Guyanese and Surinamers exhibited an apparently remarkable ability to detect Amerindian ancestry in the most un-Amerindian-looking persons. Other symbols were language; attitudes; and behaviour. In the case of Oreallans, with the exception of some elderly persons who could converse in Arawak or Warao few people could speak their native language. Attitudes and behaviour often helped identify a person as Amerindian when his phenotype suggested membership of some other racial group and his language was Guyanese English or Surinamese.

In initial interaction Oreallans and non-Amerindians acted as members of different racial groups. Behaviour often expressed opposition or hostility. Guyanese associated Amerindians with shy, diffident behaviour. But this was characteristic of Amerindians when they were on the Coast, where they were rare, and often temporary, residents away from their social and geographical milieu and surrounded by non-Amerindians who often treated them with contempt. When they were away from the Coast, in their communities or in the Bush or on the river, they would openly express their prejudices. Here it was the non-Amerindian who was a member of a numerical minority, and if he was not associated with authority he might find himself treated with hostility and contempt.

However, if Oreallans and non-Amerindians were interacting constantly in the Bush, usually working together or in some other economic relationship, they often chose to act in the idiom of Mattie as this enabled work to proceed smoothly and in an atmosphere of companionship. Appeal was to Mattie as Humanity, implying that the parties had bridged the Buck:non-Buck boundary. On both sides behaviour was confident, vocal, aggressive and self-assertive. But they recognized that use of the Mattie idiom often was instrumental, a useful way of achieving common ends rather than an expression of belief in common identity. If the parties were of different ages they might apply the appropriate kinship terms to one another and act in the idiom of Manners and Respect. If interaction continued for any time ties of Mattie could become more genuine and less purely instrumental. In rare cases individuals from the opposite sides of the Buck:non-Buck boundary might become close friends and apply the term Mattie to each other in the sense of 'best friend'. One Orealla man had such a Mattie, an East Indian from Springlands. When the Oreallan died his aged wife left to live with his Mattie's family. Significantly, my Amerindian informant said that she never learned how he used to cheat her husband. The informant could not accept that the man's East Indianness could allow him to act towards an Amerindian as a Mattie should. Instead he used the relationship to Advantage his Amerindian friend.

This type of interaction was possible because, as well as belief in the importance of racial difference, Amerindians and non-Amerindians professed a belief in Humanity. Both were expressed in different applications of Mattie. But even when individuals developed cordial relationships they remained influenced by racial identity. Oreallans usually subordinated Mattie to racial identity. Ultimately the non-Amerindian was a member of a racial group first and a person second because it was believed that his racial group Advantaged Amerindians. And even if a non-Amerindian had genuine relations of Mattie with some members of the community others would continue to be openly hostile towards him because of his racial identity.

Case 6:14 During part of the period of fieldwork two young East Indian men from Skeldon were employed as teachers at Orealla village school. They were appointed to their posts by the Ministry of Education in Georgetown. Being young and of pleasant disposition they made friends among the young men and women of the village, but ultimately they were regarded always as East Indians first and friends second and most villagers did not accept their presence. They considered them East Indian nuisances who had been foisted on the village by the government and had no right to be there. Attempts were constantly being made to make them aware they were unwelcome and people complained about their behaviour (in particular about them having sexual relationships with girls and married women) to the Captain, the priest, and the ADO in attempts to have them removed.

Non-Amerindian men working in the Bush not only established degrees of Mattie with Amerindian men. Through their relationships with Amerindian men they came to have relationships with Amerindian women. They also established relationships with women more directly by having sexual relations, particularly with unmarried women and girls. Unmarried girls usually led permissive sex lives and had a reputation for sexual eagerness. Men visiting Orealla tried to establish casual relationships with girls for sexual purposes. They bought them drinks and tried to make them tipsy in order to achieve this, but the girls might require little persuasion. Once they were experienced they wanted sexual intercourse, and the personal relationship between a girl and a non-Amerindian man might be irrelevent to her willingness to have sexual relations with him. Some racial groups had a particular physical appeal. Black men were believed to have large sexual organs and be good copulators. Europeans had a particular attraction because of their high racial status. (Children by White men were admired for their light skin.) However at Orealla the number of children by casual relations with non-Amerindians was less than appeared from superficial observation, and than Oreallans themselves believed the case.

If his relationship with an Amerindian woman developed a man might establish a domestic relationship and come to live in the community. Older persons claimed inter-racial marriage was a recent development. This was certainly untrue, although its incidence might have increased in recent years. Their claim was influenced by their critical view of the young generation.

By the time he established a domestic union a non-Amerindian man usually had relations containing a degree of Mattie with some of the villagers. Marriage established relations of Manners and Respect with many members of the community, and his continuing presence resulted in further relationships involving Mattie. Interaction with the community resulted in increased recognition as a person. But because of the association of community membership with the Indian Right, and hence with Buck, to all but a small set of close relatives and friends ultimately he remained an outsider. He could not truly become Mattie.

Whereas Arawak and Warao identity had come to have little importance for interaction, Amerindian identity remained important for the way Oreallans viewed relations with members of non-Amerindian Nations and influenced interaction with them. For Corentyne river Amerindians the boundary between Buck and non-Buck was the important social boundary.

9

In June 1967 Oreallans considered there to be seven non-Amerindians living at Orealla in domestic unions with Amerindians, six men and one woman. The men were two Africans, three Coloured (Afro-European), and one East Indian. Oreallans classed the two Africans and the three Coloured together as 'Black'. (The African ancestry of the Coloured men was prominent in their skin, features, and hair.) The men's ages ranged from 21 to 58 years and between them they had 13 children at Orealla.

Five Orealla women had been in domestic unions with non-Amerindians which had broken up, and their ex-spouses had left the village. The men were two East Indians, two Coloured, and one 'Doogla' (Afro-East Indian)[31]. Two Orealla men had been in domestic unions with non-Amerindian women on the Coast, an African and an East Indian. Both had returned to Orealla and married Amerindians. I was able to trace eight persons from the village who were living elsewhere in domestic unions with non-Amerindians, most in Suriname. Only one was a man, a police constable married to an East Indian. With the exception of one woman married to a Chinese all the women were in unions with Africans or Coloured men, including light-skinned Coloured. There were probably other women living with non-Amerindians away from the Corentyne river of whom I have no record, and undoubtedly there were other women living away from the village who had had domestic unions with non-Amerindians which had broken up.

Miscegenation and marriage with non-Amerindians were mainly the result of relations between Amerindian women and Coastal men. There were few Coastal women living in the Bush. Coastal people regarded the Bush as a dangerous place. It had even less attraction for women than it had for men, and there were few occupations for women available in the Bush. However, those few single women who went into the Bush were unlikely to engage in liaisons with Amerindian men. Their status as Bucks made them unattractive as mates, and on the Coast the stigma suffered by a Coastal woman who married a Buckman was greater than any suffered by a Coastal man who married an

Amerindian woman. Consequently the rarity of matings between non-Amerindian women and Amerindian men was not a mere reflection of demography. It was influenced by social factors. However, there were two non-Amerindian women in domestic unions with Amerindians at Orealla. Since these were unusual cases they merit some attention.

Case 6:15   Coolie Jane (34) was an East Indian, a married woman from the Springlands-Skeldon area. She lived with an Amerindian from Orealla who worked on Skeldon sugar estate and managed to make the accommodation to Coastal life. Even so, when she left her husband for the Amerindian it caused great amusement in Springlands-Skeldon. They lived together for several years before coming to Orealla in 1966, where Coolie Jane started a shop. The people complained about a Coolie woman living in the village and objected even more when she opened a shop, saying she was Advantaging them. But as she was living with a man from Orealla she could not be prevented from doing so. Jane had six children by her Amerindian keeper and two by her East Indian husband. All lived at Orealla.

Case 6:16   The other case was a Portuguese woman who was more than seventy years of age in 1967. She was born on the English Shore of the Corentyne when it was sparsely inhabited. She said she fell in love with an Amerindian from Orealla and came to Orealla to live with him as a young girl. She became thoroughly Amerindianized, learned to speak both Arawak and Warao, and still dressed in the traditional manner for an Amerindian woman, in a long dress knotted over one shoulder. She had become accepted as an Amerindian by the villagers. That a Portuguese woman should marry an Amerindian was unusual, but she lived in what was then an out-of-the-way, unsettled part of the colony. She had three children resident at Orealla, and many grandchildren.

In these two cases prejudice against the couple from Coastal people was removed by the simple expedient of moving from the Coast.

Three Orealla men had domestic unions with non-Amerindians, all on the Coast. They illustrate the special circumstances under which such unions could develop. One left Orealla at three years of age and was brought up by rich non-Amerindian relatives in Georgetown. He had two children by a Black woman. He returned to Orealla when he was twenty-two to teach at the village school, but left the job to drive a tractor in the Bush because he prefered a happy-go-lucky life and enjoyed working with machinery. He married at Orealla. Another became a seaman on a ship working between Georgetown, Paramaribo, and the West Indian islands. He had children by an East Indian woman in Georgetown. He returned to Orealla and married. The third became a police constable on the Coast, married an East Indian, and remained on the Coast. These examples show that on the Coast improved socio-economic status could counter anti-Buck prejudice sufficiently to enable domestic unions to be established with non-Amerindian women. (I know of other examples, where the Amerindian was a schoolteacher or had a similar position, but they were not from the Corentyne river.)

The majority of domestic unions with non-Amerindians were with persons of African ancestry. Despite their more derogatory stereotype, certain factors made it easier for Blackpeople to establish domestic unions with Amerindians than it was for East Indians. East Indians working on the Corentyne said there would be considerable family opposition to their establishing domestic unions with Amerindian women, although this did not prevent them trying to get sexual relations with them. In addition, Black men working on the Corentyne river were less likely to have occupations Amerindians considered exploitative than were East Indians. They were more likely to be loggers, sawmill workers, and boatmen than sawmillers or buymen, boat owners, and tractor owners. Because East Indians were associated more directly with Advantage, relations with Africans tended to be more easy going than they were with East Indians.

It is an apparent paradox that although women had relations with non-Amerindian men, with the consequence that some men might have difficulty establishing domestic unions, in arguments women accused men of sexual relations with outsiders, whereas men did not accuse women. In particular, they claimed that their spouses had relations with Black women. In fact these were ritual forms of complaint, stereotyped expressions of structurally generated conflict between the sexes. This was most developed in the domestic relationship, and tended to be one-sided in the sense that women were more dissatisfied with the behaviour of men than vice versa. In a community in which race symbolised hostility and danger, which was set in a national environment in which race symbolised status and conflict, it was to be expected that ritual complaints would adopt racial themes; and throughout the national society the Black woman symbolized sensuality.

Men's attitudes to unions with Black people and East Indians were disapproving. Persons who entered such unions were the subject of critical comment about people marrying members of these Nations and bringing them to live in the village. Criticism usually concerned the Indian Right. People marrying outsiders, Blackpeople and East Indians in particular, were believed to be promoting erosion of the Indian Right. Women who had married non-Amerindian men and gone to live with their spouses outside the local community were not criticized in this way. Their husbands were not usurping The Right.

Women's attitudes to such unions appeared to be more ambivalent than those of men. They held derogatory stereotypes of Blackpeople and East Indians, but were less likely to condemn domestic unions with members of these groups. Amerindian women often were jealous about their non-Amerindian spouses, and it appeared that non-Amerindian men would have no difficulty finding new spouses if their unions broke up. During the period of fieldwork two Orealla women with Black keepers had disputes with women whom they accused of having affairs with their keepers. In one of these the spouse accused the other woman of trying to steal her keeper in order to marry him. The other, in which the accusation of sexual relations was justified, led to the non-fatal stabbing of the offending woman by the jealous spouse. Despite the stabbing the affair continued until the aggrieved spouse left her keeper, took their baby, and returned to live with her relatives. A year later the young man, a tractor driver, was about to undergo a church marriage with yet another Orealla girl!

Discussing sexual relations and domestic unions between Amerindian women and non-Amerindian men on the Pomeroon river, Drummond defines these relationships as 'ethnic hypergamy'[32] because within the Coastal society other racial groups have higher status than Buckpeople. In terms of the social structure of Guyanese society this is undoubtedly a correct definition, but it must not be assumed that Amerindians believed in their inferiority. On the Corentyne, and in other Coastal Amerindian communities with which I was familiar, Amerindians recognised that other groups were given higher status than themselves and that this influenced the behaviour of non-Amerindians towards them, but they did not consider the current system of racial ranking to be natural or just. Whatever the Coastal society's views, they considered themselves racial superiors to Blackpeople and at least racial equals to East Indians.

Differential ranking of racial groups affected the possibility of unions with non-Amerindians. Women could mate and marry non-Amerindians. Men rarely could. On the Coast Amerindian women took advantage of this situation. Orealla girls working on the Coast frequently entered domestic unions with non-Amerindians and remained there[33]. They were not subjected to any strong negative sanctions. Men could not do so. They were subjected to anti-Buck prejudice, and while many Orealla men travelled widely in Guyana and Suriname almost invariably they returned to live in Amerindian communities. Within the Amerindian community itself and away from the Coast there would not be the same pressures on women to enter unions with non-Amerindians. Within the community Amerindians often refused to accord the outsider superior status on the basis of race. However the existence of racial ranking appears to have influenced choice of spouse in less direct ways. Marriage with a non-Amerindian could be one means of leaving the community for the Coast. Young persons, exposed to demands and wants propagated by the national society, constantly expressed dissatisfication with life at Orealla and expressed the desire to seek a brighter life elsewhere. They frequently did so, girls seeking work as domestics at Springlands-Skeldon or Nickerie, and young men going to other regions of Guyana or Suriname for Bush work. For girls one way of securing the chance to leave was to establish a union with an outsider who was likely to move in his work or in search of work and who would not suffer the discrimination accorded a Buck. Two of the non-Amerindian men in domestic unions at Orealla regarded themselves as temporary residents, and some of the women living elsewhere with non-Amerindians had begun their unions at Orealla when their spouses were working on the Corentyne river.

Another factor that made non-Amerindians attractive as spouses was the fact that they were often in regular employment. This also was a consequence of their higher racial status. Of the six non-Amerindian men at Orealla two were tractor drivers, one was a sawmill worker, and one the ADO's boatman and had worked previously as boathand and sawmill worker. At the same time, unlike Oreallans, they were unlikely to throw up their jobs just because the fancy took them. Consequently often there were economic attractions to union with a non-Amerindian.

The attitude of women towards marriage with outsiders involved a dialectic between belief in racial superiority plus belief in exploitation by non-Amerindians on the one hand, and recognition of the advantages accruing from the outsider's higher racial status in the wider society on the other. Consequently women's attitudes were ambivalent. For men there was almost no opportunity to benefit from the fact that non-Amerindians were accorded higher racial status, so their attitude was unreservedly condemnatory. Both condemnation and justification of marriage with non-Amerindians was expressed in terms of Mattie. Criticizers stressed Mattie at the level of Buck. Women who married non-Amerindians justified their actions by appealing to Mattie at the level of Mankind.

I do not wish to imply that women saw marriage in purely instrumental terms. On the contrary, they established domestic unions with non-Amerindians because they had come to know and like them as individuals, because they had established relations of Mattie with them. But these factors helped them counter their racist beliefs. A young woman's parents might oppose her establishing a union with a Black or East Indian man, but if she wished to do so neither they nor any other members of the community could do anything effective about it. If her parents objected the couple went to live with someone else. The villagers could bring no effective sanction against the outsider because they would not act together for common aims and there was a strong belief that one should not interfere in another person's private affairs. The villagers expected the Captain and District council to oppose outsiders coming into the village, but these local government authorities were ineffective and the administration accorded a non-Amerindian living with an Amerindian the right to live in an Amerindian community.

10

Oreallans believed non-Amerindians living in the village to be exercising a form of Advantage. They were usurping the Indian Right, and it was feared that they were establishing a precedent that could enable other racial groups and their governments to take away Amerindian rights and privileges. When I was taking a census of the village the Captain said he thought I should not include non-Amerindians living with Amerindian women, as they were doing so in order to obtain The Right. He was afraid the census could be used to validate their claim to village membership. A non-Amerindian very rarely came to be accepted as a member of the community even by many of his closest friends and affines.

In arguments with villagers non-Amerindians might be insulted by having their ancestry and racial characteristics denigrated. Non-Amerindians married to villagers usually were not criticized in this way, except by persons who disliked them as individuals. Instead they were told they had no right to live in the village. They had relationships of varying degrees of Mattie with many members of the village, and their kinship relationships brought them under the code of Manners and Respect. This removed them from much racist criticism. But they could only become Mattie to a limited degree.

Manners and Respect was the idiom of inter-status relations. Mattie was the idiom of belonging. Mattie not only implied the existence of a boundary; it was the idiom for crossing the boundary. In interactions with the villagers the non-Amerindian resident stressed Mattie, to show that he thought of himself as a villager and was offering himself as one. He might try to validate his claim to village membership by claiming Amerindian ancestry. In discussion he sided with the Amerindian against the government and against political parties associated with non-Amerindian racial groups. When outsiders visited the village he might put himself forward publicly as a spokesman for the community. These were all claims to Mattie; to belonging.

Case 6:17   Austin Johnson (42) and February (32) were two Black men living at Orealla in domestic unions with two sisters. Austin was legally married to his spouse and they had six children. In 1967 he had lived at Orealla for at least 13 years. He had been made the ADO's boatman, an appointment which engendered considerable criticism in the village as he was not an Amerindian. February was keeping his spouse. (He had a legal wife, a Black woman, in Georgetown, but they had separated.) They had a baby, and February had lived in the village for two years. He was a logger, sometimes worked at Deanville sawmill, and took other wage work when it was available.

Austin and February sought to strengthen their claim to village membership by claiming Amerindian ancestry. Austin said his mother was an Arawak and February said his grandmother was a Warao. Both claims were probably untrue and were rejected by the villagers.

One Sunday morning several men were sitting by the riverbank, drinking bottles of beer and 'gaffing' (chatting idly). They started discussing the 1963 strike at the bauxite works at Kwakwani, on the Berbice river. Some of the men had been working around Kwakwani at that time. They said the strike lasted three months and claimed it was the longest strike in the history of the West Indies. It was in support of the unskilled workers in their fight for a minimum basic wage. The workers had struck because the cost of living was so bad that they needed a minimum wage in order to live. Austin complained that the cost of living had got worse, thanks to the policies of the PNC government. (The government was identified by Amerindians and other Guyanese and Surinamers as a Black government.) He said the people of Guyana should all strike against the government as they did in 1962 over Dr Jagan's PPP government's budget proposals. If the people struck in 1962 to try and bring down the government because things were bad they should all come out on strike now, because the present government was making things even worse.

These attempts to claim Mattie were recognised as such by Oreallans, who rejected them. Instead they were interpreted as attempts at Advantage; attempts to obtain access to the Indian Right to the Amerindian's detriment. Oreallans believed it was the duty of their Captain to prevent non-Amerindians settling in the village. They constantly complained that he failed to do so. When, in the mid 1960s, an association was formed in Guyana to organise Amerindians politically, one reason why many Oreallans joined was because they believed it would operate to expel non-Amerindians from Amerindian communities. Such actions demonstrate that Oreallans' complaints were expressions of deeply held concern about this matter.

Case 6:18   In March 1967 the Captain informed the villagers that Philip Duncan, an Amerindian MP and a member of the Peoples' National Congress, the dominant partner in the coalition government, was coming to Oreala to discuss the people's problems with them. It was assumed that one of the things that would be discussed was the question of non-Amerindians residing in the village. This developed into a rumour, encouraged by the Captain, that Mr Duncan would order all non-Amerindians to leave. The villagers were jubilant, and discussed among themselves who would have to go. Frequently the comment was heard that Rupert Vlet and Joseph Cotton, two Black Oreallans of African fathers, were all right because they had been born in the village and everyone knew their mothers were Amerindians. They could stay. But nobody knew who Austin Johnson's and February's parents were and they had no right to live in the village. People said it was not only non-Amerindian men who would have to leave. So would non-Amerindian women with Amerindian spouses. This was aimed at Coolie Jane. Some people also said that mixed Amerindians not born in the village would have to go, as they were not really villagers. Spouses and children of people to be expelled could go or stay as they pleased. They were Oreallans, and Amerindians with a claim to the Indian Right.

It was not just enemies or distant affines of non-Amerindians who said they should be made to go. Jacob Vlet (55), Austin's wife's maternal uncle and a member of the Family of households to which Austin belonged, told me emphatically — and spontaneously — that Austin owned nothing in the village. Pointing to Austin's house he announced passionately that it did not belong to him. Nor did his farms. Nor anything else. He was not a villager and could own nothing in the village. When Philip Duncan came he would be made to leave.

On the other hand Austin's wife's maternal grandparents, also members of the same Family, said the Captain was making himself an ass by saying things which obviously were untrue. Austin and February, who was keeping another of their grand-daughters, could not be made to leave the village as their wives were Oreallans. That gave them the right to live there.

The outcome to all this excitement was an anticlimax. The people weeded the village in preparation for Mr Duncan's arrival. Coolie Jane supplied the drinks to reward the villagers for their labour — a claim to

Mattie. Mr Duncan never came. Had he done so he would have expelled no-one. Non-Amerindians in unions with Amerindians were given the right by the administration to live in Amerindian communities with their spouses and children.

In practice there were rare exceptions to the principle that the non-Amerindian could not become a villager. This was possible only under exceptional circumstances, since it involved the outsider changing his racial identity and becoming accepted as an Amerindian.

Case 6:19   Franklin Arupa was a light skinned Coloured (Afro-European) man of 54 who had lived at Orealla since he was a small child. His Black ancestry was not evident in his phenotype – at least not to me! His physical appearance was similar to that of many villagers who were regarded as pure Amerindians by their fellows. His parents brought him and his older brother from the Dutch Shore to attend the village school. Both brothers grew up in the village and took Amerindian wives. Over the years the fact that they were not of Amerindian ancestry largely became forgotten, as no symbols remained to retain its meaning within the context of Orealla life.

Franklin became incorporated into the village not only through marriage and kinship, but also by developing Amerindian patterns of behaviour and adopting Amerindian attitudes to other groups. He publicly presented himself as an Amerindian. He had no good word for the Black Nation that provided some of his ancestry, and condemned the government of Guyana as a 'damn Black government' because he believed its policies were designed to assist Blackpeople at the expense of Amerindians. To all except a few persons who remembered his childhood, and who also disliked him, he was an Amerindian. But despite his long residence at Orealla and his initimate relations with the villagers he could not have achieved such total acceptance had his phenotype been more readily identifiable with other Nations.

Despite Franklin's opposition to Blackpeople two of his daughters married Black men (Austin Johnson and February, Case 6:17). Franklin opposed both unions because the men were Black, and both daughters eloped to live with their keepers at Deanville sawmill because of his opposition. Franklin said he was so angry that in both cases he thought of taking his shotgun to shoot the man. He said he was gradually reconciled to the unions and could not wish for better sons-in-law.

Although Franklin was Coloured by ancestry, when Oreallans said his Black sons-in-law should leave the village they did not then add that so should Franklin. He had become an Amerindian by Nation. Nor did they blame him because his daughters took Black husbands. It was not his fault; a man cannot control the behaviour of his grown up children. In fact Franklin's initial opposition to his daughters' marriages probably was more extreme than would have been that of many other Oreallans, which may have reflected his awareness that he was not by ancestry an Amerindian. It was a statement to the community that he was Mattie.

Franklin's brother, who died in the early 1960s, also became an Amerindian, through the same process. He was actually made village Captain, by the priest of Orealla at that time. Most of the people who talked about him as Captain did not say he had not been an Amerindian. They contrasted his performance of his duties with that of the present Captain, to the latter's detriment.

The aged Portuguese lady (Case 6:16) had also become an Amerindian. But her Portuguese ancestry was remembered more than Franklin's Coloured ancestry. It was not because she was considered an outsider. Her ancestry was remembered because of the way she became an Amerindian. Portuguese:Amerindian unions were rare on the Corentyne, and this involved a Portuguese woman who came to live with an Amerindian in the Amerindian community. Her non-Amerindian ancestry was remembered not because it evoked criticism, but because her union with an Amerindian was regarded as a form of compliment to Poor Bucks. Her phenotype fell within the range that could be classed as pure Amerindian, and she had Amerindian sons and daughters who were admired for their light skin.

11

In 1948 P. Storer Peberdy, Field Officer for Amerindian Affairs, described Oreilla as 'a half-caste town'[34], implying that a large portion of its population had a significant, and visible, degree of non-Amerindian ancestry. In June 1967 I calculated that there were 29 Amerindians resident at Oreilla who had a non-Amerindian parent. The racial composition of this category is given in Table 6:1.

The ages of these persons were from one to over seventy years. Thirteen were under 10 years of age, and of these approximately one quarter were the product of casual sexual relations.

I calculated that there were 61 Amerindians with a non-Amerindian grandparent but without a non-Amerindian parent. This figure undoubtedly was an understimate, although it was unlikely to be so by more than ten per cent. Twenty-four of these persons were below the age of ten. Forty-two were below the age of twenty. The oldest was over sixty. Racial composition is given in Table 6:2.

Table 6.1 Persons with one non-Amerindian parent.

Sex of parent	Race of parent	Number of persons
Father	African	6
	Coloured (Afro-European)	9
	East Indian	2
	Doogla	1
	Chinese	2
Mother	East Indian	6*
	Portuguese	3**
Total		29

(* Children of one mother.)
(** Children of one mother.)

Table 6.2.   Persons with a non-Amerindian grandparent (i.e. parent half-Amerindian.)

Race of grandparent	Number of persons
African	32
Coloured (Afro-European)	10
Chinese	8
Portguese	11
Total	61

There were a few persons with both one non-Amerindian parent and one half-Amerindian parent. These have been counted in Table 6:1 only, so the two tables are mutually exclusive. Among the 61 persons in Table 6:2 are a few with two half-Amerindian parents. They have been counted once only, and the 61 persons in Table 6:2 are 61 different individuals.

Beyond this genealogical depth racial mixture was unlikely to have any significance for the mixed Amerindian's relations with other members of the community. Non-Amerindian ancestry usually was significant only when it was recognizeable in the individual's appearance. Beyond the second generation this rarely was the case.

If we compensate for persons who may have been overlooked and include non-Amerindians who were in domestic unions with Amerindians, there were about 110 persons resident at Orealla with at least a grandparent of non-Amerindian race out of a resident population of 797, or about 14 per cent[35]. While this was a significant figure it could not qualify Oreglla for Peberdy's 'half-caste town', and it is significantly lower than Drummond's figures for Amerindian:other race births on the Pomeroon river in the late 1960s[36]. (On the Pomeroon contact between Amerindians and the Coastal population was more intense, and the distance between Amerindian communities and Coastal settlement much less, than on the Corentyne.) It is possible that most Oreallans had some non-Amerindian ancestry, usually African, but the majority looked 'pure' Amerindian and were classed as such by themselves and their fellows, even where the fact of non-Amerindian ancestry was vaguely remembered.

The position of the mixed Amerindian was more equivocal than that of the non-Amerindian. Oreallans' ideology was that persons with Amerindian ancestry and raised in Amerindian communities were Amerindians, fully entitled to the Indian Right. In this they agreed with the interpretation of the officials who administered the Amerindian Ordinance. Discussing concepts of descent with Oreallans I argued that since a person took his tribe from his mother, then someone whose mother was Black and whose father was Amerindian should be Black. The people were adamant that he was Amerindian.

However, in practice Oreallans made a racial distinction between persons raised at Oreglla or in its vicinity and born from matings between Amerindians and non-Amerindians, and those born elsewhere to such parents and coming to reside at Oreglla or in its environs when adult. The former, whom I will categorize as mixed Amerindian insiders, were regarded as Amerindians. The latter, whom I will categorize as mixed Amerindian outsiders, had a more ambiguous status and often were regarded as non-Amerindians. People did not articulate this distinction, they said all mixed Amerindians were Amerindians, but it tended to be observed in practice.

When Oreallans argued each might use any ammunition at his disposal to disparage the other. If one party was a mixture his non-Amerindian ancestry was likely to be used against him. He would be told he was not an Amerindian and had no right to live in the village. But if he was raised in the village the accusation was an expression of conflict between persons, not of opposition between the community and the mixture. In fact the accuser recognized that he was an Amerindian with an inalienable right to live in the village and full claim to the Indian Right.

The type of mixture influenced the importance attached to the fact of mixture in any particular case. If it was with White or Portuguese the mixed Amerindian was unlikely to be insulted, because it did not produce an undesirable phenotype. Indeed, if it lightened his skin he would be admired for it. On the other hand mixture with African tended to produce the most obvious, and undesired, deviation from the 'typical' Amerindian phenotype and was most likely to promote derogatory comment during argument. But mixtures suffered no disability in finding mates and establishing domestic unions because they were mixtures. If one did it was because women believed that as an individual he possessed undesirable personal qualities.

Case 6:20   Rupert Vlet's (45) father was an African headmaster at Orealla who had an affair with a married woman, and Rupert showed his African ancestry strongly. He was born and raised at Orealla and all the villagers were his relatives. He was admired as the best Bushman in the village — in other words as the best Amerindian in a craft in which Amerindians prided themselves — and was married to an Amerindian and had six children.

Rupert owned two heifers which he kept in the village pasture. The pasture had been neglected and the posts and wire were broken, and the animals got out and ruined a farm the Captain had planted in cassava and plantains. The Captain went to Rupert and asked for compensation, but Rupert said the Captain had made his farm too close to the pasture and must take responsibility for what had happened to his crops. The Captain retorted that the pasture had been condemned and Rupert should not keep his heifers there. If he attended village meetings he would know village policy. The two parted on bad terms.

Immediately after this incident the Captain was sitting in his yard with several friends who had come to attend his matrimani. They were commiserating with him and deploring Rupert's behaviour, and again and again the phrase was repeated, 'Look what go happen when he race be over we'.[37] They were implying that Rupert was a Blackman, not an Amerindian, but none of them believed it and few would have insulted him with it to his face. To the people he was an Amerindian, and it was only because they were in dispute that the Captain designated him a Blackman.

Case 6:21   Caleb McIntosh (59) was born at Orealla and had lived there most of his life. He had moved recently to Sipuruta to work for the forest ranger station. His mother was Amerindian and his father a Blackman, and his Black ancestry showed itself strongly in his phenotype.

One night Caleb went to a drinking party at Orealla which was also attended by Theodore Williams (59), an Oreallan who disliked him. Theodore insulted Caleb and told him to get off the village as he had no right to be there. He was not an Amerindian. He shouted that Caleb claimed he was an Amerindian, but he (Theodore) had never seen an Amerindian with woolly hair.

The next day all the people were talking about the incident. They said Theodore was wrong to insult Caleb, especially as he had given no provocation. Theodore had no right to say he did not belong to the village. Caleb was an Amerindian who had lived all his life with his relatives at or near Oreallla.

In Case 6:21 note the Guyana use of hair rather than skin colour as the indicator of African ancestry, even though Caleb also had very dark skin. Theodore's claim that he had never seen an Amerindian with such hair was untrue. There were other persons with negroid hair in the village whom he would not think of calling non-Amerindians. Hair was being appealed to as the symbol of non-Amerindianness because to do so suited Theodore's purpose.

The position of the mixed Amerindian who was not raised in the village was more equivocal. In contrast to the mixed Amerindian insider, when people said he was not an Amerindian and had no right to live in the community they often meant it. The criticism was an expression of opposition between the community and the outsider. Mixed outsiders usually were living in domestic unions with Oreallans and were regarded, to a lesser degree, in the same manner as were non-Amerindians with Amerindian spouses. This was true even when their Amerindian genealogy was known to the villagers. Frequently in such cases people would pretend ignorance of the mixed outsiders genealogy.

Case 6:22   Paris Simmons (44) and his older brother Joseph (47) had a Warao mother and a Chinese father, both deceased. They were born in Paramaribo, where they received a better education than most Amerindians, but had lived on the Corentyne river most of their adult lives, at Wassiabo,where their uncle was Captain, and at Oreallla. They had many relatives on the Corentyne, and were married to Oreallla women and had children. However although the people knew their kinship links both were considered outsiders and many people professed ignorance of their genealogical ties. The villagers said they were Chinese, not Amerindians, and should not be allowed to live in the village.

Paris was widely disliked because he used his knowledge and education to humiliate people in argument and make them look foolish. People said he thought he was too clever and sarcastically nicknamed him 'The Curator' for it. When he walked past, children sometimes shouted after him that he liked to hear the sound of his voice, a criticism they had heard their parents make. These comments were not made about Joseph, who was more popular, but he was widely spoken of as an outsider and a non-Amerindian.

One afternoon Paris was criticizing Amerindians. He said Buckpeople were stupid because they would not get together to defend their rights. The Amerindians present told him he was not a Buckman, he was a Chineeman, so he had no right to call them stupid. With what appeared to be genuine feeling Paris replied that he did not know what he was.

Case 6:23   Corlette Sabajo (35) was mixed Black and Carib. He was from Suriname and lived at Orealla with an Orealla woman, and they had five children. One night Corlette and a friend had been drinking and they went to Coolie Jane's shop to buy more drink. The shop was shut and Jane was away, and her young son refused to open and serve them. Because they were drunk the two men pulled some of the manicol slats out of the wall and reached in and took some bottles of wine, intending to pay the next day. Before they could do so Iris complained to the ADO, and Corlette and his friend were accused of taking the wine and damaging the shop. They did not deny the charges, but pleaded mitigation and the ADO and a visiting police inspector, who together heard the case, accepted that they had acted with good intentions. They ordered the two men to pay $15 to Coolie Jane for the wine and the damage. The story became celebrated at Orealla as a case of 'break and enter'. The people said Jane had made exaggerated claims about the number of bottles of wine taken and the damage done. They said that instead of coming to Orealla to make trouble she should have stayed in Skeldon. Because the behaviour of Corlette and his friend had been well-intentioned, and because Jane was a Coolie, they considered them innocent.

Two weeks later Corlette was at a birthday party when he became involved in an argument with the old man in whose house the party was being held. The old man ordered him to leave. Drunk, Corlette protested and Rupert Vlet tried to persuade him to leave before the argument caused trouble among the drunk party goers. But before he could go one of the old man's adult granddaughters, a domineering woman, bustled up to support her grandfather and started insulting Corlette. She asked Corlette if he was going to hit the old man and told him he was always getting into trouble. Corlette replied he had only been in trouble once, over the break and enter, and left the house.

Just outside he was accosted by Philbert Benjamin (25), an aggressive young man who had a hostile relationship with him, who called him a 'Black dog' and threatened to take a knife and stab him.

The stress on the term 'Black' left no doubt that it was intended as an insult. The two drunk men stood in the night insulting each other, calling one another 'raas' and 'dog', surrounded by intoxicated Amerindians from the party. They were kept apart by Joshua James (47), Philbert's uncle and a shopkeeper. He stood between them, at the same time supporting Philbert and criticising Corlette, who he claimed owed him money on goods bought from his shop which he refused to pay. The feeling among the onlookers was against Corlette, who was considered to be disrupting the party. One man said to me, 'Look how this one Doogla[38] fellow spoil the party.'

Corlette went away but returned a short time later and re-entered the house to a flurry of excitement. One of his friends had a drink with him and said the people should not argue as they were all Buckmen. Corlette replied that he no longer considered himself a Buckman; from now on he would be Black. Myself and a friend, Lionel, led him out to take him home.

Instead of going to Corlette's house we went to Lionel's house to drink tonic while Corlette complained that people in the village disliked him. He said it was mainly because he was Black, but also because he was Dutch and a Carib. They had been informing on him to the police and the ADO, saying he had brought spirits from the Dutch Shore and was selling them at Orealla, contravening Guyana's customs regulations. The ADO had called at his house to warn him. But it was a lie. Drink cost so much on the Dutch Shore that he could not possibly sell it at Orealla and make a profit. (Prior to this I had observed mainly good feelings towards Corlette, and I do not believe he had more enemies than other people. Currently he was working as a boatman with a Dutch development company working on the Dutch Shore, a job which gave him a good steady salary and may have occasioned some envy and complaint that because he was Dutch the company was biased in favour of employing him rather than other persons.)

Corlette left to go back to the party. I wanted to go after him and dissuade him but Lionel said to let him go; if he wanted to get into a fight that was his affair. A short time later we were returning to the party when we heard a violent quarrel and found Corlette in an argument with Joshua James' younger brother Joseph (45) and his wife. He had bought two bottles of Scotch Ale, and on passing Joseph's house he turned aside to insult him because he was Joshua's brother. Again we led him away. As we did so he threw an empty Scotch Ale bottle at the James, who shouted after him why didn't he go and marry his 'wife'? (Corlette was 'keeping' his spouse and was not legally married.)

Corlette wandered off and we continued on our way towards the party. On the path we met the village Captain. As part of his office he was a rural constable and responsible for law and order. He was walking away from the party, although his house was next door to the party house and he could not have failed to hear the arguments and fighting. We were some distance from it and yet we could hear the sound of violent argument. We stopped and talked and the Captain said he was going up the hill, where he had some important business. We said goodnight and as we continued on I remarked that the Captain was going in the opposite direction to the trouble. Lionel laughed and said that was always the case.

If Amerindian mixtures were brought up in Amerindian communities they learned to think of themselves as Bucks. They grew up in the Bush and learned Amerindian skills, and adopted Amerindian attitudes towards the national society. If Amerindian languages were widely spoken they learned those languages. They established domestic unions in the community with Amerindians and reared Amerindian children.

Writing of the mixed Amerindians of the Pomeroon river, Drummond records that if men left the community to live in a Coastal milieu they often changed their racial identity and became Black instead of Amerindian[39]. Contact between the Amerindian villages of the Corentyne river and the Coastal society of the Corentyne mouth appears less intensive than that between the Pomeroon down-river Arawak population and the Coastal settlements of the Pomeroon river[40], and mixed Amerindian men raised on the Corentyne river were unlikely to cross the racial boundary in this way. If they went to reside on the Coast they rarely remained for long because they disliked other racial groups and felt insecure in a hostile Coastal milieu, away from Amerindian companions. They would react as Amerindians to members of Coastal Nations, with uncertainty and suspicion, so if their Amerindianness was not evident from their physical type it would be from their behaviour and people would treat them accordingly. But the constraints on crossing were not all negative. As Amerindians they professed to be superior to Africans and East Indians, and they enjoyed the security of the Indian Right.

But the mixed Amerindian raised in one locality, where he was accepted as an Amerindian, and who moved to another, might find his racial status become more ambiguous as large numbers of Amerindians rejected his claim to be Amerindian. Full acceptence into the Amerindian group came not to himself but to his children. If they were phenotypically Amerindian they were fully accepted

On the other hand women with non-Amerindian spouses

sometimes left Corentyne river Amerindian communities to live on the Coast, and women going to the Coast to find work established domestic unions with non-Amerindian men. Their children were brought up with their fathers' people on the Coast and were raised as non-Amerindians, members of their fathers' Nation. As with Arawak and Warao tribal membership, the most important influence on the racial affiliation of the mixture was upbringing.

Non-Amerindian ancestry was unlikely to be of significance beyond the second generation and might be unimportant in that generation, particularly if the ancestor was not African and consequently the non-Amerindian characteristics were less obvious. Some Oreallans said they knew they had some African blood but that it was of no consequence. It was not expressed phenotypically and was not a matter brought up in argument. In any case, as genealogical remembrance was so shallow then if a great-grandparent was of other race it would be remembered only in a vague way. An Oreallan might know a great-grandparent had African ancestry. He was unlikely to know to what degree. He would simply know his ancestor was 'from the Black'.

Case 6:24   David Benjamin (44) told me he had some Black blood. His maternal grandmother was from the Black. But now in David it had come alright. He said, 'Now the hair has come straight', and he wanted nothing to do with other Nations, Black or Coolie. He said there were Black persons in Suriname who were his relatives, but he wanted nothing to do with them. All his Amerindian relatives visited their Black relatives when they were in Suriname, but he did not do so. He did not want to know about them.

Case 6:25   Gilbert Johannis (44) told me he had Black blood. He said a maternal aunt told him his grandmother had Black ancestry and if he had a daughter with African hair he was not to beat his wife for being unfaithful. It would be his Black ancestry expressing itself in his children. What his aunt said had come true. His four-year-old daughter had frizzy hair.

In these two examples note again how hair is used as the indicator of Black ancestry. Comments like 'Now the hair has come straight' smack of having got rid of a pollution. It is probable that many, if not most, Oreallans had some Black ancestry, but for the majority of these it had no social significance.

Notes

1 M.N. Menezes, (1977), p. 18; M.N. Menezes, (1979), p. 4.
2 Many East Indians have some important values and behaviour patterns they regard as Indian rather than European. L. Despres, (1967); cf. R.T. Smith, (1962), pp. 98–143, and R.T. Smith, (1967).
3 R.T. Smith, (1982) pp. 108, 112.
4 On the Corentine river I was told this by Amerindians (critically) and Blackpeople (proudly).
5 Menezes has recently questioned the belief that Amerindians hold hostile stereotypes of Africans (M.N. Menezes, (1979), pp. 5–6, 22–23). I can only document the situation as I found it not only on the Corentyne but elsewhere among Coastal Amerindians in Guyana.
6 Rogue. The Guyanese term is much stronger than the English.
7 This may be a fairly widespread misapprehension. Drummond records that the Amerindians of the Pomeroon river believe that the Amerindians of the Corentyne river are powerful obeahmen and sorcerers (L. Drummond, (1974), p. 406).
8 For accounts of East Indian culture see L.A. Despres, (1967); R.T. Smith and C. Jayawardena, (1959).
9 For details of lower class African culture see e.g. L. A. Despres, op. cit.; R.T. Smith, (1956).
10 See for example R.T. Smith, (1967).
11 *Goupia glabra*.
12 Porters.
13 For a sociological account of this development see R.T. Smith, (1966); R.T. Smith, (1967).
14 Make suffer. The term is much more embracing than the English 'to punish'. It can be either transitive or intransitive.
15 Blackman.
16 Anaconda (*Eunectes murinus*).
17 Menezes records these attitudes for Amerindians in nineteenth century British Guiana, and points out their historical basis in the exploitation of Amerindians by White officials. (M.N. Menezes, (1977), pp. 90, 191).
18 P. Kloos, (1971), pp. 238–63, and personal communication with Dr Kloos.
19 The ultimate West Indian swear word!
20 A.L. Epstein, (1978), p. 103.
21 Corentyne river; St Cuthberts, Mahaica river; Moruka river.
22 cf. C.Jayawardena, 1963, who frequently writes as though East Indian sugar workers think of *mati* as a set of rules or laws.
23 V.W. Turner, (1974), p. 274.
24 C. Jayawardena, (1963), p. 49. For a discussion of *mati* among East Indians see C. Jayawardena, (1963), pp. 48–52.
25 C. Jayawardena, (1968), p. 422.
26 C. Jayawardena, (1963), p. 48.
27 Ibid., pp. 48–9.
28 Ibid., pp. 139, 141; C. Jayawardena, (1968), p. 425.
29 See for example Mayer's précis of Jayawardena; '*mati* (matey) is the notion that people doing the same work are equal in status and prestige.

Any action that can be construed as indicating superiority thereby breaches *mati* and is an 'eye pass" (A.C. Mayer, (1967), p. 177).

30 C. Jayawardena, (1968).

31 'Doogla' is a term colloquially used in Guyana for a racial mixture, usually East Indian:African. It is not an officially recognised term.

32 L. Drummond, (1974), pp. 265–7.

33 This is shown by the numbers of females resident at Orealla compared to males. In June 1967 these were 377:420. The discrepency was particularly marked in the age cohorts 10–19; 20–29; 30–39. The numbers for Sipuruta in the same month were 43:53. (A.D. Sanders, (1972), pp. 39–42.)

34 P.S. Peberdy, (1948), section XV.

35 I have not included a number of persons with a non-Amerindian grandparent who were not resident at Orealla but whom the villagers considered to be Oreallans.

36 L. Drummond, (n.d.).

37 This was a few months before Guyana achieved independence.

38 In fact Corlette was not a Doogla as the term was generally used on the Corentyne (i.e. an East Indian:African mixture). The colloquial Guyanese for an Amerindian mixture was Boviander — a term rarely used at Orealla. The man was employing the term Doogla to stress that Corlette was not an Amerindian.

39 L. Drummond, (1974), p. 243–5; L. Drummond, (n.d.), p. 14.

40 L. Drummond, (1974).

CHAPTER 7

The Village as Competitors
Eyepass

1

Case 7:1   One day I was sitting talking with an Amerindian friend outside his house. He had a number of fowls which were scratching around his yard searching for food and among them was one of a type I had not seen before. Instead of walking and running like the others this particular specimen waddled like a duck. Intrigued, I asked my friend what kind of fowl it was. He replied that it was an ordinary chicken. When it was young someone had broken its back. It had survived, but was crippled and could not walk properly. By way of explanation he said that Orealla people were jealous of one another and if anyone acquired something other people would try to destroy it.

While it was not true that Orealla was full of people who crept around trying to kill one another's chickens out of spite, this kind of idiom typified one of the Oreallan's models of his community. He believed much Amerindian behaviour to be motivated by jealousy and suspicion, and that this was an important reason why Amerindians did not co-operate together. They were jealous of one another and suspicious of each other's intentions. When asked why they marked tools and utensils with their initials, instead of saying it was to identify them if they were mislaid Oreallans often said it was to recognize them if other people stole them, adding that people were dishonest and would steal from you if they got the chance. In fact the amount of theft at Orealla was small, but again this was one of the ways in which people saw relations within their community.

The theme of stealing recurred in Oreallan's accounts of the community and of their lives. People might claim that in the past they had obtained unique and valuable items which could have changed radically the quality of their lives, but that they had been stolen. These might be magical items. In the Corentyne river lived spirits known as Water Momma which were sometimes seen as beautiful naked white women. Occasionally they were seen combing their hair. If you found a Water Momma's comb you could bargain with her for wealth in exchange for it, and the names of wealthy outsiders who did so were quoted at

Orealla. One was the agent with the balata concession on the Dutch Shore, a Coloured man who lived in Nickerie and had Amerindian relatives at Orealla. Oreallans sometimes claimed they found such a comb but subsequently lost it, or had it stolen, or were afraid to take it. Consequently they remained poor.

Poisoning was another theme that recurred in life histories and discussions of village relationships. It was believed people sometimes attempted to harm the persons or livestock of those of whom they were jealous by resorting to poison. An old lady whose grandfather, a Warao, had been village Captain told me he gave it up because someone tried to poison him for it. She said the present Captain's father, an Arawak, wanted the captaincy for the Arawak. He made some poison and asked his wife's nephew to administer it to the Captain as he would not suspect him. Curious, the nephew tasted it to see if it really was poison and nearly died. When the Captain learned what had happened he took his family and left for Apoera. When he died his son was asked to be Captain but he refused, saying people would try to poison him. Much of this may have been exaggeration, but it illustrates the theme of poisoning. An authenticated case occurred in the early sixties when a shopkeeper's cow died through drinking from a basin of cassava juice. The shopkeeper claimed the poisoning was deliberate. This was denied by people who saw it happen, but certainly they made no attempt to stop the cow drinking from the basin.

The idea that people tried to harm those of whom they were envious was strongly expressed in magical beliefs. Oreallans believed people might throw jumbie arrows on those they disliked. In the past people knew more magic and were able to kill in this way, but now they could only cause pain. A person might acquire a bacro[1], a small but very dangerous spirit. If buried in a bottle beneath the house of an enemy it caused him great pain; his foot twisted and the women of the house became barren. There were bad 'passwords' (spells) which could be put upon a person to make him ill, causing headaches and fever. Oreallans claimed to know the names of people who used these techniques for anti-social purposes, and a person who became ill might think someone had harmed him and believe he knew who was responsible. Persons who were particularly successful sometimes were believed to have attained their success by magical means, and envious persons might claim these means were anti-social. But no-one was openly accused of practising anti-social magic, for the same reasons that no-one would have been accused of being kanaima. People who used anti-social magic might not direct it at anyone in particular. For example, they might bury jumbie arrows in the ground so that anyone walking over them was afflicted. This was done purely out of malice.

But there was also the belief that wickedness was dangerous and brought its own retribution. There was the danger that your own wickedness would kill you. Ronald McIntosh, the kanaima, was said to have been killed by his own wickedness (Case 3:2). If you knew a bad password you had to use it on someone or it would work back on you and kill you. If you had a bacro you had to take care of it and feed it well or it would turn on you and kill you.

Case 7:2   The most graphic account I received of wickedness killing its perpetrator concerned a man my informant claimed threw jumbie arrows. He died of a mysterious illness in the early 1960s. My informant said he threw a jumbie arrow on a man who had it taken out, placed in a split papaya fruit[2], and buried. As the papaya rotted so did the thrower. His skin peeled off leaving him red, like a deer. His family took him to Springlands and Nickerie, to the doctor to try to cure him, but it was no use. They took him to an obeah man who said he could do nothing because the man's own wickedness was killing him. He was a shopkeeper and widely disliked in the village, and although not everyone told the story of the jumbie arrow and the papaya it was widely believed that he was killed by his own wickedness.

There were many kinds of charms and spells which might be used to protect from harm, or to turn harm back on its sender. Some promoted harmonious relationships. Passwords were written on house beams to prevent fighting in the house. Chalk crosses were drawn on doors and near windows to keep out evil spirits. A leaf with a red centre was a bina[3] which when rubbed on your lips and forehead made your enemy lose his enmity when you met. People might wear various charms and talismans for the same purpose. The forms taken by these practices were of many kinds and drawn from many sources. Binas and passwords from traditional Amerindian beliefs. Creole beliefs about jumbies[4] and vampires. Talismans from Old Moore's Almanack to ensure luck. Psalms from the Bible or from European and American almanacks, used for a variety of purposes. There were many others.

Concepts of luck and fate were well developed and were one explanation for personal success or failure. Men had lucky days on which to go hunting, revealed through personal experience. From past experience people also learned whether they had good or bad luck when they worked together logging and hunting. A person who had several unsuccessful domestic unions, or whose life had been unsuccessful in some other way, might claim to have been born with bad luck, blaming this on some factor such as his Zodiac sign. People obtained charms to achieve luck, and there were binas for numerous kinds of activity.

People were believed not only to harm each other's persons and property. They also tried to destroy each other's relationships and reputations, by spreading scandal about one another; telling lies; and trying to humiliate one another.

2

One way in which grudges and jealousies were expressed was in the practice of informing to the authorities. Someone who infringed the laws of Guyana or Suriname was likely to be informed on. When asked about informing Oreallans said, 'that is the Amerindian way', meaning that was the way Amerindians behaved and they had to accept it. They implied an inevitability about it all. Amerindians were jealous of each other and because of this they informed on one another. The practice had a long history at Oreallan. It was said that some useful obeah practices, such as turning old cigarette packets into five dollar notes and making empty tobacco tins fill with tobacco, were stopped through individuals informing on the practitioners to the police and the Customs and Excise.

Living on the Guyana-Suriname border provided ample scope for informing. Much informing concerned the smuggling of small items of contraband, such as drinks and tobacco, into the village from the Dutch Shore without passing through the Customs and Excise at Springlands. White Ox, a cigarette tobacco from Suriname, was used widely by Amerindians on the Corentyne river and brought to Oreallan illegally from the Dutch Shore. Police from Springlands raided shop-keepers when informed they were selling White Ox or other Suriname commodities. (Oreallans were cynical about the identity of informers in these cases, believing shopkeepers informed on each other to try to eliminate competition.) Other offences which often led to informing were gathering forest products from Suriname, such as dalibana palm leaves or Brazil nuts, without a license or for commercial purposes. Here informing was to the 'Dutch police' and the victim was in danger of arrest if he ventured on the river, a much more drastic consequence. When criminal offences such as fights, assaults, and attempted rapes occurred at Oreallan the police might first learn about them from informers and come up-river to investigate.

People complained constantly that others did not fulfil the obli- gations of their relationships with them. Each party invariably blamed the other over relationships which had broken down. This was evident, for example, in the way people talked about their ex-spouses. I remember only one person being complimentary about an ex-spouse. Discussing his domestic life a man referred to an ex-keeper as 'a good woman'. His comment was so unusual that it stood out from the volume of data I had collected on marital relationships.

Oreallans could be said to take a pragmatic approach to life, being influenced strongly by the particular circumstances of any situation in which they found themselves. In the recent past houses were abandoned when a death occurred in them, because of the mystical danger created by death. Now that houses were more substantial, permanent, and expensive structures this had become less common. The belief that death was dangerous remained and people took measures to protect themselves from its effects, but they were unlikely to abandon a house unless they had evidence that they were in danger if they remained. Then they would move, but they would try to dismantle the house and take it to a new site. Decisions such as where to live and with whom to reside were often decided on practical grounds. People chose to work in activities such as logging and balata bleeding which brought relatively quick returns rather than take off a few days each month to work on village projects which promised larger long-term economic rewards. One reason they gave was that they were poor people who had to 'hustle for a living' in order to earn money to support their families and pay their debts. This attitude was one reason for the failure of all village development projects, and it rested on a sound material basis. Oreallans needed ready money to buy Coastal commodities, and were always in debt to local shopkeepers.

Oreallans took a fatalistic view of many of their activities and relationships. They expected to be unlucky or let down, and when they were they cursed and complained but often believed that they could do nothing about it. Rice had come to rival cassava as main food staple, and was eaten with most meals. It was bought from village shops or directly from Springlands. Some persons had tried to grow their own rice but their efforts were usually unsuccessful as they lacked the necessary skill. They accepted failure fatalistically, and it was probable that most would not try again. Oreallans often did not expect to be successful, especially when they tried a new enterprise. Some men made their rice fields too close to the river and the plants were eaten by capybara[5]. They accepted it resignedly as fate. Parents expressed the same attitude when talking about the death of children. Most parents had lost at least one child through illness or accident, and when they discussed their deaths their attitudes were fatalistic. A man of 44 who had lost several of his children said of his youngest child, a baby a few weeks old, that he was not counting it yet but would wait a while to see if it lived before he did so, in case it died like the others. Oreallans were particularly fatalistic about their relations with outside individuals or groups. They suspected them of Advantage and expected them to be acting in their own interests and those of their Matties, which were unlikely to be those of Amerindians.

Oreallans believed it wrong to interfere in another individual's affairs. They were his 'story' and it was wrong to 'mix in another man's story'. They were a matter for the individual concerned, although close relatives were expected to assist, advise, or criticize because they were kin; and close friends could do so because of the strength of the friendship tie between them. Disputes should be the concern of the parties involved unless they threatened serious trouble, when the local government authorities were expected to intervene. If two persons got into a fight no-one tried to stop them who was not a close relative or friend, unless there was danger of serious injury. Instead they sent for relatives or friends of the antagonists to intervene.

Case 7:3   The only case of possible incest that came to my notice illustrated this attitude towards other peoples' affairs. An old man told me how a deceased friend had had a son by a casual affair with a married woman. He was told about it by the father, who informed a small group of his friends when they were working together in the Bush. No-one else knew it was his child, including the mother's husband. When the boy grew up he entered a domestic union with his biological father's daughter, not knowing they were brother and sister. Their biological father was dead and none of the men who knew of their supposed relationship said anything, as it was not their story. (The names of brother and sister were given to me. Both were living in the village, although no longer in a domestic union together.)

Although one model Oreallans had of their community was of persons in mutually hostile relationships, their behaviour towards one another usually was not surly or vindictive or overtly suspicious. Typical behaviour was jocularly aggressive. Oreallans constantly joked with one another, and interaction between friends was characterised by jocular criticism of each other's behaviour. People joked about themselves and about others, and one's own and other people's misfortunes were turned into jokes which revealed a deep sense of irony. Sexual and racial themes were important topics in joking, and unsocial behaviour was not only criticized, it was joked about at the expense of the unsocial individual who could find himself saddled with an unflattering nickname in consequence. A young man who became notorious for drinking other people's shop-bought drinks without buying his round became known as 'Bug' because he 'sucked'. Because he was called Bug his younger brother, who did not behave this way, came to be called *Kayaba* (Arawak, Flea). A man who was called

'Cassey' because his name was Charles became notorious for beating his wife when he was drunk. When Cassius Clay became a famous boxer people started to say that Charles must have been nicknamed Cassey because he was such a great fighter of women!

3

Except in their common relationship as Bucks to the wider society, Oreallans did not believe that all villagers were of equal social standing. Some were entitled to greater esteem than others because they filled more adequately certain deference-entitlements.

Gossip revealed an intense concern with personal reputation[6] and was the mechanism whereby most reputations came to be maintained at a relatively equal level. Much Orealla gossip was slander, talk intended to discredit rather than pass information for its own sake[7]. It was used by individuals to criticize others, thus implying that the criticizer was a better, more moral, person.

Oreallans saw themselves as competitors for esteem. This was illustrated by their attitude towards the performance of their children at school. Most parents took little interest in their children's academic performance, kept them away from school to help with domestic tasks, and did not bother to find out if they were playing truant. However, when the schoolchildren received their annual marks parents suddenly became intensely interested. All the marks were released the same day, and by that night most parents had discovered the relative performances of all the schoolchildren in the village. A child who did badly would be volubly told off by its parents and usually threatened with a beating. They would tell it that it must do better next year *for their sakes*, and draw unfavourable comparisons of its performance with those of children of other parents. They saw a child's performance as influencing the reputation of its parents within the community, and they sought to know the performances of the children of other people. After a few days the marks were forgotten and parents ceased to be interested in their children's academic performance until the same time the following year. The same attitude was revealed in reactions to the school Christmas party. When a small boy failed to win any of the prizes his mother was very angry and abused the headmaster as a thief because she had donated money for the prizes. But she was also angry with the boy for not trying hard enough and told him he must try to win something next year, *for her sake*. In both cases parents saw themselves as being in competition with other parents, through their children, for esteem within the community.

Oreallans recognized a number of criteria as entitling an individual

Boy with iguana

to deference. All were achieved criteria. For men, many were concerned with occupational success. A man should maintain himself and his dependents at a reasonable living standard, which meant being a hard worker and a good income earner and not spending so much of his income on sporting that his dependents' living standards suffered. Technical skill in performing Bush tasks and occupations was admired, and as all Oreallans were good Bush and river men to be outstanding in this sphere of activity meant to demonstrate very high standards of Bushmanship indeed. There were a few specialist occupations in the village, which could be achieved by very few, which should give the holder high esteem. They carried special responsibility; were salaried; and required special knowledge or ability for their attainment and performance. They included schoolteacher and village Captain. (There were a number of other posts which their holders claimed entitled them to special respect, but the claim was not recognized by other Oreallans. They included village councillor, church councillor, and village catechist.)

Behaviour contrary to that required for these deference-entitlements carried negative deference. Laziness and wasteful spending were condemned. Both were usually associated with what Oreallans considered to be excessive drinking, which was defined by its consequences and not by amounts drunk. Excessive drinking was spending so much time and income on drinking that your standard of living and that of your dependents suffered in consequence.

Being legally married carried higher esteem than being in a consensual union, as this was the only truly respectable form of domestic union[8]. (This did not apply to persons who had recently entered domestic unions, or to persons who could not marry because one partner was already legally married.)

The qualities that should give a woman esteem were mainly domestic qualities. A woman should be hard-working and carry out her domestic and farming tasks efficiently. She should not engage in extra-marital affairs. Women considered marriage a more important status-indicator than did men. In consequence a woman would hint to her keeper that they should marry, as she believed it would increase her social standing, whereas he was often unconcerned[9]. Laziness and drunkenness destroyed a woman's reputation. A woman who was thought to drink heavily was criticized more than was a man, and usually women drank only at parties and matrimanis and on public holidays.

Because Oreallans saw themselves as being in competition for social standing a person's success in terms of one deference-entitlement often was turned into criticism by other villagers, who claimed it was achieved in immoral ways. Or a person who was successful in terms of one set of criteria was critized in terms of other criteria by which he was less successful, thus reducing his reputation. Economically, shop-keepers were the most successful members of the community. But far from being respected for their ability and success they were derided as having achieved their supposed wealth at the expense of their fellow villagers. They obtained their income by overcharging their fellow Bucks. They Advantaged them. The man who occupied a position which should carry esteem, such as schoolteacher or village Captain, had his standing reduced by criticisms that he performed his job badly, used his position for his own gain, and attained it through favouritism. Achievement was counteracted by criticisms of immoral behaviour. One's social standing consisted of other people's manipulations of contrasted sets of values. People's reputations were diminished by appeals to Manners and Respect and accusations of Advantage.

The pattern of behaviour required by Manners and Respect included respect for age, refraining from violence, controlling one's drinking so that it did not interfere with one's domestic responsiblities or cause arguments or fights, and following a code of respectable sexual conduct. This was not only the ideal pattern for the community, it was that propagated by the church and the administration. It was the only ideal pattern for women, but men had an additional set of values, antithetical to Manners and Respect, concerned with what men considered manly behaviour. Their successful pursuit should entitle men to esteem among their fellows. They included drinking and sexual conquest. On the other hand men were contemptuous of those men who were braggarts and liars ('liard mouth').

To men drinking was not only a recreational activity and a stimulating act. It was a manly activity. A man should be able to consume large amounts of drink while comporting himself as a man, retaining enough self-control to stop himself behaving foolishly or anti-socially. Men prided themselves on their sexual conquests, and their sexual exploits provided much of the conversation of men working together in the Bush. Men said it was good to have an 'outside wife', by which they meant a mistress, but one must be careful not to let one's spouse find out. But one man would condemn another's sexual exploits when they caused trouble; or if they were with his spouse or the spouse of a close friend or relative; or if he was jealous of the individual concerned. In this set of values blame was allocated situationally, not because the act was intrinsically immoral.

Women judged each other's reputations, and were judged by men, in terms of Manners and Respect. Women disapproved of men's pursuit of masculine values and criticized them in terms of Manners and Respect. They made constant complaints and criticisms about the behaviour of men in general and of their spouses in particular. But in their endeavours to raise their own reputations men also criticized other men's masculine behaviour. They could do so in two ways. They could criticize manly behaviour *per se*, because it was opposed to Manners and Respect; and they could criticize manly behaviour when its performance, as it almost invariably must, brought about a dramatic breach of the values of Manners and Respect – when drinking resulted in a fight or in some other stupid or anti-social behaviour, or when a man was caught with someone else's wife and there was trouble – in other words, when a man failed to behave as a man pursuing manly values should, and brought about a public breach of Manners and Respect.

Men thus criticized other individuals when they pursued masculine values, while pursuing them themselves. But older Orealla men criticised young men in general for their masculine behaviour, for their drinking, fighting, and sexual behaviour. At Orealla there was no ritual or prescribed age to mark the transition from social child to social adult. At 16 a person was a child. By 20 he or she was recognised as adult. During the intermediate period was a time when the child was asserting claims to adulthood that were rejected by its parents and by the community. Children started behaving in ways they considered adult. They had sexual relations and boys drank and fought. Because of the lack of any institutionalized transition to adulthood these attempts by young people to claim adult status caused inter-generational conflict. Young people cheeked their elders and refused to obey them. Youths roamed the village in small gangs looking for drinks. They were criticized by their elders because they were 'small boys' trying to act like 'big men', and because they got drunk, made themselves sick, fought, and insulted their elders.

Even after their adulthood was recognised young persons were criticized by the older generations. They were criticized for being lazy, wasting their money on clothes and sporting, and behaving disrespect-fully. In fact young people had different values from older persons. They had worked for their money and they wished to enjoy themselves drinking and having sexual liaisons before they entered domestic unions and took on family responsibilities. They had different patterns of expenditure. Because they had no responsibilities they were able to spend their money on gay clothes, dresses, trousers, leather shoes, and sun-glasses. Young persons ideal models were not the hardworking responsible family person but the attractive young woman and the dashing young man. Young men took masculine values to greater extremes than did older men. They were more ready to fight and they prided themselves on being good fist fighters. But when they entered domestic unions and settled down they rejected the ultra-masculine values of their recent past.

The older generation complained that youth no longer had Manners and Respect and claimed this was a recent development. However, information collected from life histories suggested that at Orealla young people's behaviour had not changed significantly during this century and that in their youth older people had behaved just as irresponsibly. Old men particularly took pride in recounting the drinking and sexual exploits of their youth.

In the competition for esteem a 'pure' Amerindian might criticize a mixed Amerindian, particularly one who on some criteria was deserving of higher social standing than himself, by inferring that he was not an Amerindian and therefore had no claim to the Indian Right and so was removed from the competition.

As there were no protected statuses in which individuals could invest any success, people were unable to elevate themselves above the competition taking place in the village and their reputations were constantly reduced through criticisms of their behaviour. There were a few individuals who did not fulfil adequately many of the deference criteria. They were regarded contemptuously by most of the community. They were lazy individuals who spent much of their time drinking rather than working. Because of their reputations they might have difficulty obtaining credit from the village shops. Men in this category might have difficulty finding people to log with them as it was believed they would not do their share of the work, and they were unlikely to enter domestic unions as those qualities which gave them their bad reputations made them undesireable as spouses. However the majority of villagers filled adequately most of the deference criteria and attained and maintained the same general standing. But no-one was able to achieve a reputation outstanding from the others. It was not a situation in which a few persons became elevated above the mass; instead a few were put below. Oreallans could not compete for social standing in the wider society and were given none. They competed intensely for esteem in their community, but achieved little or none.

An individual who openly claimed superiority in a confrontation with another was likely to be criticized. Such an assertion might contravene the pattern of Manners and Respect appropriate to the age and kinship relationship between the parties. It would certainly be construed as an insult by the person against whom it was made and so was likely to provoke a serious argument or a fight — behaviour that contravened Manners and Respect and for which the person making the claim was likely to be blamed. Many members of the community might consider his claim unjustified by his general behaviour. He was no better than the person he challenged, and by doing so he showed that he had 'ideas above his station' — that he professed to be better than his behaviour proved him to be.

It has long been recognized that joking can be a way of coping with contradictory social pressures[10]. Aggressively jocular behaviour appears an appropriate mode of adjusting to the problems imposed by concern with reputation on the one hand, and the negative consequences overt public claims to superiority can have for one's reputation on the other. By acting in this way people are able to criticize others, but make their criticisms a joke rather than an open confrontation in which they claim superior moral standing. If the victim of joking behaviour loses his temper this suggests he feels the criticisms are true and is ashamed of his behaviour. On the other hand by replying equally jocularly he both gets his own back and asserts his own claim to status. Oreallans applauded the ability to argue jokingly at the expense of one's opponent, but it was easy for such behaviour to go beyond propriety and become an overt claim to superiority, and even easier for your opponent to believe you had gone beyond propriety and meant to insult and humiliate him[11]. When this happened fights and serious arguments took place. This could happen between friends, but friendship was often strong enough to withstand occasional altercations. It was much more likely between enemies, and people who had hostile feelings toward one another often tried to avoid each other because of the likelihood of trouble arising between them.

4

Oreallans called a deliberate attack by one person against another's reputation an 'Eyepass'. An Eyepass was a form of assault against someone or something. Oreallans said camoodi (anaconda) Eyepassed deer, because anacondas wrap themselves around swimming deer and drown them. Used in this sense, Eyepass was a deliberate, aggressive attempt to curtail or reduce someone else's being. In jocular arguments the parties jokingly called Eyepass the pretended insults they made to profess that the other was foolish, did not behave properly, or was socially lacking in some other way. Eyepass could be used as a general term for an insult, and any action construed as a deliberate insult, under any circumstances, could be called Eyepass. However, in common usage the term was restricted to what were believed to be deliberate attempts by one person to humiliate or belittle another by claiming some form of moral superiority.

The term was rarely used for example to describe behaviour in domestic quarrels. Conflict between spouses was so common that it must be regarded as an aspect of the marital relationship. It was generated by structural factors. A wife was dependent on her spouse for money to support herself and her children, and women were critical of the masculine values held by men and of the way they spent their time. Conflict in the husband:wife relationship was a more intense expression of a wider pattern of conflict within the community, that between men and women. More intense because it took place within an inter-personal relationship defined by common residence, norms of authority and subservience, and detailed patterns of rights and obligations and constant reciprocal exchanges.

In their frequent quarrelling spouses accused each other of failing to fulfil their family responsibilities or carry out their domestic duties, but they rarely interpreted the many insults that flew as Eyepass. They had a ritual nature and were for private consumption. They were not seen as deliberate attempts to reduce the general standing of the individual within the village. When discussing other people's domestic quarrels Oreallans rarely said the couple had been Eyepassing one another. They might say they had been 'calling' each other. Or if one or other spouse was believed to have gone too far in his insults he or she might be said to have been 'stupid' or 'foolish' or 'playing bad'. Or some similar term was used; rarely Eyepass.

Case 7:4   Mathew Klaverweide (46) and his keeper Abigail (51) had been to a birthday party. They returned home after they had been drinking for some time, arguing loudly. Abigail, a Warao, kept shouting that Mathew was a lazy worthless Arawak who did no work and he should get out of her house. (The house was built by her legal husband. He left Orealla with another woman and so the house belonged to her.) After they had been home arguing for some time Mathew's younger brother Alexander (42) arrived. Alexander was a shopkeeper and he and Mathew were close friends who visited constantly and attended each other's matrimanis. But Alexander had also been drinking, was more drunk than either Mathew or Abigail, and was acting aggressively. Mathew, angry from his argument with his keeper, told him he should go home and sober up. This angered Alexander and he started insulting his brother, abusing him as 'poor' and 'hungry'. This made both Mathew and Abigail (who until Alexander arrived had been insulting Mathew with almost identical terms of abuse!) very angry. They told Alexander he should show Mathew respect because he was Alexander's older brother. Alexander continued insulting Mathew, and finally Mathew hit him and he left crying and shouting abuse. The next day when he was sober Alexander could remember nothing of the argument. He said drinking was bad, it made you do bad things. He must go to Mathew and beg his pardon because he was his older brother, so accepting his wrong in Eyepassing his brother.

Case 7:5   Lionel Francois (34) and I were drinking at a village shop, where several men were gathered outside drinking. I had just bought bottled beer for myself and Lionel when Arnold Gordon (36), a man towards whom Lionel was hostile, entered the shop. Lionel was tipsy and accused Arnold of coming to scrounge a drink. Arnold angrily replied by accusing Lionel of scrounging drinks from me. Lionel exploded in anger, threw his bottle out of the door, leapt on Arnold, and they both rolled out of the shop and started fighting.

I appealed to the men outside to help stop the fight but they were friendly with both antagonists and refused, saying it was not their story. At that moment James Gordon, Arnold's younger brother, came up and tried to stop the fight. But Lionel accused him of coming to help his brother and began fighting both brothers. One of the onlookers had been to fetch Lionel's wife and she and I managed to get the antagonists apart and drag Lionel home, where he sat and complained that the two brothers had started the fight by attacking him.

A few days later Lionel told me he thought he had been wrong about the fight. He now believed he had caused it and not the Gordon brothers, but although he thought he was in the wrong he would not go to Arnold and apologize because he did not like him. But he and James had a drink together to show there were no bad feelings between them.

In the first example the insults exchanged between Abigail and Mathew were considered by neither to be Eyepass, but when Alexander called his brother 'poor' and 'hungry' this was immediately construed by both Mathew and his keeper as Eyepass. Alexander was claiming superior social standing to Mathew by in effect saying he was poor through his own fault and did not support his family properly.

In the second case Lionel's comment to Arnold was intended as, and immediately interpreted as, Eyepass. He was stating that he considered himself morally superior to Arnold, that Arnold scrounged for drinks and did not work for the money to buy them, and did not buy his round as a man should[12]. But when Lionel attacked James this was not because he thought James was Eyepassing him. He believed, wrongly, that James had come to fight for his brother.

The term Eyepass was usually used to describe attempts by one person to reduce another's reputation in some way or demonstrate that he cared nothing for the other, that he thought him inferior. The term had the connotation of looking past or through someone; of ignoring someone as though he were not there. Oreallans, with their flair for descriptive phraseology, a flair they shared with other Guyanese and Surinamers, sometimes alluded to the concept without using the term itself as when one person would warn another, 'Not you take you blasted eyes and pass mine'.

An Eyepass was intended to make the other party 'Shame', to humiliate him by drawing attention to his anti-social or immoral behaviour or to his personal failings. Shame meant approximately the same as 'ashamed' does to an Englishman. It carried the implication of retreating, withdrawing, hanging your head because you were ashamed of your moral condition. In the Guianas there is a small plant with pinnate leaves that slowly curl up when they are touched. Oreallans called it 'shame bush' because its action reminded them of a person withdrawing in Shame. When I showed them a photograph of my Black maid holding my baby son Oreallans' first comment was that she was Shame. She was looking away from, not at, the baby, and they interpreted this as showing she felt ashamed of her Blackness in contrast to the appearance of the Whiteman's baby.

Shame was an important influence on Oreallans' behaviour. Concern with reputation meant Shame was easily felt for actions which reflected adversely on one's social standing. It was felt not only for one's own actions, but also for the actions of others which it was felt might reflect adversely upon oneself. When a child was accused of stealing another pupil's pen at school its parents were Shame and took it away from the school. They left the village for a while, ostensibly going into the Bush to farm and fish. A man who was strict about his daughters' sexual conduct was Shame when it became common knowledge that his fifteen-year-old daughter had stayed out all night with a young man. Most fathers would have beaten her and not been much concerned, but because he was widely disliked the incident occasioned much gossip and amusement in the village and he was Shame and withdrew her from the village school. Stupid or anti-social acts were shaming, the degree depending upon how bad the act was judged to be. Many shaming acts took place when people were drunk and lost control of themselves. To lie in the path in a drunken stupor, in view of passersby, was silly behaviour which caused amusement in the village. It was shaming but quickly forgotten. For a drunk man publicly to take off all his clothes and lie comatose was more amusing and more silly, and more shaming because it would be remembered longer. A drunken attempt at rape was far more serious and far more shaming. Others would remember it a long time and allude to it in arguments.

Not all attempts by one person to make another Shame constituted Eyepass. When a parent admonished grown up sons or daughters, drawing critical attention to their behaviour, perhaps publicly, in order to make them Shame for their actions, ideally this did not constitute Eyepass. It was a duty a parent owed a child, part of the norms of Manners and Respect, and usually was recognised as such by the recipient. Some persons had the right to rebuke other persons because of the norms appropriate to their age and kinship relationship. Older relatives might rebuke younger relatives for their bad behaviour. Other persons might claim the right because they were close friends or relatives and believed the tie between them was strong enough to prevent their action being interpreted as Eyepass, and they might feel that because of their relationship the admonished's actions had also shamed themselves.

I write 'ideally' and 'usually' because in fact any criticism might be interpreted as Eyepass, from whatever quarter. It depended on idiosyncratic factors in the situation of admonishment such as the personal relationship between the parties; the criticized's feelings of the moment; and whether or not the criticized was drunk. A person who was drunk and angry might interpret any rebuke, from anybody, as Eyepass. However in the examples given in the previous paragraph the admonisher would be unlikely to be making an Eyepass, and any audience would be unlikely to consider it such.

What characterized Eyepass was that it was a deliberate act to make someone Shame in order to claim higher moral standing than the shamed. That this was the aim of Eyepass was shown by the responses of people to Eyepass, both the immediate response of the person Eyepassed and the responses of the villagers when they discussed an Eyepass after it had occurred. Insults exchanged in a domestic quarrel were not Eyepass because they were ritualized complaints, not claims by one spouse to higher standing than the other. If a man attacked someone because he believed he had had sexual relations with his spouse he obviously believed there had been a deliberate infringement of his sexual rights, but the wronged husband would not consider it an attempt to claim higher social standing than himself. Eyepass was a claim to higher standing than another, detectable because it was done in a sneering, aggressive, or otherwise contemptuous manner to draw attention to the other's failings in order to humiliate him. Because it was performed for selfish reasons, ideally Eyepass constituted an immoral action. The claim usually was made in a confrontation between the parties, and Eyepass generally took the form of some kind of criticism of the behaviour of one party by the other rather than a statement that one's own standing was higher, a statement which would be likely to be construed as having ideas above one's station. A person of whom it was said 'he (she) has ideas above his (her) station' was believed to be claiming esteem to which he was not entitled.

An act considered Eyepass usually had three characteristics. It was believed to be deliberate. It took place between individuals. It took place in a face-to-face confrontation. Three examples of accusations of Eyepass follow.

Case 7:6   Lewis Highman (40) and Lionel McIntosh (45) had a relationship of enmity. At a birthday party one night a small group of drinkers, which included Lewis, Lionel, and myself, were sitting outside the birthday house, drinking and talking. I got into a discussion with Lionel in the course of which Lewis interrupted to draw Lionel's attention to my status, saying I was a professor and knew what I was talking about. I was educated, so Lionel should listen to what I was saying. Lionel misunderstood, believing Lewis to be claiming to be educated and saying that he was not. He took this as an Eyepass and told Lewis he was as well educated as him, and told the company that Lewis had been a notorious dunce when he was at school. The argument was getting heated so Lewis' wife came and took him away into the house, where he became drunk and abusive and was finally taken away by his wife and daughter. When he had gone Lionel derisively asked the company what right had Lewis to pretend he was educated. Everyone knew he was just an Amerindian and had only been to the village school, and was a dunce even there. Lewis was born on the Berbice river and Lionel jokingly told me he was a kanaima[13].

This is an Eyepass in the usual usage of the term. Lionel believed Lewis was claiming to be better than himself. He denied the claim and accused Lewis of having ideas above his station.

Case 7:7   One day I was at matrimani drinks following a morning matrimani to prepare a field for planting. William Fraser (66), also present, and myself had been asked to help with a small matrimani that afternoon to cut down a locust tree[14] on a farm newly cleared from the Bush. We left when it became cooler in the late afternoon and returned after the tree was felled. As we entered the house yard where the drinking was continuing Nathan Williams (63) got up from among the drinkers and walked away. William thought, incorrectly, that Nathan had done this deliberately to ignore me. He went after him and stopped him and they started arguing with William saying several times, 'You must not Eyepass this man'.

This is also a standard Eyepass. William thought Nathan was deliberately and ostentatiously snubbing me; showing publicly that he considered me of no worth.

Case 7:8   Nathan Williams was an old man with a reputation for drinking heavily and behaving foolishly, especially when he was drunk. Because of his poor reputation he was often treated with a degree of contempt by all but his close relatives. When teased or insulted he usually fell back on his age in order to demand respect, but this was generally ignored.

One night Nathan was drunk at a birthday party and instead of going outside to urinate he stood against a wall and relieved himself inside the house. Several people saw that he was doing and shouted at him to go outside. Nathan retorted angrily that they were Eyepassing him.

In this example it may be that the drunk Nathan, sensitive about his poor reputation, thought the onlookers were deliberately trying to draw attention to his reputation by publicly pointing out his bad behaviour, so claiming to be better than himself. On the other hand the circumstances suggest he may simply have considered their behaviour disrespectful because they criticised him, he being older than they. They were all adults in their thirties and late twenties, and none were his close relatives. This being so he may have used the term merely in the sense of a general insult.

An Eyepass took one of three forms. The Eyepasser might accuse the Eyepassed of not behaving according to Manners and Respect, for example by criticizing him for keeping his spouse and not being properly married as in Case 6:23 where Corlette Sabajo was criticised by Joseph James and his wife. Or he might accuse him of being inadequate in some way, as in Case 7:6 where Lionel thought Lewis had called him uneducated. Or he might slight him to show he considered him of no worth, as was believed in Case 7:7.

Eyepass was an interpretation by one person of the actions of another towards him, and my observations suggested the interpretation was often mistaken. Frequently no insult appeared intended. The accuser was over-sensitive in detecting Eyepass, an indication of Oreallans' concern about their reputations. Because Eyepass was a personal interpretion of someone else's behaviour, actions were more likely to be interpreted as Eyepass when they were between persons who were hostile towards one another. They anticipated insults. Between friends Eyepass was not expected and the parties were more indulgent towards one another's behaviour. Also, among a group of friends when a serious argument appeared to be developing between two of their number others often were able to divert their attention, so that the potential conflict failed to develop.

Case 7:9   A small group of friends was playing troopchall (whist) at matrimani drinks. Lewis Highman was losing consistently and began to get annoyed. One of his friends, Buto, was teasing him about his ragged trousers. Already angry because of his bad luck with the cards Lewis began to lose his temper with Buto. The other players then joined in teasing Lewis about his trousers, pulling and poking them so that all his attention had to be directed at trying to stop them pulling them off, causing him to forget his annoyance with Buto.

It is no coincidence that the examples involve situations where people were drinking. In this situation of heightened sensitivity and decreased self-control people were more likely both to make and assume Eyepass. The most serious Eyepass confrontations occurred at gatherings such as birthday[15] and wedding parties, where large numbers of people were drinking together. They were occasions when people who disliked each other participated in the same activity and were intoxicated. Eyepass consequently not only created a confrontation, it usually created a public confrontation. Not because this was an intrinsic aspect of Eyepass[16], but because the circumstances usually ensured a public. When Eyepass took place in public being made Shame was felt particularly strongly as one's humiliation became public knowledge.

The usual response to an Eyepass could only be called explosive. Two persons would be talking or arguing together, often as part of a small group engaged in animated conversation, and suddenly one accused the other of Eyepass and they were both abusing each other and cursing each other at the tops of their voices while other people tried to hustle them away from each other. If they were not closely related, relatives of one or the other were likely to take his or her side and abuse the other party in like fashion, while simultaneously trying to lead their relative away. The normal reaction of an individual detecting Eyepass against himself was interesting. It could be defined as a 'what makes you think you are so good yourself that you can accuse me...?' type of response. Instead of rejecting the other's criticism outright he accused him of behaving in a similar manner, implying that in fact the accused's behaviour was worse than his own and therefore he had no moral right to criticize. In Case 7:6, when Lionel McIntosh believed Lewis Highman had Eyepassed him by claiming to be better educated he retorted that Lewis only had the same education as himself, and even then he was a dunce at school. When the story spread through the village that the Black nurse insultingly told an Amerindian patient that Blackpeople had to teach his ancestors to wear clothes the villagers angrily rejected her claim. Whitepeople taught their ancestors to wear clothes. She belonged to a Nation that had never taught anyone anything. In the example that concludes this chapter (Case 7:17), when the shopkeeper Jeremiah James denounced the Captain and the catechist from the pulpit they rejected his claim to pass judgement on them by counter claiming that his behaviour as a shopkeeper showed him to be a thief, immoral, and a hypocrite.

The reaction of people to Eyepass often suggested they believed, or feared, the accusation to be true. It was not a denial of the accusation but an objection to being made to appear Shame and a denial of the superior moral standing claimed by the accuser. The nature of the reaction meant it would almost certainly be interpreted by the presumed accuser — whether or not he was innocent of the intention to Shame — as an Eyepass in its turn, which accounted for his equally strong response.

If the sober response to an Eyepass could be described as explosive the reaction when people had been drinking was even more explosive, Eyepass often precipitated a fight. People were drinking and talking, often in an animated crowd at a birthday or wedding party, when suddenly one person was screaming abuse at another while at the same time hitting him, and the other immediately responded in kind. Fights were generally of short duration because usually many people were present when there was drinking and some would drag the contestants apart and hustle them away. But while they lasted they attracted an enthusiastic crowd of (mainly drunken) spectators, and were the subject of gossip for many days afterward.

Fighting was bad behaviour. It was condemned as anti-social and most people were able to restrain themselves sufficiently when sober to prevent arguments turning into fights. The majority of fights took place when people had been drinking. They were common at parties, and I believe there was none among the many parties I attended at Orealla where there was not at least one fight. They were rare at matrimani drinks because there were fewer drinkers and they were usually friends.

Eyepass was not the only cause of fights. Most sober fights were the result of sexual or domestic disputes. Fights between spouses usually were over domestic matters. When two sober men or women fought it was because of sexual jealousy or because one believed the other to have had sexual relations with his or her spouse. Drunken fights might result from Eyepass; from domestic or sexual quarrels; from conflicting interests, such as ownership of a piece of moveable property; or simply from a mistaken belief that someone was about to hit you.

Case 7:10 Two weddings had been held on the same day and a group of men were carousing at Joshua James' shop, as a break from carousing at the wedding parties. It was a boisterous, light hearted gathering with everyone buying rounds of bottled beer. After the group had been drinking for some time Kenna, a boy of sixteen, entered the shop and bought a beer. He had been involved in an incident a few days before when he had been one of a group of young boys who had been drinking. They had stopped the Captain, Kenna's paternal uncle, on the main village path, insulted him, and threatened to fight him. The incident quickly became the village talking point. It was condemned by adults, who took the Captain's side. They said young people no longer had any respect. One of the drinkers, Clarence Johannis (38), started telling the boy off, saying he was a small boy and not a big man. He should not drink with men, and he should respect his elders and not insult them. Kenna ignored him and kept on drinking, and Clarence became more abusive and threatening. Kenna's mother entered and when she saw what was happening she tried to persuade him to leave. Kenna insulted her, Clarence became more abusive and James Gordon (32), a mild man who was Kenna's brother-in-law, asked Clarence to leave the boy alone. It was a bad thing he had done but let them forget it while they drank. Kenna's mother hovered around agitatedly. Clarence continued to insult the boy, swearing and threatening him. James' requests became demands. The atmosphere grew increasingly tense and Joshua's stepson began to close up the shop.

Suddenly James lost his temper. He leapt at Clarence and they fell from the shop veranda and rolled about on the ground, swearing and striking at each other. Several men dragged them apart and told them it was bad to fight, while they cursed and struggled to get at each other. Friends and relatives of the antagonists then led them away to their homes. As Clarence was led away James' wife ran shrieking after him and threw a lump of wood which bounced off his back. The drinking party was now broken up; the shop shut. James quickly recovered his temper and several members of the company accompanied him to his house to continue drinking. Kenna went along, but whereas he had previously been silent except to insult his mother he was now bragging about the fight. James told him he should be ashamed, it was his fault the fight had begun. At his house James said he would go to Clarence and apologise. (In fact he did not go, and Clarence came to James' house later, still drunk and angry, and the fight continued.)

In this example the fight was not a consequence of suspected Eyepass, but because Clarence was threatening James' young relative whom he felt obliged to defend. That he was prepared to go to Clarence immediately afterwards and apologise for his part in the affair shows he did not consider Clarence's behaviour to constitute Eyepass. Nor did Clarence interpret James' behaviour towards him as Eyepass.

Women also had Eyepass arguments, but they were less common than between men. Women behaved aggressively and jocularly, much as did men, but did not appear to be under the same pressure to detect Eyepass. They did not share the masculine values of men; and for them there was not the conflict between masculine values and respectable values. Fights occured between women but were rarer than fights between men, which helped explain their popularity. A fight between women always raised a good crowd and provided weeks of gossip, as it was more scandalous for women to fight than it was for men. As with public drinking by women outside of parties and public holidays, it was a more profound breach of respectable behaviour.

Case 7:11   At the August sport in 1965 three sisters — Shirley Johnson (35), Nellie Arupa (33), and their paternal half sister Amy Johannis (33) — were walking around the village together looking for drinks. They had close, friendly relations with one another. They were raised in the same Family of related households, sometimes in the same household, and although they were all in domestic unions they continued to live in the same Family. They went to drink at the house of a relative. The house was filled with people come to drink the August drinks. One of the drinkers, Iris Francois (36), was suspected by Nellie to be having an affair with her Black keeper. Iris was legally married to an East Indian but their marriage had broken up. Although she had a hostile relationship with Nellie she was friendly with her sister Amy. Everyone was tipsy and Nellie accused Iris of trying to steal her keeper. Amy did not believe the accusation and supported Iris. The argument developed into a fight between Nellie and Iris, which the spectators watched with great enthusiasm. As a result of her friendship with Iris, Amy found herself on the opposite side to her two sisters. Some men parted the contestants and Iris and Shirley left. Much to the amusement of the men present Amy sat down and cried because she had fought her sisters. The relationship between Amy and Shirley was very close, closer than that between either and Nellie, and Amy blamed Shirley for taking sides against her. She was very bitter and for ten days she pointedly ignored Shirley, even though they were in close contact every day. Other members of their Family, including their husbands, took no notice of their private feud. By the eleventh day Amy had mellowed and the two women worked together at a matrimani. At the matrimani drinks Amy asked me to take a photograph of herself and Shirley drinking together, an act of reconciliation.

Case 7:12   Isabella Wilson (50) was walking along carrying a bamboli jar on her head when she was stopped by four young women. The women, who were all close relatives, had been drinking and accused Bella of 'calling' them — spreading scandal about them in order to denigrate their reputations. Bella denied the accusation. There was a heated argument and when Bella turned away to go the women attacked her, striking her with their fists. The bamboli jar fell and smashed on the ground, and because no-one was present to break-up the fight it went on longer than one normally would. Bella was beaten and several days later was still in pain. She was examined by an Orealla 'doctor' who diagnosed that the beating had caused some ribs to overlap. He said he could not cure her because they had overlapped too far. Bella continued in pain and finally had to spend some time in Skeldon hospital. Because of her condition the police were informed about the attack. They made an investigation, and in consequence the four women were served with summonses to appear at Skeldon Magistrates Court on charges of assault.

In the first example the fight between the two women was not occasioned by Eyepass. In the second the young women believed Bella had Eyepassed them by spreading scandal about them in the village.

A woman might Eyepass a man and a man might Eyepass a woman. In Case 6:23, at the birthday party Corlette Sabajo was Eyepassed by the old man's grand-daughter who told him he was always getting into trouble. Corlette did not react by accusing her of Eyepass. Instead he admitted he had been in trouble over the 'break and enter' but denied ever being in trouble over anything else. The break and enter was still the major topic of village gossip and because of this he was still Shame for his behaviour. Consequently he neither denied the fact of having been in trouble nor began a serious argument. (Another person of course might have reacted differently.)

In one of the cases at the close of this chapter (Case 7:16), Lionel Francois contemptuously calls Albertina Klaverweide a 'scunt' (cunt). This was a definite and particularly blatent Eyepass, made without any pretence of provocation, and later Lionel gave her a bottle of beer as compensation for his behaviour.

As with Eyepass disputes between women, Eyepass disputes between the sexes were rarer than Eyepass arguments between men. Eyepass accusations between a man and woman might cause arguments between them, but they did not fight one another. No matter how drunk he was, or how provoked, I never saw a man assault a woman who was not his wife. Unless they were domestic partners men and women did not fight each other.

5

Jayawardena, in an analysis of conflict on a sugar plantation in British Guiana[17], interpreted the concept of Eyepass among East Indian estate workers as an offence against their egalitarian ideology, which was a refraction of *mati* (Mattie). When someone believes he has been Eyepassed by another claiming higher social status or prestige he appeals to the egalitarian norms of the community (*mati*). Eyepass is a breach of these norms[18]. By egalitarian norms he means the belief that all members of the community are equal in status and prestige[19]. Belief by the members of the community that they are all social equals is emphasised particularly in Jayawardena's 1963 work.

Jayawardena defined the concept of Eyepass among estate workers as: 'To eyepass someone (is) to wound his self-esteem, to belittle and humiliate him, to ignore his rights and claims. The notion of lowering a man's prestige and of depriving him of his dignity as a man by claiming an unjustified superiority (is) the essence of this offence[20].' The core of the concept is the same as my interpretation of Eyepass at Orealla, a deliberate attempt to claim superiority over another. But in his analysis of the political behaviour of sugar workers[21], Jayawardena focuses upon the importance of egalitarian norms. I did not find such norms within the Coastal Amerindian community, and in my examination I focus upon individual concern with reputation. Fundamentally Eyepass was a claim to higher esteem than someone else.

It appears that ideally Eyepass was always a wrong. Oreallans sometimes said, 'Na Eyepass Mattie', meaning it was wrong to Eyepass anyone. Eyepass was a wrong because it was done to draw attention to the faults of others for purely selfish motives. As such it offended against the human dignity of its intended victim. All Eyepass carried this stigma. Because it was intended to Shame for purely selfish ends ultimately Eyepass was an offense against Mattie, but it was Mattie as communitas, as people in the sense of being human beings. Mattie was the moral equality of being your fellow, not social equality. Most anti-social acts were offences against Mattie in this sense, and not just Eyepass. One cannot single out Eyepass as *the* offense against Mattie. The application of the term Eyepass was largely restricted to attacks upon reputation, but the term could be used for all kinds of personal attack. Ultimately Eyepass was classed together with all kinds of wrongful approach to other persons.

Oreallans regarded Eyepass as behaviour characteristic of Amerindians, and when they discussed it as such they criticized it for preventing Amerindians from acting together in accordance with Mattie in their relations with other racial groups. Amerindians did see themselves as social equals in their relations with the wider society, at the level of Buck. Here Mattie and social equality coincided. But Eyepass was not seen as the only cause of failure to act according to Mattie. It was part of a complex of attitudes and patterns of behaviour, such as concern with one's own interests and failure to co-operate for a variety of reasons.

Case 7:13   Samuel Vlet (50) was the village Captain's (47) older brother. One day they both attended the same matrimani and at the matrimani drinks Samuel told me what a good man the Captain was. He had to respect him because of his office even though the Captain was his small brother.

Shortly after this an argument broke out between the matrimani convenor and his wife and developed into a fight between the convenor and his wife's brother, who took his sister's side. This was quickly stopped by the drinkers, but as often happened when Amerindians were drinking, one fight or argument acted as a trigger to set off others. A woman, a village councillor, told the wife's brother he should not fight but should take his complaint to the council. Then she complained to the Captain that he should have intervened to stop the fight. The Captain lamely tried to defend his inaction by arguing that as the fight was in the man's house he had no right to intervene.

Suddenly Samuel exploded in abuse against the Captain. He leapt to his feet and cursed him, pouring out a torrent of abuse, calling him a raas and shouting that he was useless and never did anything but talk. The Captain, embarrassed, retorted that he was the Captain and Samuel would have to treat him with respect or he would lock him up. He warned Samuel not to Eyepass him, but Samuel repeated his abuse and stamped away shouting. When I asked someone what was happening he told me it was a 'Families story', but it was obvious that everyone knew what was behind it.

Samuel had some logs in the Backdam and had asked for the village tractor to pull them to the river. This had not been done, but the tractor had hauled the Captain's logs which had been felled since Samuel made his request. Like other Oreallans he believed his brother to be abusing his position to Advantage the villagers over use of the tractor, which was being driven by the Captain's daughter's husband, a member of the Captain's household.

The villagers' reactions to this confrontation were revealing. Some did not consider Samuel's behaviour to constitute an Eyepass. Others regarded it as Eyepass because of the manner in which he delivered his rebuke, but did not condemn it. In both cases Samuel's behaviour was believed justified because of the Captain's misuse of his authority. The Captain being aware of the feeling against him, we may interpret his counter-accusation as an attempt to brand Samuel's behaviour Eyepass and try to place him in the wrong, but this was rejected by the villagers.

The people's judgement in this case contrasts markedly with their reaction to Jeremiah James' denunciation of the Captain in church, given at the end of this chapter (Case 7:17), even though his criticism was similar to Samuel's. Jeremiah's action was condemned as Eyepass and there was almost universal support for the Captain, despite the fact that it occurred at a time when once more there was widespread dissatisfaction with the way he was performing his duties. In this case the people's dislike of Jeremiah was greater than their dissatisfaction with the Captain.

Eyepass was an offence against Mattie as human beings. But this was a distant level of social existence and in practice the morality of Eyepass might be judged against a number of criteria, and in some cases an act judged to be an Eyepass might not be considered wrong at all. Often when people discussed an Eyepass they merely rejected the accuser's claim to the right to criticize, on the same grounds as a person Eyepassed often did during a confrontation. They claimed his general behaviour was anti-social or immoral and often worse than that of the person he Eyepassed. He had ideas above his station. When people discussed Jeremiah James' denunciation of the Captain and the catechist (Case 7:17) they condemned him as a hypocrite. Lewis Highman was also considered to have ideas above his station (Case 7:6). When Paris Simmons said Buckpeople were stupid (Case 6:22) his audience told him he was not a Buckman but a Chineeman, therefore not only did he have no moral right to pronounce upon Buckpeople, he had no right to be in the village at all!

If an Eyepass was judged in terms of any set of moral principles it usually was not directly in terms of Mattie. Rather than being treated as an act involving persons as member's of groups Eyepass usually was treated as an act between individuals, and judged accordingly. As such it was likely to be criticized in terms of Manners and Respect, the idiom of relations between persons as holders of individual statuses. Mathew Klaverweide demanded Alexander show him respect because he was his big brother, and when Alexander was sober he said he must apologize to his brother for the same reason (Case 7:4). William Fraser thought Nathan was Eyepassing me because he believed he was making a show of ignoring me and not showing me the respect which was my due (Case 7:7). In Case 7:16, when Lionel calls Albertina a 'scunt' she replies that he should respect her because she is an older relative. People discussing these three cases might also criticize them in these terms and go no farther.

Some acts which constituted Eyepass might be condemned because the act itself was anti-social of its very nature, as well as being Eyepass. To spread scandal was of this order. It was wrong, as were other acts such as cheating, lying and stealing, which may not constitute Eyepass. Discussing the case of Bella Wilson (Case 7:12), people who believed she had spread scandal would always condemn her Eyepass because the act was wrong in itself. Such a judgement could be analyzed as an appeal to Mattie as communitas, the ultimate rationale for all moral action.

In some cases criticism of Eyepass might be made simply on the basis that it was untrue, that the action was unjustified because the Eyepassed was undeservedly accused. When Lionel Francois accused Arnold of scrounging and so caused a fight (Case 7:5) his accusation was untrue, and later he was prepared to admit it. Nor was Arnold a person who scrounged, whatever else he might do. Lionel's accusation was incorrect regarding this occasion and unjust if intended as a comment on Arnold's general behaviour. In practice other persons might condemn the Eyepass for these reasons, rather than because it was Eyepass.

These points are important. If the accusation made in an Eyepass was believed true by others they might not condemn it. Some persons believed the Captain was Eyepassed by his brother (Case 7:13) but refrained from condemning the act. The Captain's wrong was greater than that of Samuel. Similarly, an Eyepass might be regarded as justified by other people even if the accusation was incorrect in the specific situation in which it was made, if it could be considered a justifiable mistake given the Eyepassed's general behaviour. In the first example at the end of this chapter (Case 7:16) Lionel Francois tells Oswald Klaverweide to leave his beer alone. Oswald replies that he has bought the beer he is drinking with his own money. In this case the Eyepass was based on an incorrect interpretation of the situation. However, given Oswald's general behaviour many Oreallans would have regarded it as a reasonable mistake to make. People discussing an Eyepass might do so simply in terms of whether or not it was justified and leave it at that. If they considered it justified it might not be condemned. If it was unjustified it might be condemned, but no further reason for condemning it might be sought.

Eyepass against a person of low esteem was often condemned less severely than Eyepass against other persons. It was treated as a comment upon someone concerning whose general behaviour there was widespread agreement. Lionel was likely to be condemned less severely, if at all, for Eyepassing Oswald and Albertina (Case 7:16) than for Eyepassing someone else. Given this, the responses of Oswald and Albertina to Lionel's Eyepass are interesting. Instead of reacting by a virulent counter attack Oswald denies the specific accusation and Albertina makes a simple appeal to Manners and Respect. From my observations this was typical of their reaction to Eyepass. They were aware of their poor reputations and appeared to accede to them. Not all persons of low esteem reacted in this manner. In fact because they knew their reputations were poor some responded particularly aggressively and were especially quick in detecting slights.

But any justification for an Eyepass could be nullified by the consequences an Eyepass could bring. A person who made an Eyepass could be condemned because it caused a fight, whereas had this not been the consequence his action might have gone uncriticized. Conversely an unjustified Eyepass might be overshadowed by its consequences. In responding to a presumed Eyepass the women who beat Bella Wilson (Case 7:12) performed an act worse than the original Eyepass.

To recapitulate. An Eyepass, if criticized at all, might be criticized in terms of any of five criteria. As an offense against Mattie. In terms of Manners and Respect. As an unjustified assumption of superiority. As an incorrect accusation. Or because it caused trouble, in which case it might not be regarded as wrong in itself but because of its consequence. An individual might apply any or all of these judgements to an Eyepass. At root Eyepass was an offence against Mattie as communitas. It was not an offence against the kind of egalitarian norms postulated by Jayawardena. But in practice usually it was treated as an offence between persons and judgement of Eyepass had a closer association with Manners and Respect than with Mattie.

The discussion of various cases in this section has treated them as though each was likely to be judged in terms of one out of a number of criteria, but in reality different persons would use different criteria and reach different judgements. Not only did individuals judge specific cases of Eyepass differently, but because of the nature of Eyepass and of the circumstances under which it was usually detected, and because of the confused nature of the little drama that ensued, usually there existed differing interpretations among the spectators as to whether or not an act constituted Eyepass and which of two antagonists Eyepassed the other. When news of the incident was disseminated by village gossip any reality became further distorted. To a significant degree people's interpretations were influenced by their relationship to the parties involved. They tended to impute Eyepass where they wished to impute Eyepass, and allocate blame where they wished to allocate blame, and the consequence of involvement in such a drama for the principals usually was to keep their reputations as before. In terms of the overall structure of the community this was on a general level with those of most other people. In Case 7:5, even though Lionel came to admit that he was in the wrong in the fight with Arnold his close relatives continued to believe the Gordon brothers had ganged up on him because of an old grudge and attacked him without any provocation on his part!

6

If my interpretation of Oreallans' concepts is correct there were actions that more directly offended against Mattie, but these were termed Advantage not Eyepass. Advantage was incompatible with Mattie, which stressed similarity, equivalence, solidarity, and mutual assistance and trust. In contrast to Manners and Respect, which was rooted in social status, Mattie could be said to be rooted in trust. Advantage was a betrayal of trust. Advantage was always recognized as unjustified in itself. No desert attached to the Advantaged; his behaviour could never justify his being Advantaged. Advantage was an offence against all the qualities which constituted Mattie, even though a specific act of Advantage might not be an offence against codes of behaviour such as Manners and Respect or the laws of Guyana or Suriname.

Advantage was the misuse of power by the stronger to exploit the weaker. Given Oreallans' suspicions of the motives of other persons, implicitly they assumed that any position of power would be abused. Because of the Amerindian's lack of economic and political power persons believed to Advantage them were usually non-Amerindians, but the term was applied to some relationships and actions within the community. Shopkeepers were said to Advantage their customers. They overcharged them and became rich at their expense. The village Captain used his office to Advantage the villagers. In fights a big man was said to Advantage a small man and a sober man a drunk man.

These actions were not in themselves Eyepass, although their performance could involve actions interpreted as Eyepass, as suggesting the Advantager felt contempt for the Advantaged. In themselves they were not attempts to reduce the Advantaged's reputation. While they infringed his rights or just expectations they were not of their nature intended to make him Shame. In contrast to the typical Eyepass, Advantage could take place outside of interaction between the parties. The sawmiller could Advantage the logger or the government Advantage the Amerindian without them ever meeting one another.

Whereas Eyepass was primarily an offence between persons Advantage could take place between groups, or between persons as members of groups. Mattie involved relations between groups, and relations between persons as members of a group. Although Advantage was an offence against Mattie in any of its refractions, Advantage between Amerindians was particularly an offence against Mattie as a bond between like persons opposed to similarly constituted groups of persons, with Mattie at the level of Buck. Other Nations Advantaged Buckpeople. Amerindians should assist one another, should work together in accordance with Mattie to protect themselves from Advantage. Advantage within the community meant exploiting your fellow Bucks, and we may deduce from this that to Advantage a fellow Buck was to behave like an outsider.

Amerindian shopkeepers provide an illuminating example. In 1967 there were six Amerindian shopkeepers at Orealla, one at Sipuruta, and one on the English Shore between Orealla and Sipuruta. Collectively shopkeepers were described as 'rich'. They were thought to obtain their wealth by offending against Mattie. They were said to 'rob the people' (i.e. persons seen as members of the group). They Advantaged them. As a category they were conceptualised hostilely, and as individuals each was criticized for exploiting the people. The act of making a purchase was a hostile one. The purchaser threw his money down on the counter, and if there was any change it was thrown back by the shopkeeper. Shopkeepers were believed generally to overcharge on their goods[22]. Their behaviour was thus of a morally inferior kind, opposed to Mattie. All shopkeepers were described as having ideas above their station — their station, in this case, referring to their status as Bucks.

As well as taking Advantage, shopkeepers had other qualities which were those of outsiders rather than Bucks. They had a degree of power. Because the villagers had to operate on credit they were always in their debt. Much of a man's income went to pay for his household's credit to its shopkeeper, and he had then to obtain goods on fresh credit. The shopkeeper thus had a degree of control over a household's earnings and expenditure.

But shopkeepers also obtained their goods on credit, from a Chinese shopkeeper in Springlands, and their overheads were high. If they were to be at all successful they had in some measure to behave like outsiders. They participated in the recreational activities of the village, and particularly in drinking, less than other persons and consequently were thought to have ideas above their station. But they had to be sober to operate their businesses effectively, and they must not drink their stock. The only shopkeeper at Orealla who was really successful had to become a real outsider within the community in order to do so (Case 7:17).

Because of their occupation and its relatively large and consistent income shopkeepers were able to support themselves and their dependents without engaging in arduous work in the Bush to the extent that other villagers had to, another characteristic distinguishing them from their fellow Bucks. They were among those Oreallans who had luxury items such as radios and sewing machines. But in fact their life styles were not markedly different from those of other Oreallans, although some had begun to invest in capital items such as livestock, and in one case a tractor (Case 7:17).

Shopkeepers, in Advantaging their fellows, were behaving in a way which was un-Buck, and this was exacerbated by other aspects of their behaviour. They behaved in some ways as outsiders did, and this strengthened the hostility felt towards them. They were professing to be something they were not; they had ideas above their station. I believe a similar interpretation could be placed upon the accusation that persons who obtained positions of administrative power used it to Advantage their fellow villagers. Between Amerindians Advantage was particularly an offence against Mattie associated with Buck identity. In this way it differed from Eyepass. It was at this level that Mattie was associated with a belief in the existence of social equality, and it was Advantage rather than Eyepass which was the offence against equality.

There was a further way in which the concept of being Buckmen, of all being equally unequal in the face of the wider society, fed back into criticisms and arguments within the community. Because of their deprived position there were certain benefits available to other Nations from which Amerindians considered themselves excluded; and there were certain patterns of behaviour they considered appropriate to themselves as Bucks. Any attempt to claim esteem by professing the have access to these benefits, or behaving in ways inappropriate to being a Buck, were criticized as showing ideas above one's station. In Case 7:5 Lewis Highman was thought to be claiming to be well educated. He was derided because this was an absurd claim for an Amerindian to make unless he was a schoolteacher. The most outstanding example of ideas above one's station at Orealla was Jeremiah James, the shopkeeper whose case concludes this chapter. By rejecting the typical patterns of Amerindian behaviour Jeremiah had voluntarily excluded himself from the social life of the community.

7

Eyepass also took place between Amerindians and outsiders. When Oreallans detected Eyepass by outsiders they often regarded it as an adjunct to Advantage. Because of his powerful position the outsider believed he could show his contempt for Amerindians openly. In practice however the two types of action could be distinguished to varying degrees, and analytically we must differentiate between them.

Case 7:14   In May 1967 the Thompson's house burned down when the cooking fire caught some thatch loosened by the wind and rain. The household consisted of 18 people. Only a young girl and two children were present at the time and they escaped unhurt, but the members lost all their goods, including clothing and luxury items such as the household head's wife's sewing machine.

There was much sympathy in the village for the homeless family, who went to live with friends and relatives until they could build a new house. The following day two men organised a village collection to help them replace some of what they lost and were given provisions, clothing, hammocks, mosquito netting and other items, and about 30 dollars in cash.

In addition the ADO went to Springlands and returned with a large amount of clothing, for all ages and both sexes. The clothes were second-hand and many were worn and patched and some had holes, but they were in the same condition as everyday Orealla wear. Particular items often did not fit the person who would wear them and socks and shoes might not match, but none of this could have been avoided and in fact the ADO had made an outstanding effort to replace the lost clothing. His effort was even more commendable when it is remembered that he took it on his own initiative and was not obliged to help in this way.

I do not know the procedure the ADO employed to obtain the clothing, but the Thompsons assumed it had been donated voluntarily by people on the Coast. While they accepted the clothing, they did not applaud the ADO's act. Coastal people were collectively conceived as rich. That they had donated worn, second-hand clothing of the wrong size was interpreted as a deliberate act of contempt. They should have given new clothes, as befitted their wealth and status. It was assumed they had not done so because the clothing was for Buckpeople and so anything would do, and the ADO had connived at their action. The Thompsons laughed and joked as they held items up for inspection or tried them on, but Jethro (56), the household head, said 'Just because we poor people is no need to make we Shame'. The act was interpreted as Eyepass. (Notice how once again the unfortunate ADO was excoriated for performing his duties in an exemplary fashion.)

Often the Oreallan's rejection of Eyepass by outsiders took the same form as with Eyepass by fellow villagers. The outsider's claim to superior status was rejected. If he was a Coolieman or Blackman he was morally inferior, and Amerindians Eyepassed Blackpeople and East Indians in arguments. This reaction characterised face-to-face encounters with individuals who did not hold office. Officials often were believed to demonstrate contempt for Amerindians as Bucks. Amerindians accepted the official's superior status, but by terming his behaviour Eyepass they denied him the right to treat them without regard, even though their powerlessness forced them to accept the fact that he did so. As a human being the Amerindian claimed the right to be treated with courtesy and consideration. Not to treat him so was an Eyepass, which supports the interpretation of Eyepass not as an offence against social equality, but as ultimately an offence against Mattie as communitas.

Case 7:15   In June 1967 the Hon. Randolph Cheeks, United Force MP and Minister of Local Government in the PNC-UF coalition government, visited Orealla. There was a public meeting at which the people were expected to discuss their problems and grievances. Questions were asked about the mail service, the water supply, Amerindian land ownership, and other village concerns. Mr Cheeks committed himself to nothing but said all the problems would be looked into. This did not satisfy the people, who believed that as a government Minister he had the power to resolve their difficulties. They presumed he was prevaricating, and this reinforced their belief that the government had no intention of helping them because they were Bucks. The government was only interested in Advantaging Buckpeople, and the Minister's approach to their questions was itself a form of Advantage. He was using his status as Minister to avoid making any commitment.

Teacher Will asked if he could get a government loan to build his house. The Minister replied that if the government gave a loan to one person they would have to give to everyone and they could not afford it. The villagers did not accept his answer and after the meeting they complained that if you could not get help from the government then who could you expect help from? What was the use of asking about anything?

Someone asked about the recently erected rain water tank and its associated system of water pipes on the Flatland. When would it be in operation? He complained that the muddy Corentyne water at the end of the big dry season sometimes caused sickness when people drank it. In his answer Mr Cheeks said the villagers should boil their water, then it would not make them sick. The people said nothing, but they considered his comment an Eyepass. Everyone knows if you boil water it can prevent sickness, but they wanted a positive response in the form of a promise of some kind of assistance. They believed his answer showed not only that the Minister did not care about their problems, but that he held them in such low esteem that he thought they were ignorant or believed he could treat their questions flippantly. For weeks a distorted version of his answer was bandied around the village as a joke — 'If you want to solve the water problem, boil the water!'

8

In this chapter I endeavour to determine the relationship between three concepts, Eyepass, Advantage, and Mattie. I base my analysis on what Oreallans said about these concepts, how they employed them, and how they appealed to them to explain their own and other people's actions. But Oreallans did not analyze their concepts to the degree that I have done, and would have had difficulty defining them and articulating their inter-relationships. There is no doubt that the concepts were less precise and their use less systematic than I may have suggested. For example, the terms Advantage and Eyepass were sometimes used as alternatives. An Advantage sometimes was referred to as Eyepass, and less frequently the reverse was true. This we might expect. People do not define concepts rigidly and both Eyepass and Advantage were at root actions of the same class, assaults upon someone else for self-gain. As such both were ultimately offences against communitas. Again, forms of insult which were not regarded as attacks on reputation were sometimes described as Eyepass, because all were offences against communitas. But I believe my interpretation to accord with the manner in which the concepts were generally used.

I wish to conclude this chapter with two examples which illustrate some of the points that have been made. The first concerns two persons who were accorded low esteem. The second was the Oreallan who had achieved greatest success in terms of the economic criteria which qualified an individual for esteem.

Case 7:16 Oswald Klaverweide (38) and his younger sister Albertina (35) were accorded low status by all members of the community. Oswald was probably the man ranked lowest in reputation by the great majority of villagers, and Albertina was certainly the woman with lowest esteem. Both were lazy and drank heavily. Oswald particularly was notorious as a drunkard who preferred to drink rather than work. Both were classed as 'poor' people within the village, and this was blamed entirely on their behaviour. They lived in an overcrowded house of ten persons which was regarded as one of the poorer households in the community. Neither had ever been in a domestic union, although Albertina had two daughters, aged eight and one years, by casual sexual relations.

Because of his very bad reputation Oswald had difficulty finding people who would log with him, as they did not believe he would do his share of work. In 1966 and 1967 he was usually working with the village Captain, a relative, who appeared to be trying to take him in hand. He could no longer get credit from village shops unless he was guaranteed by a close relative, and again this was the Captain, who consequently was keeping an eye on him and trying to ensure he made his contribution to work parties. Oswald was recognised as one of the best native doctors in the village, particularly good at curing *nara*, a common and painful stomach complaint often caused by excessive drinking while neglecting food. This ability, from which he derived small sums of money as payments for his services, was insufficient to counter his overall reputation and he was often derisively referred to as 'Doctor Oswald'.

Oswald had never entered a domestic union and never would, although he wished to do so. He would be a bad economic provider. In this respect he was only one among several Orealla men, although his reputation was so bad any woman taking him would be derided for it by the rest of the community. Albertina however was unique in being the only woman past her early twenties who had never been in a domestic union. Furthermore it was unlikely that she would ever enter one, despite the scarcity of marriageable women in the community and the number of single men who wished to enter domestic unions. Her reputation for being lazy was so bad nobody wanted her as a wife, and this was reinforced by the fact that she was extremely ugly. (Both she and Oswald had protruding upper lips and cauliflower ears.) She was criticized as immoral, particularly by women, for bearing children without being in a domestic union. This was a criticism to which young women and separated women would not be subjected as the villagers knew they would enter domestic unions.

Oswald and Albertina were often openly treated with contempt. On one occasion when both were drinking bottled beer in a village shop I observed Lionel Francois with no provocation warn Oswald not to touch any of the beers he had just bought. Oswald took this as an Eyepass and indignantly replied he had bought the beer he was drinking with his own money. He took his money from his pocket and showed it to Lionel, asking why he was trying to make him Shame. Lionel ignored him, treated Albertina with contempt, insulted her without provocation, and called her a 'scunt' (cunt) — a blatant Eyepass. Albertina became very upset, accused Lionel of trying to make her Shame, and told him he should treat her with respect because they were relatives and she was older than he. Lionel gave her a bottle of beer to acknowledge he had behaved wrongly by insulting her and to make reconciliation.

Case 7:17   Jeremiah James (39) had the longest established of the six shops at Orealla. He and his father started a shop up the hill in the early 'fifties. Although it was not the first native shop at Orealla, at that time it was the only one. They shared the profits and expenses until they quarrelled and Jeremiah demanded his share of the business. His father left him with the shop and went down the hill and built another.

Jeremiah's father died in the early 'sixties and his business was said to have been declining before his death. He died of a mysterious ailment that caused his skin to peel off, and many people said he died because of his wickedness. He was said to have been a bad man who threw jumbie arrows on people, and some people believed he made a bacro to obtain success in his business. After his death Jeremiah moved down-hill and rebuilt his shop.

Jeremiah was a good businessman who managed his shop carefully, and it prospered. Shortly after his father's death he became converted to a Jehovah's Witness while visiting the Dutch Shore, and on his return to Orealla he preached in the village, going from house to house and proclaiming the Anglican Faith a lie. The headmaster, a Coastal East Indian, re-converted him and he became a regular attender at church. He adopted the Protestant Ethic, which at least as much as his business acumen accounted for his economic success.

Jeremiah was sincere in his Christian belief. Like other shop-keepers he made much of his sales on beer but with his conversion he became opposed to drinking, which he regarded as the principal cause of the Amerindian's 'backwardness'. He stopped selling beer and closed his shop on Sundays. He diversified his stock to keep items not sold by other shopkeepers. He was for example the only shopkeeper who sold clothing.

Jeremiah's religious commitment and new life style effectively cut him off from social life in the community and the people said he had ideas above his station. Some believed he killed his father by magic because of their quarrel over the business and his conversion was an attempt to salve his guilty conscience. People believed his business prospered because he had a bacro. At night it caused the furniture to move about in his house and made noises like someone walking on his corrugated iron roof. They said he came down the hill when his father died because he was afraid of the evil spirits that infested his old site. (They belonged to himself and his father.) When he started Sunday School classes he gave the children who attended the first class a small bag of sweets each to encourage them to come again. The villagers said it was an attempt to get them to go only to his shop when they were sent out to buy things by their parents. They said he was a hypocrite who preached in church on Sunday and then Advantaged the people.

Jeremiah invested the income from his business in capital. He bought a seining net, which he proved unable to use effectively, and three heifers, which were reared for meat and which he hired out to loggers for hauling their logs. One died from drinking cassava juice, an act which if not deliberate at least was not prevented by those persons who witnessed it. He also bought two pigs, but sold them when he decided it was against his religious principles to keep unclean animals. He tried growing rice, without much success.

As his shop prospered he tightened up on extending credit because customers often took over-long to pay. He stopped giving credit to his close relatives because they were the worst offenders, believing their kin ties gave them an especial claim on his forebearance. By doing so he offended against Manners and Respect and further cut himself off from the community.

In 1966 he bought a tractor. Before buying it he worked for three months logging in the Bush to raise the money for the down-payment, an act that typified his determination and single-mindedness. He hired a driver, a Dutch Coloured man who was keeping his niece and had been a tractor driver on the Dutch Shore. Instead of charging the loggers to haul their logs to the river he bought them where they were felled, hauled them to the Corentyne, and sold them to the buyman. In 1966 he was paying 12 cents per cubic foot of timber while the buymen were paying around 65. After the royalty of 5 cents he was left with a profit of 48 cents on every cubic foot. If the logger sold direct to the buyman he had to pay 25 cents to the village tractor to haul the log to the river, and the 5 cents royalty to the government, which left him with 35 cents. Although the people complained Jeremiah was Advantaging them, many sold to him because he paid on the spot and they did not have to wait several weeks for their money. In addition they did not have the problems of waiting until the tractor was able to haul their logs out of the Bush, finding a buyman, and waiting until he could come up-river to purchase their logs. Jeremiah had to find a buyman and from his profit had to pay his driver, pay men to load hardwood logs onto the buyman's boat, meet his overheads and pay any other expenses on the tractor, and pay off the hire-purchase debt. But by early 1967 the tractor was almost paid off and he had bought a second for which he employed another driver.

In January 1964 Jeremiah was one of the successful candidates in the District council elections and was made Vice-Chairman of the council. By the end of the year he had told the council he would no longer attend meetings because its decisions were not being implemented and councillors were not interested in their duties. He was particularly critical of the Captain, whom he blamed for lack of village development. In 1965 he presented a petition of grievances against the Captain to Mr Stephen Campbell, an Amerindian MP in the coalition government and Parliamentary Secretary to the Ministry of Local

Government, and the Commissioner of the Interior when they visited Orealla with the Canadian High Commissioner and Mr S. C. Knapp, a Canadian expert on Amerindian affairs undertaking an examination of Amerindian problems for the government of British Guiana. The petition was signed by twelve persons, all hostile to the Captain. Jeremiah tried to present it during a village meeting with the officials, but was told it would have to wait until all business was concluded. After the meeting all the villagers left and he had to present the petition on his own. He denounced the Captain but Mr Campbell, the Commissioner, and the ADO supported him and Jeremiah was unable to accomplish anything.

Jeremiah had three main complaints against the Captain. He was opposed to drinking and thought the Captain set a bad example. He was opposed to East Indian tractor drivers selling rum and rations to the villagers as he believed this encouraged them to be lax in paying credit to shopkeepers, and wanted the Captain to stop them working on the reserve. He thought the Captain supported the East Indians, and claimed his complaints to Mr Campbell and the Commissioner resulted in them being prevented from operating on the Orealla reserve. Finally, he thought the Captain was incompetent and his incompetence was a hindrance to village development.

Because of his association with the church Jeremiah was made a member of the Orealla church council and became a lay preacher. The priest considered him the most progressive individual in the village and gave him his support. The priest also believed drinking to be the main block to Amerindian advance and was opposed to the Captain because he drank. He believed the government of Dr Jagan deliberately to be trying to undermine the influence of churches among Amerindians for political reasons, and regarded local government institutions as the mechanism whereby this was being brought about. Consequently he opposed the ADO and Captain because they were representatives of the threat to the churches' relations with Amerindians. When Jeremiah used the church council to pursue his criticisms of the Captain the priest supported him. When Jeremiah complained to him that an East Indian tractor was working on the reserve he wrote informing the ADO and demanding it be removed. (In fact the ADO had asked the tractor to haul on the reserve as the village tractor was overworked. Jeremiah was using his position on the church council to try to remove competition to his own tractor.)

Jeremiah usually gave the sermon on those Sundays when the priest was not visiting Orealla, and often denounced drinking and anti-social behaviour from the pulpit. The people took this as Eyepass. They said he was a hypocrite because he criticized them for their behaviour while at the same time Advantaging them, and they said he had ideas above his station.

In April 1967 a new priest was appointed to Skeldon Parish. On his first visit to Orealla he called a meeting of the church council, at which Jeremiah denounced the Captain and other members for their behaviour and accused them of being drunkards. The priest tried to reconcile the opposed individuals. Because of his bad relationship with the previous priest the Captain had ceased attending meetings of the church council. The new priest asked him back and appointed him to read the lesson at Sunday service.

In June 1967 Jeremiah gave a very provocative and scathing sermon in which he denounced people who drank and did not perform their duties. It was obvious he meant the Captain and the village catechist, who had charge of church affairs in the priest's absence. This was a massive Eyepass and was condemned by the villagers. The Captain walked out of the sermon in anger and shame and complained to the ADO, and the catechist wrote a letter to the priest asking that Jeremiah be removed from his position as lay preacher. The ADO delivered the letter and the priest visited Orealla and again tried to reconcile the antagonists. While he did not remove Jeremiah, in his morning service he told the congregation they must not use the pulpit to denounce one another — a public rebuke for Jeremiah. This was where matters stood when I left the village a fortnight later.

In 1968 Jeremiah contested the election for village Captain. He received 51 votes to the incumbent's 175, with another shopkeeper coming a poor third with ten votes.

The villagers negated Jeremiah's remarkable economic success by claiming he used evil magic to attain it, and that he killed his father. In achieving his success he had to behave in a manner which was interpreted as having ideas above his station and which contravened Manners and Respect. His behaviour was interpreted as selfishly motivated and he was seen to Advantage the people. In his attempts to achieve a condition he considered more conducive to social development people did not support him in his attacks on the Captain, even though many of them were dissatisfied with the Captain's performance, because they resented Jeremiah's behaviour, suspected his motives, and envied his success. His religious commitment was taken to indicate not his conviction but his immorality. All this was exacerbated by his indiosyncratic religious behaviour.

Notes

1 This is the spirit known on the Coast as baccoo.
2 *Carica papaya.*
3 A good luck charm (E. Im Thurn, (1967), p. 288). Binas were lanceolate leaves of various plants, for different kinds of luck.
4 Spirits.
5 *Hydrochoerus capybara.*
6 'A man's reputation is what is said about him. It is the overall response of people to both actor and role performance; an assessment not only of the results achieved but also of the manner in which they are achieved.' J. Hutson, (1971), p. 79.
7 R. Paine, (1967), p. 279.
8 A.D. Sanders, (1972), pp. 272–3.
9 Ibid., p. 272.
10 A. R. Radcliffe-Brown, (1956a); A.R. Radcliffe-Brown, (1956b).
11 See for example K.H. Basso, (1979), pp. 35–76.
12 Buying your round was an important expression of manliness and generosity.
13 Lionel's father was the reputed kanaima in Case 3:2.
14 *Hymenaea* sp.
15 Everyone's birthday was celebrated by a drinking party, no matter how young they were. Consequently at Orealla village there were often several birthday parties each week.
16 cf. C. Jayawardena, (1963), p. 141, who argues that Eyepass among East Indian plantation workers both presumes an audience and ensures one.
17 C. Jayawardena, (1963).
18 Ibid., p. 139; C. Jayawardena, (1968), p. 425.
19 C. Jayawardena, (1963), pp. 48–9; A.C. Mayer, (1967), p. 177.
20 C. Jayawardena, (1968), p. 425.
21 C. Jayawardena, (1963).
22 See A.D. Sanders, (1972), pp. 171–6, for an attempt to assess the truth of these accusations.

CHAPTER 8 | The Amerindian Community

1

Oreallans classed behaviour into four main types. These were Manners and Respect, Mattie, Advantage, and Eyepass. The degree to which they were aware of the meanings of these concepts was influenced by the manner in which they learned how to apply them. Oreallans learned the use of all four through interaction and by observing the behaviour of others. Manners and Respect was also taught more formally, as it constituted the norms of inter-status behaviour. The concept of Advantage was acquired less formally, but it was taught and people discussed it continuously. Both concepts were relatively simple and people were aware of a great deal of the meanings of both. They were often less aware of the meanings of Eyepass and Mattie. People could pronounce upon Mattie as a personal relationship between friends. Usually they could say much less about it as an aspect of the membership of groups. I believe the concepts of Mattie, Eyepass and Advantage were particularly important keys to understanding much Orealla behaviour.

Oreallans had four types of model of their community. As holders of particular kinds of rights from which others should be excluded. As occupiers of differentiated statuses in ordered inter-relationships. As persons who were jealous of each other and continually tried to do one another down. As persons sharing a common identity, and hence a form of equality which should carry mutual responsibilities.

The models revealed the assumption that inter-personal relation-ships were of two qualitatively different ideal kinds and that each person should be in both kinds of relationship with everyone else, as holders of inter-related statuses and as particular types of being, co-members of groups. From this we may deduce that Oreallans saw the groups to which they belonged as of two kinds. These were not mutually exclusive, the same group often could be viewed in both ways. It could be seen as internally differentiated, consisting of a pattern of inter-related statuses with different obligations and with differential prestige associated with the carrying out of these obligations. In this view the group was seen as from 'inside', consisting of positions whose relations were hierarchical, differentiated, competitive, and unequal. This was the field of Manners and Respect. The model was that of V.W. Turner's 'structure'[1]. The second kind of group consisted of persons of the same kind, equal and undifferentiated. Instead of being seen as from 'inside', as differentiated, the group was seen as from 'outside', as a unity, often in segmentary opposition to other unities of the same order. The model was that of Turner's 'communitas'[2]. This was the field of Mattie. A person was a member of the first kind of group because he occupied particular statuses. He became a member of the second because he was accorded a particular quality by his fellows, that of belonging, of being 'one of us'. If the first type of relationship was not reinforced by acknowledgement of the second then an individual's membership could be weakened, and he might be regarded as not really belonging to the group.

The five folk models of the community together provided Oreallans with an overall picture of their village and of its place within the wider social arena. The models of the village as Families and of the village as competitors consisted of antithetical conceptions of relations within the village. The village as Families was concerned with Manners and Respect. On the basis of genealogical relationship, sex, age, racial identity and social position, Manners and Respect could be applied to all persons with whom one came into contact. Much of the behaviour in the alternative model of the village as competitors was recognised as antithetical to Manners and Respect. Manners and Respect referred to relationships between persons as holders of statuses and members of categories such as adult, child, man, woman, male and female. Eyepass was an offence which belittled the way persons performed in these positions. The two models were used in a dialectical fashion, constantly encroaching on each other and shifting back and forth in any individual's interactions and in his view of the community. He applied them to different persons, or to the same person at different times. Neither attacked the Indian Right. Consequently there was no incompatability in their application to all persons with whom Oreallans came into contact.

In contrast to the dialectical relationship between the models of the village as Eyepass and as Families, the models of the village as Bucks and as Oreallans were complementary. They reinforced one another. The village as Oreallans equated village membership with Buck as a category, instead of with more restricted criteria such as birth or genealogical relationship. It also demonstrated that others were more powerful than Amerindians. The village as Bucks stressed that its members should have special ties with one another as a consequence of membership, and that other racial groups sought to Advantage them.

The Indian Right strengthened the idea of the community as Buck by adding a material dimension. It linked communitas with structure by making Buck a status with rights denied members of other racial groups. It stated one of the reasons why other groups sought to Advantage Bucks, and what it was they had to lose. By doing so it became the ultimate brake on the extension of Mattie across racial boundaries, influencing personal relationships and restricting community membership.

Manners and Respect and Mattie provided two ideal patterns of behaviour for the community, and the models of which each was the idiom were what Ward has termed ideological models of relationships, models of what relationships between members of the community should be[3]. Whereas Manners and Respect applied to the field of inter-status relations, Mattie applied to the field of inter-group relations and of relations between persons as members of a group. It was the proper relationship that should pertain between persons who shared a common identity. It operated at successive levels of grouping and in part was expected to operate in a form of segmentary opposition — group members acting together as Mattie against members of other groups of the same order. It stressed the existence of different kinds of person. But Mattie was also the idiom of incorporation. It crossed group boundaries to incorporate persons into one's group, or expressed membership of a wider group encompassing one's own. Consequently it was also the concept which derogated inter-group opposition. Mattie stated the equivalence of persons; ultimately of all persons. All human beings were persons and Mattie should apply to all.

However the West Indian colonial ideology of racial difference made it difficult to extend Mattie across perceived racial boundaries, as it was based on the idea that different 'races' did not consist of the same kind of persons. They were qualitatively distinct and not equivalent. The idea that members of a racial group assisted one another to Advantage members of other racial groups, which was linked to the idea of racial difference, also inhibited the extension of Mattie.

Together the complementary models of the village as Oreallans and as Buck defined the margins of the community, who belonged and who did not. In doing so they made a virtually absolute dichotomy out of many of the major sets of opposed categories of the Oreallan's social world. They equated them together to form the two halves of a fundamental division which Oreallans saw as forming their world, with the Amerindian on the disadvantaged side opposed to the rest of the society. They equated villager:non-villager with insider:outsider; Amerindian:non-Amerindian; poor:rich; powerless:powerful and exploited:exploiter. It may be that there is a sense in which we can include kinsman:non-kinsman, as the way Oreallans talked of the village consisting of Families often implied that all members were Amerindians. ('We is all Bucks from this Corentyne river and so we is all Families.') This would be consistent with their other assumptions. For most people the view of the village as Buck took priority over the village as Families. No matter how many relatives a non-Amerindian had in the village he was regarded as an outsider without rights, even by most of his closest Amerindian relatives. In this way the position of the non-Amerindian married into the village contrasted with that of the Amerindian from elsewhere who married into the village. The latter was regarded as a villager, with full rights.

Oreallans' perceptions of their community and their world created for them a fundamental dichotomy overriding tribal identity and dividing Amerindians from other racial groups. The non-Amerindian part of the dichotomy was less monolithic than the Amerindian half. It contained sub-divisions, most notably between Whitepeople on the one hand and Blackpeople and East Indians on the other. This was based on the Amerindians' (and the national society's) belief that these were qualitatively different kinds of person, and was supported by the perceived attitudes of these groups towards Amerindians.

Race was the master symbol that incorporated and represented all the oppositions of the dichotomy. Consequently it influenced relationships with the offspring of matings between Amerindians and non-Amerindians. As race was also associated with moral, natural, and aesthetic inferiority and superiority, as a symbol it had a particularly strong affective component. It was a particularly emotive symbol.

However, aspects of personal relations between Oreallans and non-Amerindians suggested that in such relations concern over the Indian Right could be more important than dislike of race *per se*. A key concept relating to the Buck:non-Buck dichotomy was that of Advantage. Advantage was the antithesis of Mattie, and the association of Advantage with non-Amerindians strengthened the expression of the dichotomy in inter-personal relationships. Culture and institutions could cross the boundary between the two parts of the Amerindian world, but the only way the non-Amerindian could become accepted was by becoming Amerindian, and being Amerindian was associated with phenotype. Belief in Advantage was particularly effective in stopping Mattie at the Buck:non-Buck boundary.

The logic of this interpretation of the meanings of Mattie and Advantage and their inter-relationship would appear to be that Advantage prevented the non-Amerindian with whom personal relationships had been established from being thought of as a person, from being considered to be like 'one of us'. In a real sense he remained a category or a stereotype. The most outstanding example of this was the non-Amerindian married into the village. Despite having genealogical ties with most villagers and being friendly with many he was never accepted as a villager as this would give access to The Right. Oreallans objected to his living in the village because they believed that by doing so he was Advantaging them, seeking to claim the Indian Right and setting a precedent for its loss. Their model of the village as Buck was concerned with relations between racial groups and their implication for relationships within the village. These relations were thought incompatible with village membership, with the model of the community as a group of persons with access to the Indian Right.

A non-Amerindian could become Families to members of the village because this involved relations between persons as holders of statuses. Similarly he could have Eyepass relations with its members. Neither pattern of inter-personal relations directly invoked group membership — Mattie as communitas. But because of his racial identity his relations with the village as an entity were perceived as relations of Advantage and consequently he could never become accepted as a member, which involved Mattie. It would be mistaken to interpret intimate relations across the Buck:non-Buck boundary, and the fact that people may interact intensively for years together, as a sign of acceptance. Relationships can be interpreted in different ways by the participants, and the very fact of interaction may be regarded by the parties involved as a form of non-integration and as having an antisocial intent.

Because village membership was based on the Indian Right it was in theory non-transactionable[4]. It was inherited by persons of the Amerindian racial group and could not be acquired by other persons. However, very rarely non-Amerindians did become villagers. They did so by in effect becoming Amerindians, as we saw in the case of the Arupa brothers (Case 6:19) and the old Portuguese lady (Case 6:16). In both cases the change probably took a long time to accomplish and was only possible because appearance did not readily symbolize Advantage. The individuals concerned either looked like Amerindians or did not look like Africans or East Indians. Because of this, in their cases, village membership became transactionable.

What happened in these situations was that the individuals concerned adopted Oreacla symbolisms and offered prestations which implied they were Amerindians. For example, in Case 6:19 Franklin Arupa curses the 'damn Black government' and violently opposes his daughters marrying Blackmen. Such prestations were offered as statements of shared identity (Mattie). When they were accepted as such and not interpreted as attempts to seek own ends (Advantage), and further prestations continued to be accepted as statements of common identity, then the supplicant had changed his racial identity and become a villager. He had established fully relationships of Mattie as communitas.

Non-Amerindians married into the community adopted a similar strategy in their efforts to achieve incorporation. They presented themselves as persons who identified with the community and its problems against outsiders and the government. In Case 6:17, although Austin obviously cannot stigmatize the PNC-dominated government as a 'damn Black government' as his father-in-law does, he publicly seeks to identify himself with the community by professing to oppose the government its members regard as his. But Oreallans would interpret his action as an attempt to usurp The Right by hiding his true intent behind pretended commonality. Even if a non-Amerindian was believed sincere in his protestations it was thought that his acceptance into the community would set a precedent allowing others to usurp, and ultimately destroy, The Right. Because of fear of Advantage his relationships could not fully be converted into Mattie as communitas.

In attempts to overcome this the outsider might claim Amerindian ancestry, as did Austin Johnson and February in Case 6:17. Since they could not change phenotype they attempted to change their ancestry, to claim Mattie and to conform with the Amerindian, and official, definition of a Buck. But this was also rejected by the villagers as a ploy to gain access to The Right.

2

In contrast to the non-Amerindian, who was on the opposite side of the Buck:non-Buck boundary, the mixed Amerindian was at the boundary. All Oreallans said mixed Amerindians were Amerindians with full access to the Indian Right. In this they agreed with the official definition of an Amerindian[5]. Yet mixed Amerindians often were identified with the racial group of the non-Amerindian parent and accused of usurping The Right. Like the non-Amerindian, but to a lesser degree, their relationships with other members of the village tended to be interpreted as Advantage and they had difficulty converting them to Mattie.

Although mixtures were in theory Amerindians, the Oreallans' model of their village as Buck ensured their position would be controversial, and this was reinforced by their model of the village as competitors. As members of a West Indian colonial society Amerindians accorded race a particular ideological importance. Race was particularly important in their conceptions of themselves. While they recognzed the existence of cultural difference between themselves and members of other groups these were not regarded as innate differences. Because of their social position Amerindians minimized the importance of such differences and stressed cultural similarities. Consequently the differences they did stress were regarded as inherent qualities, as racial differences. Race was perceived as the distinction between Amerindians and others. It was a major symbol of Amerindianness, and was typified in their stereotype of the full-blood or 'pure' Amerindian.

Consequently Amerindians had two conflicting definitions of themselves, in terms of ancestry, which accorded with the official definition, and in terms of appearance or 'blood'. Because of the importance accorded to race the definition in terms of blood was more powerful than that in terms of ancestry. Race was used not merely to stress difference, it was used to claim natural and moral superiority. In the Amerindian's perception of his relations with the wider society race was also associated with Advantage and the Indian Right. I suggest these factors constantly pressured Amerindians to attempt to force what was a very complex and fluid racial situation into line with their conceptions of race. In particular, I believe the importance they attached to preserving the Indian Right caused them to attempt to set a distinct boundary to the Amerindian group, identified in terms of race and defined as sharply as possible. They did so by attempting to deny the mixed Amerindian's Amerindianness. This was done not by rejecting the alternative definition, but by denying the mixed individual's Amerindian ancestry.

However it was only the mixed Amerindian outsider who could be treated in this way. For the mixed Amerindian born and raised in the community the definition of Amerindian in terms of ancestry took precedence over the conception of Amerindian in terms of blood. His ancestry was irrefutable. He was related by blood ties to all the village and had interacted with them from infancy. Because of the concern with reputation he would be criticized and insulted for his non-Amerindian ancestry, but this was recognised as Eyepass. The position of the mixed outsider was different. He was likely to have fewer blood relatives and it was easier to deny his Amerindian ancestry. But even where he had blood relatives and his genealogy was known to all, many people would attempt to deny it. He was classed with the non-Amerindian part of his ancestry and blamed as a threat to the Indian Right.

The position of the mixed Amerindian can be regarded as intermediate between that of the non-Amerindian, who was excluded from membership of the community, and the 'pure' Amerindian, who had the right to membership. He was partially incorporated, in the sense that some had full incorporation while attempts were made to exclude others. But knowledge of genealogical ties and existence of Families ties of blood meant that the mixed Amerindian outsider could only partially be excluded. And although the mixed Amerindian did not achieve total incorporation into the community it would be achieved by his children.

3

Oreallans' models of their community were used to interpret their relationships; to interpret the actions of others; to organize their actions; and to proffer messages concerning their intentions. All five models had representational and operational aspects. They both stated what was and provided guides for action[6]. Many of the 'facts' they contained did both. (In the model of the village as Amerindian Nations the operational aspect was not strongly developed, at least with respect to interactions between Amerindians living on the Corentyne.)

The models contained ambiguities and inconsistencies. (For example, one was Mattie to all persons and one was Mattie only to members of one's racial group. Advantage was wrong and could never be justified. At the same time Advantage was natural across racial boundaries, and in some sense laudable.) These inconsistencies, as well as the existence of conflicting folk models, presented the individual with choices and problems of interpretation and of action, including moral problems[7].

The individual's interpretation of any situation was influenced by the qualities he believed were brought to it by himself and others. These included the other's motives, and interpretation of these was influenced by racial identities; the degree of friendship or hostility between himself and the other; and such factors as sex, age, and genealogical relationship. It was also influenced by idiosyncratic personal feelings of the moment, such as drunken camaraderie or drunken aggressiveness. However he interpreted a particular situation, often it was not encumbent upon an individual to act in terms of the model which he believed described it. He could choose to act in terms of alternative models and proffer information about his intentions in terms of alternative conceptions of inter-personal relations. His actions were motivated by goals and personal interests. They were influenced not only by his interpretation of a situation, but by what he hoped to gain. He might interpret a situation in terms of one model but believe it to his benefit to act in terms of another. For example, in Case 6:12 an East Indian hauls some firewood for an Amerindian and says he has done it to help his 'Mattie Warao'. It was possible that the East Indian, working in the Bush and temporarily residing at Orealla, found it useful to profess that he and the Amerindian (and by implication all Oreallans, and all Amerindians) were Mattie, rather than that he really believed any kind of moral equivalence linked them.

As most situations allowed an element of choice people could manipulate the models in pursuit of their interests. A person might interpret his relationship with another in terms of Eyepass or Advantage but choose to present himself in terms of Manners and Respect or Mattie because he believed this would enable him to achieve his aims. Because it was recognized that people often had ulterior motives persons might be suspicious of the intentions of others and believe their behaviour masked hidden motives, which they would search for in order to interpret their actions.

4

The operation of the community was influenced by Oreallans' perceptions of their relations with their fellows and with outsiders. The formal structure of the village was defined by three sets of imposed institutions — local government, church, and school. Each was the agency of a national institution — the Ministries of the Interior and of Local Government, the Anglican Church in the West Indies, and the Ministry of Education. Oreallans' beliefs and attitudes played a significant part in inhibiting the effective operation of these institutions within the community. They also prevented the development of effective community leadership.

Traditionally the authorities at Orealla were the priest and the headmaster of the village school, a church appointee, who were concerned with all matters affecting the village, such as settlement of disputes, relations with non-Amerindians, and representing the village to outside authorities. The headmaster was also a rural constable with legal powers to detain suspected criminals and send them to the Coast for examination. They worked through the village Captain, who was appointed by the priest and whose duties were to keep the priest and headmaster informed about events in the village and act as the channel of communication between the church authorities and the villagers. The priest also appointed a church council which was concerned with village affairs generally.

In 1951 the Amerindian Ordinance placed Amerindian local government under the control of the Department of the Interior, and authorized the creation of local councils to operate under the guidance of a Department official[8]. At Orealla the fledgeling District council was guided first by the village headmaster, then by two successive VSOs[9] from the United Kingdom, and finally by the Assistant District Officer for Orealla, an office created in 1962. The offices of Captain and District councillor were made elective in 1964. Orealla District council was the formal organ of local government. It consisted of the Captain, seven councillors, and the ADO[10]. The villagers' notions of its duties varied considerably, from those who believed it existed simply to organize 'mission work' to keep the village tidy, to those who believed it should legislate against every form of anti-social activity, such as drunken fighting or loose behaviour by young girls. In fact it was empowered to make and enforce laws concerning use of village resources and maintenance of village amenities, and was intended to operate as the vehicle for village development[11]. Although it proposed development schemes and passed laws concerning the use of village resources and created taxes to raise money for the village development fund, which was used to purchase the village tractor, it never operated as a legal instrument to enforce these regulations. If breaches were dealt with at all it was through various *ad hoc* procedures.

Oreallans criticized the council as ineffective, but whenever it functioned it was likely to be accused of helping to Advantage the villagers. Its tax-raising activities particularly were resented. Although the amounts concerned were small they were regarded as a financial burden on 'poor people'. But more significantly they were seen as an attack on the Indian Right, as Amerindians were exempt from many of the revenues paid by other Guyanese. They criticized the council but ultimately they blamed the ADO, claiming that as a non-Amerindian and representative of a hostile government he used the council to institute policies which Advantaged Amerindians.

Oreallans liked to stand for the council. They believed election would enhance their prestige. Candidates did not explain their seeking office in these terms. They said they wished to fight for the people against Advantage. But unsuccessful candidates reacted as though their rejection was an Eyepass, criticizing successful candidates as nonentities and the voters as fools for electing them. If elected most took little interest in their duties. They failed to attend council meetings unless pressured by the ADO, and because the villagers criticized the council as ineffective and its policies as Advantage they often sought to distance themselves from it. They blamed its policies on other councillors, saying they were being misled by the ADO who was Advantaging the people. Frequently they resigned shortly after election and then boasted of how they fought for the people, claiming to have resigned in protest against lack of support from fellow councillors.

Consequently the council largely was ineffective and local government devolved upon the Captain and the ADO.

The key to understanding the behaviour of these two officials was the fact that they occupied inter-hierarchical offices — administrative positions in which distinct levels of social relations, organized in their own hierarchies, geared into each other. Gluckman argues that the important feature of such offices is that the holders 'occupy positions where there are major discontinuities in the total hierarchy and sets of social relations become radically different. That is, distinct subhierarchies within a total hierarchy meet in one person, who is the lowest member of the senior hierarchy and the highest member of the subordinate hierarchy[12].' Such positions are the focus of conflicting interests. Captain and ADO were subject to conflicting constraints from both hierarchies — the local community and the administrative apparatus of the state to which Amerindians were subject. How they performed their role was also influenced by idiosyncratic factors — abilities and attitudes they brought to their office. These could be expressed more easily in the case of the ADO. If he wished he could cushion himself from the community by maintaining social distance and restricting his activities to the formal competences of his office. My observations of captains from several communities and areas[13] indicated less variation in their behaviour. They could not use the rules and authority of an external bureaucracy to insulate themselves from the community, and they brought to their roles Buck ideas about relations between Amerindians and non-Amerindians.

The Captain's duties were to carry out the instructions of the District Officer and to maintain order in the Orealla Amerindian District[14]. He should report criminal offences to the ADO and, with the aid of two other Amerindian rural constables who had been appointed by the District council, arrest and detain offenders and collect evidence. It was the ADO's duty to supervise these actions and report the matter to the police.

Oreallans believed their Captain should protect their interests against the society and the administration. As any act by the ADO, the District council, or the Ministries of the Interior and of Local Government could be interpreted either as Advantage or a prelude to Advantage the Captain was blamed continually for the acts of these officials and institutions. But in the last resort the people believed that, being a Buck, he was powerless and the blame for administrative policies and acts lay with the ADO or the government. The Captain adopted the same position to attempt to divert blame for unpopular administrative decisions away from himself.

Although Oreallans believed the Captain should represent them and maintain order within the village, when he tried to interfere in their affairs — to enquire into an offence or get them to devote time to community development projects — they denied him the authority they believed he should exercise over others. Because he was a Buck like themselves they said he had no right to mix in another man's story. He was accused of Eyepass; of having ideas above his station; or offending against Manners and Respect. They expected him to act with authority while denying him that authority.

Given the Captain's position his best strategy was to try to avoid becoming involved in disputes and administrative matters. In Case 7:13, when he was rebuked by a woman councillor for not intervening in a drunken fight he argued that he did not have the right to interfere because the fight was in the assaulted man's house. He invented an excuse and presented it as though it were the law. If he could not avoid taking action he tried to place responsibliity on someone associated with external authority. Usually this was the ADO. On one occasion when he felt he had to investigate a wife beating he took along a villager who was a police constable stationed on the Coast and currently visiting his parent's home. He did so to divert responsibility onto external authority. If he must investigate a dispute he wore his hat and carried his baton, the symbols of his office, to demonstrate that it was his duty to intervene whether or not he agreed with doing so. Then he would harangue the parties and make threats, all the while stressing that it was his duty to investigate and that the law was behind him. Then, unless it was a serious offence which could not be ignored, he hoped to do nothing. His actions in disputes and offences were aimed at absolving himself from responsibility.

Similarly, at meetings of his people and the administration he postured eloquently, made strong speeches about the need for economic and social development in order for the Amerindian to advance himself, suggested development schemes and supported projects proposed by the ADO, and then did nothing unless pressured by the ADO. To his people he tried to place responsibility for administrative proposals on the administration. To the administration he sought to put responsibility for the failure of development schemes upon lack of co-operation by the people. But if a policy proved popular or a development scheme was successful, or if a dispute was resolved successfully, then he sought to claim the credit.

The Captain's strategy then was to try to avoid becoming involved in village concerns. If he had to become involved he placed responsibility for his actions upon external authority, and then if possible did nothing. Finally he claimed credit for the positive outcome of any issue in which he should have been concerned. This was not the idiosyncrasy of the Orealla Captain. It was typical of Amerindian Captains. It would appear the most effective way of coping with the constraints to which the Amerindian Captain was subjected by his inter-hierarchical role, in particular the values and beliefs of the community and his own attitudes as a Buck.

The villagers criticized the Captain for the way he performed his duties. In Case 7:13 a woman councillor criticized him for failing to intervene in a drunken fight and he was Eyepassed by his brother, who publicly accused him of always talking but never doing anything. In Case 6:23 Lionel said the Captain always walks away from trouble. These criticisms typified the villagers' attitude towards the Captain, but again this was not limited to Orealla, or to any particular Captain. It was typical of attitudes towards Amerindian Captains by their people. The Amerindian Captain was sensitive about the community's criticisms. He responded by blaming the people, claiming they would not co-operate or support him in his fight with the government on their behalf.

5

The ADO was responsible to the Ministry of the Interior and the Ministry of Local Government for supervising the operation of local government; maintaining order; and initiating and organizing community development. To perform his duties effectively he had to act in a broader capacity, and in more vaguely demarcated spheres of activity, than delineated in administrative regulations. The effective ADO involved himself in many aspects of community life and interacted personally with the villagers on development projects and in their economic activities. He organized development schemes and oversaw their operation. He acted as an entrepreneur, finding new markets and obtaining better prices for logs and balata. He went out with loggers, overseeing log hauling and the loading of hardwood logs on boats for transportation down-river. He tried to resolve disputes and settle crimes so that they would not go to the police and law courts. He had to cajole, persuade, and spend much of his time in direct and relatively informal contact with the village. He got to know many of its members personally; addressed them familiarly; lent small amounts of money to those he believed he could trust; assisted cases of personal hardship; and visited to offer condolences over bereavements. Much of this was not part of his duty. Often he overstepped the limits of his formal role so that his activities conflicted with the functions of the police or of other agencies of the state. To perform his duties effectively he had to assume a general interest in the affairs of the community and this constrained him to act in matters which went beyond his official competence and even in ways which were illegal.

Differences in the attitudes of ADO and Captain were revealed by their respective behaviour in the treatment of disputes. At Orealla a common procedure for dealing with disputes was for the ADO to try the case informally, usually with the assistance of the village Captain, and fix some minor penalty or compensation or reach some compromise between the disputants. (In Case 6:23 Corlette Sabajo and his friend were tried informally by the ADO and a visiting police inspector for 'break and enter'.) Together Captain and ADO tried to reconcile the parties to their decision by showing there was right – or more likely wrong — on both sides. In doing so their motives often differed. The ADO was concerned that disputants should not get themselves involved with the law because of the expense and inconvenience this could cost them. On the other hand the Captain usually was trying to prevent himself from becoming further involved. If he could reconcile the disputants or persuade the plaintiff to accept minor compensation then he did not have to become involved with the legal apparatus of the Coastal society. Offences which were criminal under Guyanese law and should involve the police often were tried in this manner. The ADO simply ignored the criminal nature of the offence, even a serious criminal offence such as assault with a deadly weapon, provided it had not resulted in serious damage to persons or property and was unlikely to be repeated. Disputants often were prepared to accept this procedure because they distrusted the police and courts as agencies of the government and lawyers as non-Amerindians out to Advantage Buckpeople. However the informal procedure allowed much complaint about the resolution of any case. It gave ample scope for complaints that the Captain did not do his duty or that the ADO Eyepassed or Advantaged the people.

Inevitably the ADO's actions brought him into conflict with the villagers. However he performed his duties, and however well-intentioned his actions, he would be accused of Advantage because he was a non-Amerindian and a representative of the government. We have seen examples (Case 6:5, 7:14) where in acting in an exemplary fashion his motives were questioned and he was considered to Advantage the people. Oreallans saw him as possessing power as a representative of the government. He should use this power to help them. But they believed he used it instead to help his fellow East Indians or Blackpeople, in accordance with Mattie, and to line his own pockets. And as an agent of the government his activities were believed to be aimed at the destruction of the Indian Right.

Consequently Oreallans suspected the aims of development

projects. Such projects usually were proposed by the ADO. Occasionally they were suggested by the Captain or the District council, but for any scheme to get off the ground it had to be pushed by the ADO. Even if Oreallans approved they would not work on it unless pressed. They distrusted one another and believed others would not do their share of work. They did not wish to take time off from pursuit of their short-term economic interests to work for what they saw as dubious or unlikely long-term community benefits. They would not act according to Mattie. If the ADO ceased persuasion, lost interest, or was replaced by another who did not persist with the project, it collapsed. All Orealla development projects ultimately had failed. (In the period immediately prior to Orealla receiving its own ADO development projects had been initiated and organised by a go-ahead headmaster and two VSOs. As soon as the initiators left the community their projects fell into abeyance.) Recent projects which had failed after a few months or years, or were proposed but never implemented, included a community centre; sewing classes; a pasture at the up-river end of the Flatland; a pasture in the savannah behind Orealla; a house-building scheme; building a village boat; a new medical centre; rebuilding the village stelling (jetty) after it was destroyed in a boat accident; building latrines; erecting kokers (sluice gates) at the mouths of the main drainage ditches; starting a heifer herd; pig rearing; buying a huller; starting a village rice industry; commercial production of starch; a village crèche; a village library; organizing a postal agency; a Saturday market; and a co-op shop.

6

Before 1959 the authorities at Orealla were the Vicar of Skeldon Parish and the headmaster. Subsequently they formally were made the representatives of the church and the Ministry of Education only, but like the ADO if they were to perform their duties effectively they had to be involved in many aspects of village life. Pressure on them to do so was strengthened by their traditional roles in the community. Like the ADO and the Captain they occupied inter-hierarchical statuses.

The headmaster had always been a non-Amerindian Christian Coastal Guyanese, appointed by the Anglican Church. Because he was an African or an East Indian he was viewed with a certain amount of hostility and his actions could be suspect, but this was countered by his association with the church, the traditional guardian of the Indian Right. Because of this, and the respect due to his position, villagers often asked his advice in their dealings with the institutions of Coastal society. Parents sought his help in problems and disputes involving schoolchildren. He would try to settle such disputes to prevent them from becoming legal matters. Consequently his actions could impinge on the ADO's activities, and since they could involve criminal offences might conflict with the function of the police. But the former usually welcomed his involvement and the latter were unaware of it.

In the past, when the headmaster was the village constable, he was brought more directly into such community matters as disputes and fights. This often operated to erode the respect he wished to maintain. There were instances where headmasters were assaulted when they intervened to stop fights. Loss of their previous local government functions appeared to have helped headmasters retain their authority and respect by enabling them to maintain social distance.

Because the priest visited the community for only two or three days each month he did not have the headmaster's problems regarding maintaining social distance, which was supported by the fact that he was usually a White expatriate Englishman. But if he was to carry out his duties properly he had to become involved in the community beyond the formal competences of his office and he was constrained to do so by the church's view of its traditional, and what it considered its proper, relations with Amerindians.

In 1961 Dr Jagan's People's Progressive Party government placed mission schools under the formal control of the Ministry of Education. Although churches continued to exercise *de facto* control over Amerindian education the new education policy and the new local government organization were regarded by churches in Guyana as attempts by the PPP Government to reduce their influence over Amerindians. In many Amerindian communities, including Orealla, this resulted in conflict between representatives of the church and officers of local government. (See the case of Jeremiah James, Case 7:17.) This strengthened the Amerindians' view of the clergyman as protector of the Indian Right, and complaints concerning The Right continued to be taken to the priest. But the conflict also demonstrated that the church was now ineffective against the government, and made the Amerindian see his situation as increasingly precarious.

7

At Orealla disputes could be settled through the mediation or arbitration of several external authority figures, often assisted by the Captain who, paradoxically, was acting in order to avoid his responsibilities. They were dealt with by *ad hoc* procedures which often promoted complaints of Eyepass and Advantage. An Oreallan who considered himself wronged usually wanted compensation for himself and/or punishment for his opponent[15], and a plaintiff who believed he had a strong case might by-pass the local authorities and inform the police directly, believing he would get more satisfaction from a police investigation. Usually this was done only if he believed he could gain markedly thereby. But the police often became involved in disputes and offences through receiving information from persons envious of, or hostile to, parties involved.

Just as the formal leadership of the community was ineffective at Orealla, so there were no *de facto* leaders. No individuals acquired followings which would give them support. Ability and economic success aroused envy and criticisms of Advantage, as was demonstrated by the position of shopkeepers. Successful shopkeepers were admired for their entrepreneurial skill, but they were also envied and criticized for Advantaging the people. They were said to have attained their success through cheating the people. Shopkeepers might appear to be those persons in the strongest position to become village leaders. Each had a core of customers to whom he extended substantial amounts of credit, whom he referred to as his 'Clients'. These formed a stable nucleus of customers, but did not form the basis of a personal following.

Shopkeepers were not the only Oreallans to have Clients. One's Client was someone for whom one performed a specific service. For example, Amerindian 'doctors' had Clients, persons whom they regularly treated for particular illnesses. Consequently your Client was also someone who owed you for services rendered. As a result there was ambivalence in the relationship which implied conflict. The concept had two aspects. It implied service on the one hand and indebtedness on the other, and in use might stress either aspect. Friends might jokingly address one another as each other's Clients, implying friendship was a service each performed for the other. On the other hand when it was indebtedness which was being stressed the term might be intended as an insult. For debtors may not repay their debts, and the term might be interpreted as 'beggar' or 'scrounger'. In the fight between Lionel Francois and Arnold Gordon (Case 7:5), when Lionel Eyepassed Arnold he began by saying 'Here is one of my best Clients'. By this he was implying Arnold owed him for services performed, specifically that he owed him for drinks bought which he had not repaid. He was a scrounger who did not buy his round when he drank with others, and he had come to scrounge drinks from me.

The relationship between shopkeeper and Client might not be a friendly one. The Client saw the shopkeeper as practising Advantage by overcharging for goods. The shopkeeper saw the Client as potentially an unreliable debtor, who often was slow in repaying his debts. Thus

Clients were often hostile to their creditors and would not willingly give them their support. Nor could a shopkeeper use his position as creditor to pressure a Client into giving political support, even though Oreallans professed that they often tried to do so. Any shopkeeper who did so would have been condemned by the community for Advantage, mixing in another man's story, and having ideas above his station. The attempt would have been rejected by the Client, for although the economic relationship was one of assymmetrical indebtedness it was seen as a relationship between equals. I believe any such attempt would have been regarded by the community, and by other shopkeepers, as legitimate grounds for the Client reneging on his debt and opening an account with another shopkeeper.

Attitudes towards shopkeepers often combined admiration with dislike and envy. They were criticized for Advantaging the people, but admired and envied for their economic success. In the 1968 election for the office of Captain two shopkeepers stood against the incumbent. They claimed they wished to institute social and economic development, and presented their entrepreneurial skill in business as evidence of ability which they would put to the service of the community. One of them, Jeremiah James (Case 7:17), undoubtedly was sincere in this. But despite widespread discontent with the Captain and criticism of lack of development during his eight years in office he won handsomely, receiving three-quarters of votes cast. (He was standing for re-election because of the prestige he believed derived from the office, but said it was because he wished to continue to fight for the people.) The degree of admiration a shopkeeper might command could not overcome the envy his success generated, or the belief in Advantage implied by power of any kind.

8

Orealla beliefs and attitudes inhibited the development of effective village leadership and the operation of the three sets of institutions which defined Orealla's formal structure — local government; the village church; and the village school. Although each of these institutions provided a formal framework for village activities their operation was inhibited by the villagers' attitudes to co-operation and, in the case of local government, their distrust of the outside officials who dominated these institutions. Each had been introduced from outside and operated only because it was managed by officials from outside, who were non-Amerindians. Their operation served to impress the Oreallan with his subordination, as an Amerindian, to other Nations.

For most of Orealla's history these officials were expatriate Whitepeople or Coastal Guyanese directly, and obviously, subordinate to
White officials. Traditionally the church had been the governing
institution, and as such was regarded as a safeguard of the Indian Right
and a protection against Advantage by outsiders. In the 1960s local
government became the responsibility of a Guyanised administration.
At Orealla, from its inception the new local government organisation
was under the charge of East Indian or Black local officers, identified
by the villagers with governments believed opposed to their interests.
Now even the priest was sometimes a non-White Guyanese. As a result
the Oreallan saw his traditional protection from Advantage weakened
and control of his interests handed to those he considered his racial
opponents.

Most disputes were settled by the action of external, or externally
imposed, authorities. With the introduction of local government these
were an Amerindian (the Captain) and a non-Amerindian outsider (the
ADO), and no longer a White outsider (the priest) and a White-
subordinated outsider (the headmaster). When the Captain tried to act
his authority was denied because he was a Buck. When the ADO acted
his motives were suspect because he was a non-Amerindian and seen as
an agent of the government.

The three local institutions were integrated into nationally
organised institutions which were staffed, and their policies determined, by non-Amerindians. They integrated Orealla formally into the
national society. The Anglican Church and the Ministry of Education
integrated Orealla both with other Amerindian communities and with
non-Amerindian communities. The Ministries of the Interior and of
Local Government, because of the provisions of the Amerindian
Ordinance, integrated Amerindians together for administrative purposes and separated them from the national society. The operation of
these institutions expressed and reinforced the Amerindian's subordination to other racial groups.

The rules of the Amerindian Ordinance formulated the Indian
Right. It, as its predecessor the Aboriginal Indian Protection
Ordinance, had been administered through a Department whose senior
civil servants were White; whose appointed local officers were
Whitepeople; and whose policies were subject to the 'English'
colonial administration. Whitepeople were the protectors of the Indian
Right. In recent Guyanese history the colonial administration progressively was replaced by Guyanese, non-White, governments. Defence of
the Indian Right became the responsibility of institutions operated by
racial groups believed to Advantage Amerindians and subordinated to
governments believed to Advantage them. Only the churches remained

independent, White-dominated institutions because they were international organizations. Amerindians continued to see in their churches a protection against loss of The Right, but they were made aware of the fact that churches were no longer all-powerful in their relations with national governments.

The Oreallan's involvement with each of the institutions integrating the village into the national society was mandatory, neither at the local or national level was he allowed any formal alternative. This applied even to church affiliation. Nationally, religious affiliation tended to be seen as a matter of personal choice, but for Amerindians little choice was available. Particular Christian denominations had long been associated with specific Amerindian localities and communities whose residents had little effective alternative to belonging to that denomination. However, in the 1950s and 1960s Amerindians did possess one commodity for which national organizations competed — their votes. During the period of fieldwork Guyana's government was still an elected one in fact as well as constitutionally, and the three political parties all supplicated Amerindian votes. During the period of internal self-government in Guyana their view of their position in a colony approaching independence influenced the way Amerindians used their votes, and their behaviour in national politics.

Notes

1 V.W. Turner, (1969), pp. 96–7. 'Society as a structured, differentiated, and often hierarchical system of political-legal-economic positions with many types of evaluation, separating men in terms of "more" or "less".' (Ibid. p. 96).
2 V.W. Turner (1969), pp. 96–7. 'Society as an unstructured or rudimentarily structured and relatively undifferentiated *comitatus*, community, or even communion of equal individuals who submit together to the general authority of the ritual elders'. (Ibid. p. 96).
3 B.E. Ward, (1965), p. 124.
4 F. Barth, (1966), p. 4.
5 *British Guiana*, (1951), section 2.
6 L. Holy, and M. Stuchlik, (1981), pp. 19–20; R. Jenkins, (1981), pp. 96–101, 108–9.
7 Leach, for example, has drawn attention to the manner in which folk models provide the individual with choices and alternatives. (E.R. Leach, (1954).)
8 *British Guiana*, (1951), sections 17–18.
9 Voluntary Service Overseas. The British organization.
10 *British Guiana*, (1951), sections 17, 18 part 2, 20–5.
11 Ibid., sections 20–5.
12 M. Gluckman, (1969), p. 71.

13 Corentyne river; St Cuthberts, Mahaica river; Moruka river.
14 *British Guiana*, (1951), section 15.
15 The emphasis on compensation and punishment rather than recon-
    ciliation may have been unusual for an Amerindian community as Orealla
    was a large community. Because of the importance of voluntary
    relationships in Amerindian social life individuals did not have to interact
    continually. In a smaller village necessity for intimate interaction, and
    closeness of kinship relations, might promote reconciliation. It might be
    an important aspect of Manners and Respect. (However, in Sipuruta,
    which had less than 100 residents, emphasis in disputes was also on
    recompense and punishment. But Sipuruta consisted mainly of strangers
    who had come to the Corentyne from outside, and this may have
    influenced their relationships with each other.)

CHAPTER 9 | The Powerless People

1

Oreallans' models of their community, and the way they used the concepts comprising them, had to be understood within the context of the Amerindian's relationship to the wider society. Historically Guyanese society developed an ideology stressing differences between racial groups. Members of different racial groups were believed to be qualitatively different types of persons. Oreallans expressed this in their concept of Nation. The ideal pattern of behaviour associated with Nation was that of Mattie, which meant communitas or humanity. But as well as possessing a belief in racial difference Oreallans also had an idea of the unity of Mankind, and the concept of Mattie applied to Mankind just as it applied to Nation. Because Mattie was associated with both race and Mankind it both buttressed and negated racial identity.

The idea of the moral equivalence of Mankind presumably was acquired through the interaction of the Amerindian group with the Coastal society and its progressive incorporation into the national society. Acquisition must have been promoted by factors such as Christianity and education, which while operating to support the political requirements of a White-dominated colonial society at the same time promoted universalistic values.

The extension of Mattie to include the whole of the Amerindian racial group was facilitated by the fact that Amerindians were made to see themselves as a group not only as a consequence of the social stress on race, but also because of their legal position in Guyana. Their racial status and the way they were treated by other Guyanese made them see themselves as a deprived group. This made it easier to extend Mattie to all members of the group. Mattie was based on an idea of equivalence; therefore it was readily identifiable with 'people like us'. To Oreallans this meant 'poor people'. And that meant Amerindians.

Mattie was a quality seen as inherent in group membership. Where members of different racial groups were thought to possess different inherent qualities this made the extension of Mattie beyond racial boundaries difficult. It was rooted in the concept of equivalence. Different racial groups were not seen as consisting of equivalent types of being. If we take the three groups with whom Amerindians had most contact, Europeans on the one hand and Blackpeople and East Indians on the other, there was a sense in which the former consisted of super-beings and the latter of un-persons. When a Whiteman was perceived as a person he might be allocated membership of a different racial group, so bringing him down to an accessible racial level[1]. When a Coolie or Blackman, through interaction or intermarriage, showed the characteristics of being a person he could not wholly succeed in becoming one, in becoming Mattie, because of the belief in Advantage.

Advantage was the antithesis of Mattie. It contravened all the basic qualities of Mattie. Amerindians believed other racial groups Advantaged them. In particular they believed Blackpeople and East Indians Advantaged them and that these groups wished to take away the Indian Right. This was a reasonable interpretation of their situation. They had a history of exploitation by the Coastal society, and lower class East Indians and Africans treated them with contempt. Belief in Advantage was supported by their protected status. The higher strata of the society attempted to protect them from Advantage by the Black and East Indian lower class. Amerindians extended the belief in Advantage to Guyana's nationalist parties, and to the governments formed by these parties. This was supported by the Amerindian's unrealistic conception of the wealth and power of the government, and by the fact that nationalist governments had largely ignored Amerindians while they devoted themselves to the Coast, where the country's economic and political life was located and where their supporters resided. Action by agents of these governments was interpreted as Advantage, particularly when the agents were non-White.

Both the belief in Advantage — which was in a sense a 'natural' quality — and the conception of racial groups as consisting of naturally differing populations, operated to restrict the Oreallan's extension of the concept of Mattie to his own racial group. Of the two, Advantage appeared the ultimate constraint. The Blackman or Coolie who came closest to having his individuality recognized, the individual who was married into the group or who interacted continuously with its members in a situation of equality, could not rid himself of the taint of Advantage. Oreallans thought of their village as consisting only of Amerindians. To be an Amerindian meant to be powerless, Advantaged, and poor. Beyond the Buck boundary people were powerful, exploiters, and rich.

2

This work is concerned primarily with Amerindian race relations, and is not intended to examine in depth Oreallans' intense concern with reputation. This is a complex subject, to be analyzed in the light of anthropological material on reputation, and deserves detailed treatment of its own. However I do not believe the concern was simply a consequence of Amerindians being an alienated or deprived minority. Nor was it merely a case of competitive values from a traditional 'big man' political system being perpetuated into the present.

I believe Amerindian relations with the national society were a factor influencing concern with reputation. Contact with the Coast created a situation where achievement of social standing within the community was open to all adults of the same sex, in more or less equal measure, while standing in the wider society was denied to all. Resources needed to obtain prestige within the community were available to all. Consequently if anyone failed to achieve a deference-entitlement blame often could be laid quite justifiably at his own door. This must have helped engender concern that other persons were claiming higher status than oneself. If they did so they were not just saying they were better; they were saying that given the same opportunities one had proved defective. It must also have engendered jealously. If someone was more successful than yourself it was as likely to be an indication of your failings as it was of their ability.

Hence the attempts by the less successful to demonstrate that really they were better than the more successful by seeking failure in some areas of Alter's behaviour to counter his success in others. Attempts were also made to demonstrate that another's success was due to some favourable circumstance unavailable to oneself. Given the availability of resources, often this had to be immoral use of an opportunity, but ideas of luck and fate were also used. These explained one's lack of success in terms which did not reflect adversely on oneself. Claims of Advantage by non-Amerindians could be used in the same way.

3

The position of the Amerindian group in Guyana's social structure was of the type that many sociologists and psychologists would define as a marginal one. The classic definition of the marginal individual is that of Stonequist, who defines him as the person who 'through migration, education, marriage, or some other influence leaves one social group or culture without making a satisfactory adjustment to another and finds himself on the margins of each but a member of neither[2].' More recent uses of the concept examine the influences a particular kind of structural situation may have on the behaviour or personalities of its occupants, and suggest modifications of the concept. Generally its core has come to be the exclusion of individuals or groups from desired social groups or statuses while possessing qualities which could be expected normally to qualify them for admission[3]. If we take this as the crucial factor in defining a marginal situation the position of the Amerindian group was doubly marginal, on cultural and racial grounds.

In considering what their standing in Guyanese society ought to be Amerindians took as their standards the traditional values of West Indian colonial society. They possessed many of the cultural characteristics regarded as civilised by Coastal society. While there was cultural variation within the Amerindian category, almost all communities possessed those institutions associated by the Coastal society with the civilized state, and many communities shared other cultural and social characteristics with lower class Coastal populations. Yet a reason commonly given to justify their inferior status was cultural inferiority. Amerindians believed culture entitled them to a status equal to that of other lower class Guyanese.

But Amerindians also considered themselves racially superior to Blackpeople. In a society in which superiority had long been associated with the phenotypic characteristics of the stereotyped European and inferiority with those of the stereotyped Blackman, phenotypically the 'pure' Amerindian was closer to the former than to the latter. Amerindians also followed the Coastal stereotype in attributing to Africans innate unhuman personal qualities. On racial grounds they claimed superiority to Blackpeople.

East Indians on the other hand were believed by Amerindians, and by many Coastal people, to possess an undesirable kind of personality – mean, grasping, over-clannish (an ambivalent quality), and two-faced. These were regarded as inherent characteristics. I suggest they contrasted with the ideal personality type of the colonial society which was open, generous, and honest — positive qualities of the Oreallan's stereotype of Whitepeople. Amerindians saw themselves as superior to East Indians in personal character, conforming more to the Guyanese ideal.

Despite approximating valued racial characteristics Amerindians were regarded universally as the most inferior racial group in the society. We might expect the racial aspects of their marginality to influence them to be opposed to Blackpeople and Cooliepeople and to ally themselves with those groups in the society that they associated with Whiteness, which they regarded as naturally superior. However, how groups in such a situation are likely to behave is influenced by their perception of their general situation. The most important influence on Amerindian political behaviour was their perception of themselves as a powerless group faced by Advantage from East Indians and Africans, racial groups whose members assisted each other in accordance with Mattie, and in particular from the governments they saw as representing these groups.

In the field of social action Amerindians constituted an ethnic group as defined by Barth, as a form of social organization. 'The crucial feature is...a membership which identifies itself and is identified by others as constituting a category distinguishable from other categories of the same order. ...A categorical ascription is an ethnic ascription when it classifies a person in terms of his basic, most general identity, presumptively determined by his origin and background. To the extent that actors use ethnic identities to categorize themselves and others for purposes of interaction, they form ethnic groups in this organizational sense.'[4] In the light of the last sentence Amerindians would appear to have constituted an ethnic group to a marked degree, since virtually all their interactions with non-Amerindian Guyanese were influenced by their ethnic identity because of their concern over the Indian Right. But in spite of these organizational characteristics and the fact that Amerindians were the only one of Guyana's racial groups which was a corporate group, the Amerindian group was unable to organize for common activity. Amerindians were few in number and lived in small villages widely scattered in the Interior. These demographic disadvantages were reinforced by attitudes and beliefs. Within the local community jealousies and Eyepass inhibited common action and prevented the development of leadership. Hostile tribal stereotypes and antagonisms between villages limited the possibility of inter-community activities. Because of their attitudes and beliefs Amerindians failed to act according to Mattie. Structural factors also limited the possibility of widespread action. Each local community was integrated separately into Coastal institutions which dealt with the village concerned and were controlled by non-Amerindians.

Even had Amerindians been able to organize, their unaided efforts could not have achieved political success. They were few in numbers and lacked economic power. In contrast to other lower class Guyanese such as sugar workers or bauxite workers, whose occupations also were associated with particular racial groups, Amerindian occupations were not crucial to Guyana's economy. They had no economic power to use as a lever in pursuit of national political objectives. All they had were their votes. Of all this Amerindians were aware. Any impetus from their marginal position to ally themselves with Whiteness was strengthened by their perception of their general situation, and was supported by the tenor of Amerindian relations with the Coast throughout the whole of Guyana's colonial history.

In the 1950s and 1960s fear of Advantage focused upon the Indian Right, embodied in the Amerindian Ordinance. Amerindians feared the loss of The Right; of their privileges and protections. They also feared that independent governments, freed from the restraining White hand of the British Colonial Office, could use the powers in the Amerindian Ordinance to Advantage them. Their perception of themselves as a powerless group which needed allies is crucial to understanding the behaviour of the Amerindian racial group in Guyanese national politics during this period.

4

The political history of Guyana in the 1950s and 1960s was characterized by opposition between its two nationalist parties, which developed into serious East Indian:African racial conflict. Racial tensions were being promoted by the increasing incorporation of East Indians into the mainstream of the society, particularly their entry into urban and high status occupations traditionally the preserve of the Black and Coloured groups. That they developed into racial polarization and increasingly violent inter-racial conflict was a consequence of external involvements in Guyanese politics.

There are many analyses, from a number of theoretical perspectives, of Guyanese national politics in this period[5]. Here I can give only the briefest outline of events. In 1953, in the first national elections to be held under universal adult franchise, the recently formed People's Progressive Party (PPP) won a majority of seats on the Legislative Council and formed the government. Its founder and leader was Dr Cheddi Jagan, an East Indian dentist whose main support was in the sugar plantations. Its deputy leader was Mr Forbes Burnham, an African lawyer. His power base was in Georgetown and his main support was the African working class, but he also had close ties to that element of the urban middle class which had become nationalist through experiencing British racial discrimination[6]. The PPP's ideology was Marxist-oriented and it drew much of its support from both the Black and East Indian racial groups. Three months later the Governor suspended the constitution, claiming a communist plot by the PPP to subvert the process of government[7]. A period of 'marking time' was instituted during which the British government hoped the leaders of the PPP would lose a significant amount of support. During this period Mr Burnham broke with Dr Jagan and when elections again took place, in 1957, they were contested by two PPPs, one Jaganite and the other Burnhamite. The Jaganite party won and formed the government. Mr Burnham then formed a new party, the People's National Congress (PNC), with predominantly African leadership, which he claimed would be ideologically 'socialist' as against the 'communism' of the PPP. He persuaded the leaders of the middle class United Democratic Party, which had some African support, to join his new party. Increasingly politics became racially polarized with the majority of East Indians supporting the PPP and Africans the PNC, and the language of politics became increasingly racialist, particularly at the level of local party organizations. Mr Burnham's party was joined in its opposition to Dr Jagan by the only other major party, the United Force (UF). The UF was founded in 1960 by Mr Peter D'Aguiar, a wealthy Portuguese businessman, on a capitalist, anti-communist, platform. It received support particularly from conservative elements of the middle class and from Amerindians, and had a Portuguese, light-skinned image in contrast to the PPP's East Indian image and the PNC's African image.

Politics became increasingly violent, with riots and politically motivated strikes. In 1962 Jagan's opponents combined to oppose the PPP's budget proposals. There were riots and Dr Jagan was forced to ask the Governor for British troops to restore order in his captial city. The opposition could not bring down the government, which retained an electoral majority, but the government could not govern effectively because the opposition controlled the civil service and important urban sectors of the economy. At the London Constitutional Conference in 1962 the PNC and the UF pressed for proportional representation, as their combined electoral support was greater than that of the PPP. The Colonial Secretary said the political parties should be unanimous on the constitution before independence could be granted, and said that if the position in Guyana continued to deteriorate he would consider imposing a solution. As a result the opposition supported a general strike which was successful because of CIA funding, channelled through the ICFTU[8]. Finally, at the constitutional conference of 1963 Dr Jagan agreed to let the Colonial Secretary, Mr Duncan Sandys, arbitrate a solution. The Colonial Office introduced proportional representation and set elections for 1964, to be held before discussions regarding a possible date for independence. This was interpreted both nationally and internationally as an attempt by the British government, under United States' pressure, to oust Dr Jagan from office, an interpretation that has since been confirmed[9].

A period of East Indian:African inter-racial strife preceded the election, with murders, bombings, arson, and the creation of a substantial refugee population. The election gave the combined opposition an overall majority and Mr Burnham headed a coalition government with the UF as junior partner. Although there remained considerable racial tension there was little racial violence in the period following the election, and this was the situation when the data on which this book is based was being collected. Guyana became independent in 1966. Mr Burnham was still governing in coalition with the UF but the PNC and Mr Burnham were consolidating their hold on power. A few months after I left the country in mid-1968 the UF dissolved the coalition because of cavalier treatment by their PNC partner. Elections were held in December 1968. They gave the PNC an overall majority but there was considerable evidence that they had been rigged. Gradually Guyana became what was effectively a highly centralised one-party state under PNC control, using socialist rhetoric but with a highly personalised leadership, with Africans in most positions of power and East Indians largely excluded from government.

The importance of external factors in influencing the form and outcome of this conflict is not in dispute[10]. The British Conservative government removed an elected nationalist government which contained both East Indian and African leaders with widespread popular support, and then worked to divide the nationalist leadership in order to weaken 'extremist' elements in the movement. The government of the United States pressured the British government for Dr Jagan's removal, to prevent the establishment of a pro-Soviet state in South America. Government and anti-communist interests in the USA[11] helped foster and support opposition to Dr Jagan within British Guiana, and the British government imposed proportional representation in order to exclude Dr Jagan's party from office. Covert external influence in Guyana's pre-independence politics is now a matter of record[12]. Political conflict was exacerbated and its outcome decided by external factors[13], but these were building upon racial tensions already present in the society.

The stratification analysis of Guyanese politics, which is followed here, is associated with the work of R.T.Smith[14]. The analysis argues that Guyana has widely accepted status orders. Growing acceptance of these by the East Indians and their increasing inroads into them were felt as a threat by the Black and Coloured sectors of the population. Racial conflict was not a result of the existence of different cultural sections; the high degree of acceptance of common values was more significant. Marked cultural differences exist between Africans and East Indians at the lower class level and both racial groups have their own sense of identity, but in the towns young East Indians are adopting the life styles of other Guyanese, which itself is changing towards a kind of Mid-Atlantic Anglo-Americanism[15]. Rather than race expressing cultural difference, increasing involvement of all racial groups in a common social and cultural system strengthened their sense of racial identity. Competition for common ends and values led to the stressing of racial identity. It does not follow that this was in itself a retrogressive development. In the process of rejecting the colonial pattern of subservience to Whiteness the different racial groups of Guyanese society had to stress their distinctiveness in order to affirm their own racial worth. Tragically, largely through the actions of external forces, this resulted in large-scale racial conflict.

Amerindians did not participate in national politics until the introduction of the universal adult franchise in 1953. They had not been involved in the nationalist movement or in other Coastal political developments. When they became voters they supported anti-PPP and anti-PNC candidates until the formation of the United Force, when overwhelmingly they gave their support to the new party. The Amerindians' view of their relationships with the different racial groups of the Coastal society, in the nationalist period of Guyanese politics caused them to ally with the non-nationalist, non-radical elements of the national polity. From this alliance they expected improvements in their economic condition and changes in their social status.

At Orealla the villagers wanted higher living standards, better services, and more, higher paid, and easier work. They also wanted protection for their traditional rights. They were more ambivalent about what they believed their racial standing should be. At the least they wanted equal standing with Blackpeople and East Indians. But they often talked as though they believed they should have higher status than Africans. There was more ambivalence concerning whether or not they ought to have higher status than Cooliepeople.

The great majority of Oreallans supported the UF and voted for it in the general elections of 1961 and 1964. When asked why they did so either they said it was because it was the only party that tried to help the Amerindian, or that the two other parties had failed the Amerindian. Mr Stephen Campbell, Guyana's first Amerindian MP, was a UF MP, and this strengthened their support for the party. But the nature of their support was more fundamental than this. While the UF presented itself as a democratic capitalist party opposed to the 'communism' of the PPP and the suspect 'socialism' of the PNC, Amerindians saw it as a non-Black, non-Coolie party, and often as an anti-Black and anti-

Coolie party, despite the prominence of Black and East Indian members such as Randolph Cheeks, Minister of Local Government and Amerindian Affairs in the PNC-UF coalition government, and Fielden Singh, who was to succeed Mr D'Aguiar as leader.

Consequently Oreallans believed it provided the only political protection against loss of the Indian Right in the pre-independence and post-colonial periods. They interpreted its aims in a racist fashion. But often it was thought of not simply as anti-Coolie and anti-Black, but implicitly as a White party. In the same breath Oreallans would say that only the Whitepeople supported Amerindian interests and only the UF were fighting for the Amerindians. This appeared to be largely because its founder and first leader was Mr D'Aguiar, and we have seen that Mr D'Aguiar was often implicitly regarded as White rather than Portuguese.

The UF was aware of the crucial role of Ameridian support for its electoral success, and cultivated the image of itself as the party which was interested in Amerindian problems and represented their interests nationally. Amerindian policy was given prominence in the UF election manifesto[16]. Mr D'Aguiar was presented as the national leader of Amerindians. The party supplicated Mr Campbell to stand as a UF MP, and made political capital of his membership of the party. In the 1964–8 PNC-UF coalition government the UF received the crucial post for Amerindian affairs, the Ministry of Local Government and Amerindian Affairs. Mr Campbell was made Parliamentary Secretary to the Ministry of Local Government with special reference to Amerindian Affairs. His official role was to liase between Amerindians and the government. The party's weekly newspaper, 'The Sun', devoted much space to Amerindians. There were frequent articles on Amerindians generally and on the UF's special relationship with Amerindians[17], on Amerindian problems[18], and on projects by the UF to provide aid and assistance for Amerindian communities[19]. When Mr Randolph Cheeks was Minister of Local Government and Amerindian Affairs the newspaper gave prominence to his position, always stressing he was Deputy Leader of the UF[20].

None of the political parties had a permanent presence at Orealla. During the 1964 election campaign the Captain was recruited by the UF to canvass the village on its behalf and was taken by the party to St Cuthbert's Anglican mission, an Amerindian village on the Mahaica river, County Demerara, to canvass, but the party had no representative at Orealla[21]. This typified its attitude towards Amerindians. For the UF, understandably, politics was concerned mainly with the Coast and Coastal issues. Until near the close of the 1964–8 government's term of office it appeared so sure of its Amerindian support that it did little to maintain contact with Amerindian communities. Amerindians believed its political opponents were opposed to the Indian Right. Mr Campbell was a UF MP until his death in 1966. Many prominent members of the party, such as members of the Harte and Melville ranching families of the North Savannahs of the Rupununi[22], had influential relationships with Amerindian communities. The churches, ideologically opposed to the alleged socialism of the other two parties, and particularly the PPP, and angered by recent actions of Dr Jagan's government, openly supported the UF. At Orealla the church canvassed for the UF in the 1964 election.

The PPP and PNC maintained no representative at Orealla, out of pragmatic recognition of their lack of electoral support. But although most Oreallans voted UF in the 1961 and 1964 general elections a few supported the PPP. They appeared to have been influenced by East Indian friends and acquaintances working on the river, and because the Corentyne Coast was predominantly East Indian PPP agents occasionally visited Orealla to canvass for their party. There were no, or very few, PNC supporters, which reflected the Amerindian's more derogatory stereotype of the Blackman.

The change to proportional representation for the 1964 general election gave Amerindian voters a power they had never had before. Because the electoral support of the government and the opposition parties was closely balanced all votes were important. The value of Amerindian votes was recognized by the political parties and each sought to attract them by promises of Amerindian development[23] and by placing an Amerindian candidate relatively high on its list of candidates. All three Amerindian candidates were elected, but in the case of the PPP and PNC this was not due to Amerindian support. This went to the UF.

The PNC-UF coalition government formed after the 1964 general election commissioned Mr S.C. Knapp, a Canadian expert in Amerindian affairs, to undertake an examination of Amerindian problems and make proposals for their resolution. In his report Mr Knapp stressed Amerindian fears about ownership of their lands[24]. Recommendations of the Knapp Report were incorporated into the government's seven year Development Programme, which estimated $(Guy)2,065,000 as capital expenditure for Amerindian health, education, land development, and water supply; and a further $(Guy)918,000 for specific facilities in certain districts. The Canadian government would supply Agricultural Extension Officers to instruct Amerindians in modern agricultural techniques, and Community Development Advisers to assist in local government and marketing organization; and by providing training in these fields for Guyanese officers working among Amerindians[25].

At the 1965 Independence Conference in London it was agreed the government of Guyana grant Amerindians legal ownership or rights of occupancy to areas or reserves, or parts thereof, of which they normally were resident. It would grant other legal rights with respect to areas where traditionally they had enjoyed freedoms and permissions. A commission would be appointed to examine the extent of occupied areas and reserves, and the nature and extent of rights to land that Amerindians currently enjoyed[26].

In December 1963 six sophisticated Amerindians living and working in Georgetown founded an association they called the Amerindian Association of Guyana (AAG). Their intention was to form a pressure group, independent of any political party, to represent the Amerindian people and pressure the government into resolving common and local problems. Full membership was restricted to Amerindians, with associate membership for persons married to Amerindians or interested in Amerindian problems[27]. In 1965 a Working Committee was formed to get the Association off the ground. The six committee members gave their occupations as UF Assemblyman and Parliamentary Secretary to the Ministry of Local Government; PNC Assemblyman; surveyor; printer; security officer; and engineer. Five were Arawaks, indicative of the greater sophistication found in Coastal Amerindian communities and their relative closeness to Georgetown. In a letter to Amerindian villages in 1966[28] the President said that in the past Amerindians were always divided against each other and would not help one another. Now was the time for them to come together and act as one. (In other words, to act according to Mattie.) The association's pennant symbolized this coming together[29]. Nine stars represented the nine tribes of Guyana on a green background representing the forest. A tenth, gold, star symbolized the coming together of the tribes and their integration into Guyanese society.

The Association stated that its ultimate aim was the integration of Amerindians into an independent Guyana with the same rights and opportunities as other citizens. Among policies advocated to achieve this were an intensive campaign of Amerindian education and accelerated local government and development programmes. It proposed the setting up by government of a Board of Amerindian Affairs to examine Amerindian problems[30].

During 1965 executive members of the AAG travelled widely to establish local branches. The main issue on which they canvassed for members was Amerindian land ownership and their slogan was 'No independence before the Amerindian land question is resolved.' When members visited Orealla and Sipuruta they received an enthusiastic welcome. Oreallans and Sipurutans regarded the association as a protection against Advantage and a means by which they could compete with Blackpeople and Coolies. When Orealla's Captain introduced the members at an open meeting he said Amerindians now had their own organization to fight for them, like all other races. At a later meeting, when the executive members were gone, he repeated this and linked the association specifically with the UF, saying only Whitepeople and the UF were fighting for Amerindians.

By the end of 1965 the AAG had a membership of many hundreds at a subscription of $2.25[31]. The first Congress, held in December 1965 at Kabakaburi mission on the Pomeroon river, was attended by 65 persons as well as members of the executive, many of whom were representatives of local branches[32]. For a few months it sought to publicize issues involving Amerindians. Its spokesmen were reported by the press and received by the administration, though with little effect.

However, AAG membership remained a paper membership. Effectively it consisted of a few sophisticated Amerindians and some local activists. In spite of developing Amerindian disillusion with politicians and the UF they were unable to form the association into an effective pressure group. The history of the Orealla branch appears to have been typical. It never held any meetings. Within a few months the members had become sceptical, and within a year had practically forgotten its existence. This cannot be blamed solely on community structure and Amerindian attitudes. AAG leaders never maintained meaningful contact with the local organization.

In 1965 Oreallans believed the social and material lot of Amerindians would improve because the UF was a partner in the new coalition government, although for many people their optimism was tempered by a fair degree of scepticism. By 1967, when no changes had taken place there was widespread disillusion with the UF and with politicians generally. People said politicians only Advantaged them, lying and making all kinds of extravagant promises at election time to get their votes. Once they were in power they did nothing for the Amerindian. When Mr D'Aguiar wanted their votes he had promised to fly to Orealla to deal with their problems. Now he was in office he ignored them. The Captain, who had canvassed for the UF, said the party had lied to get the villagers' votes. It had promised the government would build a road along the English Shore to connect Orealla with Crabwood Creek, but the project never was begun. Old people said Mr Burnham and Mr D'Aguiar both promised to raise the old age pension, but they had not done so. Many villagers were so disillusioned with politicians that they said they would never vote again. Some said they would vote UF one more time, to see if they would keep their promises. A few said they would change from the UF to the PPP and see if they would work for the Amerindian people better than D'Aguiar.

The Amerindian Association proved unable to exploit this disillusion. Chronic fragmentation of the leadership inhibited any potential and increased the scepticism of the membership. In September 1965 Mr Campbell was deposed as President. The executive stated this was because he was inactive and dictatorial, but it appears that prominent among the reasons for his removal were fears that he was linking the AAG too closely with the UF[33]. The UF denounced his removal as unconstitutional, the result of a conspiracy to destroy his influence in the Association because he was a member of the UF[34]. Two more Presidents were expelled. They left denouncing the executive and claiming they represented the real AAG. Increasingly it fell under the incompetent direction of an Englishman, Mr Michael Wilson, Public Relations Officer, and a Portuguese Guyanese, Mr Anthony Chaves, who became General Secretary[35]. Both were married to Amerindians.

The causes of the fragmentation of the leadership appear to have been policy disagreements and fear of domination of the Association by one or other of the political parties. As all nationally known members of the executive were expelled or left, the AAG ceased receiving press coverage and was no longer taken seriously by the administration or the political parties, although they kept an eye on its leaders as potential trouble makers. Churches in the Interior were hostile to the Association and administrative officers were ordered to bar its leaders from entering Amerindian reserves. All this further weakened its operations and its credibility among Amerindians.

In April 1967 the AAG held a secret convention at Kabakaburi mission[36]. It was attended by about 36 Amerindian Captains and councillors, mainly from western Guyana. Attendance was by invitation. News of the conference, soon dubbed by the newspapers 'the Pomeroon pow-wow'[37], broke to the Guyanese public on April 14, and as the days passed the revelations became increasingly sensational. It was claimed that the convention had been funded by a Venezuelan diplomat who was present at the meeting. It resolved Amerindians immediately claim existing reserves as their property. It passed a resolution supporting a recent Venezuelan proposal for joint development of the 50,000 square miles of Guyana west of the Essequibo river which Venezuela claims is part of her territory, which was signed by the Captains and councillors. But the most sensational report was that this resolution also endorsed the Venezuelan territorial claim.

Two days after the news of the Kabakaburi conference the government named the five members of the commission which was to examine the question of Amerindian land tenure. The PPP opposition denounced the government for its attitude to 'the Amerindian question'. It had promised to settle the problem of land tenure before independence. It was now a year after independence and it had only just announced the formation of the Lands Commission, under pressure from the Kabakaburi conference. The Ministry of Local Government issued a warning against anyone trying to use Amerindians for personal political ends, and particularly for attacks on Guyana's territorial integrity. On April 24 the Parliament of Guyana in special session passed the Expulsion of Undesireables (Amendment) Bill. Mr Michael Wilson was deported and a vice-consul at the Venezuelan embassy was asked to leave the country. The Venezuelan ambassador issued a denial that Venezuela was involved in the Kabakaburi conference, but said he intended to inform his government of the resolution on joint development as it involved his country's interests.

All three political parties condemned the conference and Venezuelan involvement. The UF re-declared itself the champion of Amerindians and said it was the only group with the right to speak and act on their behalf because it received their votes in the 1964 general election. It believed the promises given on Amerindian land rights were sacred and had ensured that the Lands Commission would contain persons familiar with Amerindians and their problems. It had proved itself the champion of Amerindians in the past and they could have confidence it would continue to do so. It was the only restraining influence standing between two ideologically extremist parties, and it was successful because it had Amerindian support. It claimed that because of proportional representation the Amerindian people had become the key to Guyana's fate — that was why attempts were being made to divorce them from the UF[38].

Alarmed by the Kabakaburi revelations of Amerindian disillusion with the UF, UF teams began canvassing the Interior and establishing or rejuvenating local branches, paying particular attention to Amerindian areas. As the 1968 general election approached the party newspaper concentrated increasingly on the UF fight for Amerindian land tenure, claiming sole credit for the UF for defending Amerindian land rights at the 1963 and 1965 Constitutional Conferences in London[39]. In mid-1968 'The Sun' reported a visit by a UF team to Orealla[40]. It criticised Orealla's useless water tank, and mentioned Oreallans' complaints about drinking water; communications; health services; and education. (UF Minister Mr Cheeks had received these complaints a year and a half previously! Case 7:15) It reported that the main concern was ownership of the reserve. The article ended by saying Oreallans believed only the UF was genuinely concerned about their problems. They were following eagerly the great fight Mr D'Aguiar was putting up to ensure they would receive rights to their lands. The paper printed a photograph of a member of the team with the Captain and another villager who was holding a UF emblem — in fact he was one of Orealla's few PPP supporters, and they got his name wrong!

The Amerindian Association foundered upon the inadequacies of its leaders and on the rock of international politics, in addition to the difficulties inherent in trying to organize Amerindians. After the Kabakaburi drama it lapsed into a discredited obscurity. In March 1968 a group of Amerindians, mainly from the Pomeroon and the North West District, formed a new political party, the Guyana National Party (GNP), to fight the 1968 general election[41]. It was a party formed 'to represent specifically the interests of Amerindians'[42] and believed the only way they could secure their interests was by obtaining their own political representation. It would work to promote the welfare of Amerindians and ensure they received title to the lands they occupied. The party spokesman claimed Amerindians had been exploited and deceived by other parties and said 'We have been particulary disillusioned by Mr D'Aguiar and his United Force[43]'. At its founding the GNP claimed a membership of 15,000 Amerindians, an obviously concocted figure.

The twelve members of the party executive were more typical of Guyana's Amerindians than the sophisticated individuals who founded the Amerindian Association. Most were Coastal Amerindians from the Pomeroon and the North West District. The party was centred upon Kabakaburi and undoubtedly had strong associations with the Kabakaburi Convention of the previous year. It declared in favour of joint development by Guyana and Venezuela of the region west of the Essequibo river, and applauded the Guyana government's recent move to set up a mixed commission with Venezuela to examine the question of joint development of the area. This it claimed would help Amerindians. It was sceptical about the Amerindian Lands Commission.

Several years later an anthropologist carrying out fieldwork among the Amerindians of the Pomeroon river had no doubt Venezuela played a significant role in the formation of the GNP. He also noted that several of its leaders were mixed Amerindians with Black ancestry and their Amerindian opponents used this in attempts to discredit them, claiming they were not real Amerindians[44]. Whereas the Amerindian Association was formed as an attempt by sophisticated Amerindians to create a pressure group to act on the Amerindians' behalf, the GNP appears to have been an attempt by Venezuela to organize the fears and discontents of Guyana's western Amerindians for its own purposes.

As the election approached the GNP issued a pamphlet saying it, like other parties, had the right to ally itself with foreign sources for financial and other assistance to develop its supporters and their country. It claimed some of its officials had been arrested, and blamed the UF[45]. Certainly a careful eye was kept on GNP activists. An Amerindian schoolteacher at Orealla who became associated with the GNP was immediately transferred to the Coast. However, for whatever reason, the Guyana National Party failed to register for the 1968 general election.

The election was held on 16 December 1968. The results were PNC, 30 seats; PPP, 19 seats; UF, 4 seats. The PNC acquired an overall majority and UF representation was cut by half. The results, as of subsequent elections, have been widely recognized to be fraudulent. The true results would probably have been as in 1964, the PPP having the largest number of seats, possibly with a slight increase in its representation because of the increase in East Indian voters, but without an overall majority.

In the absence of an attractive alternative, as in 1961 and 1964 Amerindians appear to have voted overwhelmingly for the UF. In spite of their disillusion I suspect most Amerindians voted, in the hope that this time the UF would keep its pledges and to vote against the Black and Coolie parties. Had the GNP been contesting the election it might have attracted significant support from western Amerindians who believed their condition would improve if they joined Venezuela. Its Venezuelan links probably would have been more important than the fact that it claimed to be exclusively an Amerindian party. However the election of 1968 destroyed the very limited possibility of Amerindians becoming any kind of independent political force. From then on they were to come increasingly under the control of the PNC government.

On 2 January 1969 an insurrection was attempted in the North Savannahs of the Rupununi District. The Rupununi lies some 250 miles from Georgetown and communication with the Coast is by air. In 1969 it had a population of 12,000 of whom 10,000 were Amerindians living in scattered villages. The main industry was cattle ranching, carried on in the North Savannahs by two large and inter-related families of private ranchers, most of whom were White with some Amerindian mixture. Some Amerindians worked as ranch hands while the rest obtained income by collecting balata[46].

The insurrection[47] was organised by a number of private ranchers who distrusted the government's attitude to their grazing rights and were afraid land was to be taken and given to Coastal immigrants. They intended to secede the Rupununi from Guyana and establish political association with Venezuela or Brazil, and were assisted in organizing the insurrection by Venezuela. They declared an independent Rupununi Republic with Mrs Valerie Hart, a UF candidate in the

December election, as president. Those active in the rebellion appear to have been a number of ranchers and their Amerindian ranch hands. The great majority of Amerindians were not involved. However if the insurrection had persisted successfully for a few days the numbers probably would have increased. One reason why so few were involved appears to have been the rebels' belief that if they could hold out for three days Venezuela would allow volunteers to cross the border to fight for them. Consequently they kept their numbers small to maintain secrecy in planning[48].

The rebels took over the administrative centre and local airstrips, killing six persons, but were unable to prevent news of the insurrection being radioed to Georgetown. A contingent of the Guyana Defence Force was flown into the area and put down the rebellion in two days. The leaders fled across the border into Brazil and Venezuela, where Mrs Hart appealed to the Venezuelan government for assistance, claiming the Amerindians of the Rupununi considered themselves Venezuelan citizens. Venezuela did not act on her appeal.

The Rupununi was declared a restricted area, which cut the UF off from a large proportion of its Amerindian support. Clergymen working among Amerindians had to leave. There was a significant movement of Amerindians into neighbouring territories[49] and the behaviour of the Guyana Defence Force increased bitterness and resentment among the Amerindian population, although the number killed in the suppression of the rebellion appears to have been very small. The Venezuelan government settled the ranchers in the Gran Sabana, and the Amerindians who fled to Venezuela were settled in the region of the Upper Cuyuni[50]. Twenty-eight persons were taken to Georgetown to be charged with offences concerning the rebellion. Charges soon were dropped against eighteen and the rest, mostly Amerindians, later were released or acquitted. In February 170 Amerindian Captains signed in Georgetown a six-point resolution drawn up by the government, pledging their loyal support to the government of Guyana and agreeing to resist any aggression or intrusion into Guyana's national territory[51]. All three political parties condemned the insurrection, but the United Force re-declared itself the champion of the rights of all Amerindians[52].

In the nationalist period of Guyanese politics the Amerindians' perception of themselves as powerless caused them to vote for what they saw as a 'White', anti-Black and anti-Coolie party, regarded as heir to their traditional White protectors. When they became disillusioned with the United Force some sought an alliance with Venezuela, which they regarded as having a more enlightened Amerindian policy than that likely to be pursued by any of their national parties, and which they also regarded as 'White', causing a new problem in Guyana's international relations.

Notes

1 In my case many Oreallans rationalized that I was not a real Whiteman as I had grey hair. Everyone knew Whitemen have blond hair, so I was a little Mixed.

2 E. Stonequist, (1937), pp. 2–3.

3 For example, A. Antonovski, (1956). p. 57; H.F. Dickie-Clark, (1966); E.C. Hughes and H.M. Hughes, (1952); A.C. Kerckhoff, (1953).

4 F. Barth, (1969), pp. 13–14.

5 For example, see *British Guiana* (1962); L.A. Despres, (1967); L.A. Despres, (1975); C. Jagan, (1966); G.K. Lewis, (1968), pp. 257–88; P. Newman, (1964); P. Reno, (1964); R.T. Smith, (1962), pp. 165–83; R.T. Smith, (1971); R.T. Smith, (1976). This sample contains a variety of analyses of the conflict, including stratification analyses, Marxist analyses, and plural society interpretations.

6 R.T. Smith, (1976), p. 209.

7 *British Guiana*, 1953b.

8 R.T. Smith, (1976), pp. 213–14.

9 A.M. Schlesinger jr, (1965), pp. 664–9.

10 Ibid.; R.T. Smith, (1976).

11 These interests usually are said to have been the CIA, the US labour movement, and the Christian Anti-communist Crusade.

12 A.M. Schlesinger jr, (1965), pp. 664–9.

13 R.T. Smith, (1976).

14 See particularly R.T. Smith, (1966); R.T. Smith, (1967); R.T. Smith, (1971); R.T. Smith, (1976).

15 R.T. Smith, (1971), p. 24.

16 *New World (Guyana)*, (1969a).

17 For example, 6 July 1968, 'The United Force and Amerindians. The man who leads the fight for Amerindians'; 5 October 1968, 'Amerindians in Mazaruni/Kamarang want a UF Government'; 31 August 1968, 'United Force hold sway. Amerindians boycott Dr Jagan.'; 17 February 1968, 'Amerindians future. D'Aguiar gives four-point plan.'; 22 August 1970, 'PNC first, Amerindians last.'

18 For example, 19 October 1968, 'North-West Amerindians bare problems.'; 23 August 1969, 'Amerindians at Mathew's Ridge being squeezed out.'; 1 June 1968, 'Amerindian pupils need school books.'; 18 May 1968, 'Amerindian girls lured into sex racket.'; 27 July 1968, 'Give the Amerindians assurance on lands.'

19 For example, 9 November 1968, 'Amerindian Committee exhibition successful.'; 5 April 1969, ''Twas a grand sale day...to help Amerindians.'; 6 January 1968, 'United Force brought cheer to Amerindians.'; 20 December 1969, 'Would you be the one to put that extra smile on the faces of Amerindian children this Christmas?'

20 For example, 3 June 1967, 'Cheeks calls on Amerindians to remain United.'; 6 January 1968, 'New Year message to Guyana's Amerindians.' (Cheeks); 17 February 1968, 'New Amerindian rest shelter.' (Cheeks);

22 April 1967, 'We will not tolerate attempts to bribe or intimidate the Amerindian people.' (Cheeks).

21 This may have been less true of some communities. For example, my observations suggested the Captain of Santa Rosa, Moruka river, had a closer tie with the UF than any individual at Orealla.

22 M. Swan, (1961), pp. 125–99.

23 *New World (Guyana)*, (1969a).

24 S.C. Knapp, (1966), p. 1.

25 *British Guiana*, (1966), chapter X.

26 *New World (Guyana)*, (1969b).

27 *Amerindian Association*, (1965a).

28 *Amerindian Association*, (1966).

29 *Amerindian Association* (1965b).

30 *Amerindian Association*, (1965a); *Amerindian Association*, (1965b); M. Wilson and A. Chaves, (1966).

31 I have records of 759 persons from 39 villages and locations for early 1966, which was not the total membership at this time.

32 *Amerindian Association*, (1965b).

33 *Amerindian Association*, (1965a); *Amerindian Association*, (1965b); *Amerindian Association*, (1966); M. Wilson and A. Chaves, (1966).

34 *The Sun*, 29 April 1967; M. Wilson and A. Chaves, (1966).

35 Ibid.

36 The following account of the Kabakaburi conference is based mainly on *The Sun*, 22, 29 April 1967; *Guyana Graphic*, 14, 15, 16, 18, 19, 20, 22, 25, 26, 27, 28 April 1967; *Sunday Graphic*, 23 April 1967.

37 This typifies the Coastal society's view of Amerindians.

38 *The Sun*, 29 April 1967.

39 *The Sun*, 23 March 1968; *Evening Post*, 20 March 1968.

40 *The Sun*, 6 July 1968.

41 Data on the GNP and related events are from *Guyana Graphic*, 15, 18 March 1968; *Evening Post*, 20 March 1968; *The Sun*, 23 March, 12 October 1968. I have other newspaper cuttings from March 1968 on these events, but unfortunately I failed to record their specific dates.

42 *Guyana Graphic*, 15 March 1968.

43 Ibid.

44 L. Drummond, (1974), pp. 322–3.

45 *The Sun*, 12 October 1968.

46 T. McCann, (1969); R.F. Salisbury et al., (1968).

47 Among contemporary reports of this rebellion I have relied particularly upon *Sunday Times*, 19 January, 28 March 1969; *The Times*, 6, 8 January 1969; *The Guardian*, 5, 18 January 1969; *New Statesman*, (1969); *New World (Guyana)*, (1969c); *New World (Guyana)*, (1969d).

48 Information given me at the time estimated the number of Amerindians persuaded to join the revolt as approximately 100.

49 *Amerindian Lands Commission*, (1969), p. 19.

50 Dr Audrey Butt Colson, personal communication.

51 M.N. Menezes, (n.d.).

52 *The Sun*, 31 January 1969.

Afterward

I find it difficult to obtain information on recent developments among Guyana's Amerindians, although this is more likely a consequence of my current location than evidence of any attempt to hide such information.

Since independence the Guyanese state has become increasingly centralized and authoritarian. The PNC has used rigged elections and a rigged referendum to justify remaining in power and making fundamental constitutional changes. The ruling party has been made paramount over the government; the President (until his death in 1985, Mr Forbes Burnham) given absolute powers; and the judiciary subordinated to the political executive. This has taken place within a developing economic crisis, brought about by the crisis in the world economy and exacerbated by the government's political and economic policies. Repressive measures and constitutional changes are justified by appeal to socialist rhetoric.

However there is evidence that opposition to the government's policies and to the form of the Guyanese state is developing into class opposition which cuts across racial boundaries between Africans and East Indians. Evidence for this is the emergence of the Working People's Alliance (WPA), a left-wing party which has combined with the PPP in political and trade union actions against the government; and strikes which have received the support of both African bauxite workers and East Indian sugar workers. What appears to be happening is the re-emergence of class issues which became obscured by appeals to race in the pre-independence period[1].

In April 1976 Amerindian communities received title to 4,500 square miles of the lands they occupied. Title was given in accordance with the recommendations of the report of the Amerindian Lands Commission[2], under the Amerindian (Amendment) Act of 1976[3]. The Act contains provisions entitling the government to take back lands whenever it considers this to be in the national interest. The Amerindian villages of the Mazaruni-Potaro-Cuyuni region of western Guyana (Carib, Akawaio, and Arekuna) were not given title to lands on the grounds that the area was to be used for the Upper Mazaruni Development Project and consequently many of its inhabitants would be re-settled; and because much of the region had been declared mining

205

districts. The Upper Mazaruni Development Project, intended to produce hydro-electricity, has been aborted, but the Amerindians of the area still have no title to its land. The Waiwai and the Barama river Caribs also received no land titles[4].

In 1985 the Guyana Human Rights Association reported the migration of Akawaio and Carib Amerindians across the Cuyuni into Venezuela and noted that all but one of the villages which existed on the Cuyuni river twenty years before had gone into Venezuela. The migration of Akawaio was being encouraged by Venezuela who regarded it as valuable evidence supporting her claim to Essequibo. The Barama river Caribs had been encouraged to move to Venezuela by the fact that they had received no land titles in Guyana[5].

However, the main threat to Amerindian settlements, way of life, and living standards identified by the 1985 Guyana Human Rights Association report was mining. For reasons convenient to the government, uncontrolled mining exploration was being encouraged and was spreading into areas occupied by Amerindians, creating population movement, poverty, and social and cultural breakdown. The problem was particularly acute in west-central Guyana and had reached 'disaster proportions' among the Akawaio and eastern Patamona. Government discussions were under way with international companies regarding large-scale exploration and mining in the Mazaruni-Potaro-Cuyuni region, none of which took account of Amerindian interests[6].

Writing of the early 1970s, Drummond stated that the term 'integration' had come to have a new meaning to the Coastal Amerindians of the Pomeroon river area, and presumably to other Amerindians. It was taken to mean the absorption of the Amerindian racial group into the Black group through miscegenation. They believed the government's policy was to excise 'the Amerindian problem' through mating between Black men and Amerindian women. They interpreted this as the rationale for establishing Guyana Defence Force camps and pioneer co-operatives near Amerindian villages[7]. However the 1985 Guyana Human Rights Association report states that the Guyana Defence Force has in general a good record in its relations with Amerindian communities, but allegations of brutality have been made against the police and police inefficiency causes much inconvenience and suffering to Amerindians subjected to detention on remand[8].

On the Corentyne river the West Suriname Project, a Suriname development project based on the mining and processing of the bauxite reserves of the Bakhuys mountains, was to involve the building of a city at Apoera. A harbour planned at Apoera was to be linked by rail to the bauxite fields. In spite of Amerindian protests the land was appropriated as *domeingrond* and concessions sold to Dutch and American companies. Development went ahead without consulting the local people and I am informed that the results have been socially disastrous. The traditional economy was disrupted; there was increased marital breakdown and venereal disease; and the consumption of drink reached 'awful proportions'. Amerindian men were employed at inflated wages on temporary jobs, but no money was invested in Amerindian long-term social and economic developments[9]. Hira reports that Apoera is now 'totally erased from the map of the area', with a resulting drift of Amerindians from the Dutch Shore of the Corentyne river to the city life of Suriname's Coastal society[10].

The manipulated Guyana general election of 9 December 1985 was contested by the United Force, which was granted two seats. The party has no organisation, no office, no publications, and its manifesto remains that of 1964. All parties but the PNC condemned the election results as fraudulent, but the UF accepted its two seats. According to the government most of the UF's support came from Amerindian areas[11].

Notes

1 D. Bartels, (1981); R.T. Smith, (1976), pp. 216–24; C.Y. Thomas, (1983).
2 The Amerindian Lands Commission reported in August 1969. Its basic recommendations were, all villages be deemed Local Authorities; adequate areas of land be granted freehold to Local Authorities; Local Authorities to distribute land to households or individuals on terms approved by the government; a central authority be set up to devise, direct, and control a system of local government suitable for Amerindian villages; Local Authorities to obtain approval from the central authority before disposing of land to a non-Amerindian; Local Authorities to obtain the approval of their electorate before disposing of land to a non-Amerindian; District councils to be set up, responsible to the central authority, to deal with matters of common interest to their component villages; Amerindians residing outside Amerindian villages to be granted title to their area of occupation to a maximum of 30 acres; Amerindians holding land freehold to have the legal right to possess and extract minerals to a maxmium depth of 50 feet; Amerindians to benefit from any sub-surface mining on their property (*Amerindian Lands Commission*, (1969), pp. 68–70). The commission also made specific proposals for Amerindian communities (Ibid., pp. 71–208).
   In 1970 the PNC government held a conference of Amerindian Captains to ratify the report. There was criticism by non-PNC bodies of the manner in which the conference was held and the document agreed by the Captains, which in effect gave the government control over Amerindian lands and their designation and occupation. (See for example, *The Sun*, (14 February 1970); *Ratoon*, no. 4, (March 1970); W M. Ridgwell, (1972), pp. 246–8.)

3 *Guyana*, 1976.
4 *Amerindian Lands Commission*, (1969); *Guyana Human Rights Association*, (1985), p. 17; M.N. Menezes, (n.d.); Dr Audrey Butt Colson, personal communication.
5 *Guyana Human Rights Association*, (1985), op. cit.
6 Ibid., pp. 18–9.
7 L. Drummond, (1974), pp. 322–6. I found no evidence of this belief on the Corentyne in the mid and late 1960s.
8 *Guyana Human Rights Association*, (1985), p. 19.
9 S. Hira, (1983), pp. 169, 176, 179; Ms Lesley Forrest, personal communication.
10 S. Hira. (1983), p. 179.
11 *Guyana Update*, no. 17, p. 4.

Bibliography

1 Books and articles

Amerindian Association of Guyana. (1965a) President's report of 1965; for the branches of the Amerindian Association of Guyana. Unpub. ms.

Amerindian Association of Guyana. (1965b) Minutes of the first congress of the AAG held at Cabacaburi Mission, Pomeroon river, on Sunday, 19 December 1965 at 1.30 p.m. Unpub. ms.

Amerindian Association of Guyana. (1966) President's letter to Amerindian villages, 15 March 1966. Unpub. ms.

Antonovski, A. (1956) 'Toward refinement of the marginal man concept', *Social Forces*, 35, pp. 57–62.

Bartels, D. (1981) 'Catastrophe theory and dialectical change in Guyanese race and class relations', *Current Anthropology*, 22, pp. 435–6.

Barth, F. (1966) *Models of social organisation*. London: Royal Anthropological Institute Occasional paper no. 23.

Barth, F. (1969) 'Introduction', in F. Barth(ed.), *Ethnic groups and boundaries: the social organisation of culture difference*. London: George Allen and Unwin.

Basso, K.H. (1979) *Portraits of the Whiteman*. Cambridge: Cambridge University Press.

Bernau, J.H. (1847) *Missionary labours in British Guiana*. London.

Brett, W.H. (1968) *The Indian tribes of Guiana*. London.

Butt, A.J. (1954) Religious belief and social structure. PhD thesis, Cambridge University, Unpub.ms.

Butt, A.J. (1956) 'Ritual blowing: Taling — a causation and cure of illness among the Akawaio', *Man (OS)* no.48, pp. 1–7.

Butt, A.J. (1965) 'The Guianas', *Bulletin of the International Committee on Urgent Anthropological Research*, no.7, pp. 69–90.

Butt, A.J. (1965–6) 'The shaman's legal role', *Revista do Museu Paulista*, nova serie, XVI, pp. 151–86.

Colson, A.Butt. (1969) Comparative studies of the social structure of Guiana Indians and the problem of acculturation. (Paper prepared for the Berg Wartenstein Symposium.) Unpub.ms.

Daly, V.T. (1966) *A short history of the Guyanese people*. Georgetown: Daily Chronicle Ltd.

Despres, L.A. (1967) *Cultural pluralism and nationalist politics in British Guiana*. Chicago: Rand McNally and Co.

Despres, L.A. (1970) 'Differential adaptations and micro-cultural evolution in Guyana', in N.E. Whitten and J.F. Szwed, *Afro-American anthropology*. New York: Free Press.

Despres, L.A. (1973) 'Ethnicity and ethnic group relations in Guyana', in John W.Bennett, (ed.), *The new ethnicity: perspectives from ethnology*. Proceedings of the American Ethnological Society, pp. 127–47.

Despres, L.A. (1975) 'Ethnicity and resource competition in Guyanese society', in L.A. Depres(ed.), *Ethnicity and resource competition in plural society*. The Hague, Paris: Mouton.

Dew, E. (1978) *The difficult flowering of Suriname*. The Hague: Martinus Nijhoff.

Dickie-Clark, H.F. (1966) *The marginal situation*. London and Boston: Routledge and Kegan Paul.

Drummond, L. (1974) The outskirts of the Earth; a study of Amerindian ethnicity on the Pomeroon river, Guyana. PhD dissertation; Department of Anthropology, University of Chicago.

Drummond, L. (1981) 'The cultural continuum: a theory of intersystems'. *Man (NS)*, 15, pp. 352–74.

Drummond, L. (n.d.) Abstract: Kinship and ethnicity among the Pomeroon Arawak of Guyana. (Paper presented at the session 'Indians of the Guianas', at the XLI International Congress of Americanists, Mexico City, 2–7 September 1974.) Unpub.ms.

Epstein, A.L. (1978) *Ethos and identity*. London: Tavistock.

Feinberg, R. (1979) 'Schneider's symbolic culture theory: an appraisal'. *Current Anthropology*, 20, pp. 541–60.

Fock, N. (1963) *Waiwai: religion and society in an Amazonian tribe*. Copenhagan: The National Museum.

Foster, G M. (1961) 'The dyadic contract: a model for the social structure of a Mexican peasant village'. *American Anthropologist*, 63, pp. 1173–91.

Foster, G M. (1963) 'The dyadic contract in Tzintzuntzan II: patron-client relationship'. *American Anthropologist,* 65, pp. 1280–93.

Geertz, C. (1973) 'Thick description: toward an interpretive theory of culture', in C. Geertz, *The interpretation of cultures*. New York: Basic Books.

Geertz, C. (1977) '"From the native's point of view": on the nature of anthropological understanding' in J.L. Dolgin, D.S. Kemnitzer and D.M. Schneider (eds.), *Symbolic anthropology*. New York: Columbia University Press.

Geertz, C. (1979) 'Deep play: notes on the Balinese cockfight' in P. Rabinow, and W.M. Sullivan (eds.), *Interpretive social science: a reader*. Berkely, Los Angles, London: University of California Press.

Gillin, J. (1936) 'The Barama river Caribs of British Guiana', *Papers of the Peabody Museum of Archaeology and Ethnology,* 14, no.2, pp. 1–274.

Gillin, J. (1963) 'Tribes of the Guianas', in J.H. Steward (ed.), *Handbook of South American Indians*, vol III. New York: Cooper Square.

Gluckman, M. (1969) 'Inter-hierachical roles: professional and party ethics in tribal areas in south and central Africa' in M.J. Swartz (ed.), *Local-level politics*. London: University of London Press.

Guyana Update (1986) no.17, January-February 1986. Box BCM 7934, London WC1N 3XX.

Hanson, F.A. (1975) *Meaning in culture*. London and Boston: Routledge and Kegan Paul.

Henfrey, C. (1964) *The gentle people*. London: Hutchinson and Co.

Hira, S. (1983) 'Class formation and class struggle in Suriname: the background and development of the coup d'etat', in F. Ambursley and R. Cohen (eds.), *Crisis in the Caribbean*. Kingston, Port of Spain, London; Heinemann.

Holy, L. and Stuchlik, M. (1981) 'The structure of folk models', in L. Holy and M Stuchlik (eds.), *The structure of folk models*. London: Tavistock.

Hughes, E.C. and Hughes, H.M. (1952) *Where peoples meet: racial and ethnic frontiers*. Glencoe: Free Press.

Hutson, J. (1971) 'A politician in Valloire', in F.G. Bailey (ed.), *Gifts and poison*. Oxford: Basil Blackwell.

Im Thurn, E. (1883) 'Between the Pomeroon and the Orinoco,' *Timehri*, 2, pp. 211–39.

Im Thurn, E. (1884) 'The Spanish Arawaks of the Morooka', *Timehri*, 3, pp. 366–70.

Im Thurn, E. (1967) *Among the Indians of Guiana*. New York: Dover Publications Inc.

Jagan, C. (1966) *The West on trial*. London: Michael Joseph.

Jayawardena, C. (1963) *Conflict and solidarity in a Guianese plantation*. University of London: Athlone Press.

Jayawardena, C. (1968) 'Ideology and conflict in lower class communities', *Comparative studies in society and history*, X, pp. 413–46.

Jenkins, R. (1981) 'Thinking and doing: towards a model of cognitive practice', in L. Holy and M. Stuchlik *The structure of folk models*. London: Tavistock.

Kerckhoff A.C. (1953) An investigation of factors operative in the development of the personality characteristics of marginality. PhD thesis: University of Wisconsin.

Kirchoff, P. (1963) 'The Warrau', in J. Steward (ed.), *Handbook of South Amerincan Indians*, vol III. New York: Cooper Square.

Kloos, P. (1971) *The Moroni river Caribs of Suriname*. Assen: Van Gorcum and comp.

Kloos, P. (1972) 'Amerindians of Surinam', in W.Dostal (ed.), *The situation of the Indians in South America*. Geneva: World Council of Churches.

Kobben, A.J.F. (1976) 'The periphery of a political system', in A.J. Aronoff (ed.), *Freedom and constraint*. Assen: Van Gorcum and comp.

Leach, E.R. (1954) *Political systems of highland Burma*. London: Bell.

Leach, E.R. (1973) 'Structuralism in social anthropology', in D.Robey (ed.), *Structuralism: an introduction*. Oxford: Clarendon Press.

Lewis, G.K. (1968) *The growth of the modern West Indies*. New York: Monthly Review Press.

Mair, L. (1969) *Witchcraft*. London: Weidenfeld and Nicholson.

Marcus, G.E. and Fischer, M.J. (1986) *Anthropology as cultural critique*. Chicago and London: University of Chicago Press.

Mayer, A.C. (1967) 'Patrons and brokers: rural leadership in four overseas Indian communities', in M Freeman (ed.), *Social organization: essays presented to Raymond Firth*. Chicago: Aldine.

McCann, T. (1969) 'The Rupununi, its peoples and its problems', *New World (Guyana)*, 1, no. 1, pp. 30–1.

Menezes, M.N. (1972) 'Amerindian captains and constables: a system of alliance for security and control', *Release*, October 1972, pp. 55–67.

Menezes, M.N. (1973) 'The Dutch and Indian policy of Indian subsidy: a system of annual and triennial presents', *Caribbean Studies,* 13, no. 3, pp. 64–88.

Menezes, M.N. (1977) *British policy towards the Amerindians in British Guiana, 1803–73*. Oxford: Clarendon Press.

Menezes, M.N. (1979) *The Amerindians in Guyana, 1803–73*. London: Frank Cass.

Menezes, M.N. (n.d.) 'From protection to integration: the Amerindians of Guyana vis-a-vis the Government, 1803–1973'. Unpub.ms.

Milton, K. (1981) 'On the inference of folk models: discussion and demonstration', L. Holy and M. Stuchlik (eds.), *The structure of folk models*. London: Academic Press.

Newman, P. (1964) *British Guiana*. London: Oxford University Press.

New Statesman. (1969) 'The Amerindian plight in Guyana', *New Statesman*, 28 March 1969, p. 434.

New World (Guyana). (1969a) 'Parties plans for Amerindians — a summary', *New World (Guyana)*, 1, no. 1, pp. 28–9.

New World (Guyana). (1969b) 'Amerindian land tenure. Report of the British Guiana Independence Conference, 1965', *New World (Guyana)*, 1, no.1, pp. 32–3.

New World (Guyana). (1969c) 'A note on "Rupununi"'. *New World (Guyana)*, 1, no.1, p. 9.

New World (Guyana). (1969d) 'Excerpts from Mr Burnham's statement on revolt', *New World (Guyana)*, 1, no.1, p. 10.

Ortner, *S.B.* (*1984*) 'Theory in anthropology since the 'sixties', *Comparative studies in society and history,* 26, pp. 126–66.

Outhwaite, W. (1975) *Understanding social life*. London: George Allen and Unwin Ltd.

Paine, R. (1967) 'What is gossip all about? An alternative hypothesis', *Man (NS)* 2, pp. 278–85.

Peneux, F. (1961) History of education at Orealla 1838–1961. Bain Grey Essay. Georgetown Teacher Training College, Guyana. Unpub.ms.

Radcliffe-Brown, A.R. (1956a) 'On joking relationships', in A.R. Radcliffe-Brown, *Structure and function in primitive society*. London: Cohen and West.

Radcliffe-Brown, A.R. (1956b) 'A further note on joking relationships', in A.R. Radcliffe-Brown, *Structure and function in primitive society*. London: Cohen and West.

Reno, P. (1964) *The ordeal of British Guiana*. New York: Monthly Review Press.

Ridgwell, W.M. (1972) *The forgotten tribes of Guyana*. London: Tom Stacey.

Riviere, P. (1969) *Marriage among the Trio*. Oxford: Clarendon Press.

Riviere, P. (1984) *Individual and society in Guiana*. Cambridge: Cambridge University Press.

Rodway, J. (1891–4) *History of British Guiana, from the year 1668 to the present time*. 3 vols. Georgetown:J Thompson.

Roth, W E. (1915) 'An enquiry into the animism and folklore of the Guiana Indians', *30th annual report of the Bureau of American Ethnology, 1908–9*. pp. 103–386. Washington: Government Printing Office.

Roth, W E. (1924) 'An introductory study of the arts, crafts, and customs of the Guiana Indians', *38th annual report of the Bureau of American Ethnology, 1916–7*. pp. 25–745 Washington: Government Printing Office.

Roth, W E. (1929) 'Additional studies of the arts, crafts, and customs of the Guiana Indians, with special reference to those of southern Guiana', *Bulletin of the Bureau of American Ethnology*, no. 91. Washington: Government Printing Office.

Rouse, I. (1963a) 'The Arawak' in J.H. Steward (ed.), *Handbook of South American Indians*, vol. IV. New York: Cooper Square.

Rouse, I. (1963b) 'The Carib' in J.H. Steward (ed.), *Handbook of South American Indians*, vol. IV. New York: Cooper Square.

Rowland, E.D. (1892) 'The census of British Guiana', *Timehri*, 6, pp. 40–68.

Runciman, W.G. (1972) *Relative deprivation and social justice*. Pelican books.

Salisbury, R.F., Dummett, J.A., Mills, T., Cook, D. (1968) *Ethnographic notes on Amerindian agriculture*. McGill University Savannah Research Project. Savannah Research Series no.9.

Sanders, A. (1972) 'Amerindians in Guyana: a minority group in a multi-ethnic society', *Caribbean Studies*, 12, pp. 31–51.

Sanders, A.D. (1972) Family structure and domestic organization among Coastal Amerindians in Guyana. PhD thesis: University of London. Unpub.ms.

Sanders, A.D. (1973) 'Family structure and domestic organization among Coastal Amerindians in Guyana', *Social and Economic Studies*, 22, pp. 440–78.

Schlesinger jr, A.M. (1965) *A thousand days*. London: Andre Deutsch.

Schneider, D.M. (1968) *American kinship: a cultural account*. Englewood Cliffs, New Jersey: Prentice-Hall.

Schneider, D.M. (1977) 'Kinship, nationality, and religion in American culture: toward a definition of kinship' in J.L. Dolgin, D.S. Kemnitzer and D.M. Schneider (eds.), *Symbolic anthropology*. New York: Columbia University Press.

Schomburgk, R. (1922) *Travels in British Guiana, 1840–44*. (Translated and edited with geographical and general indices and route maps by Walter E. Roth.) Georgetown: Daily Chronicle.

Shankman, P. 1984 'The thick and the thin: on the interpretive theoretical program of Clifford Geertz', *Current Anthropology,* 25, pp. 261–80.

Skinner, E.P. (1960) 'Group dynamics in social stratifiction in British Guiana' in V. Rubin (consulting editor), *Social and cultural pluralism in the Caribbean*. Annals of the New York Academy of Sciences, 83, art. 5, pp. 904–11.

Smith, M.G. (1965) *The plural society in the British West Indies*. Berkely and Los Angeles: University of California Press.

Smith, M.G. (1974) *Corporations and society*. London: Duckworth.

Smith, R.T. (1956) *The negro family in British Guiana*. London: Routledge and Kegan Paul.

Smith, R.T. (1962) *British Guiana*. Oxford: Oxford University Press.

Smith, R.T. (1966) 'People and change', *New World (Guyana Independence Issue)*, pp. 49–54.

Smith, R.T. (1967) 'Stratification, cultural pluralism, and integration in West Indian societies', in S. Lewis and T.G. Mathews(eds.), *Caribbean integration*. Puerto Rico: Institute of Caribbean Studies.

Smith, R.T. (1971) 'Race and political conflict in Guyana'. *Race,* 12, pp. 415–27.

Smith, R.T. (1976) 'Race, class, and political conflict in a postcolonial society' in S.G. Neuman(ed.), *Small states and segmented societies: national political integration in a global environment*. New York: Praeger.

Smith, R.T. (1982) 'Race and class in the post-emancipation Caribbean' in R. Ross (ed.), *Racism and colonialism*. The Hague, Boston, London: Martinus Nijhoff.

Smith, R.T. and Jayawardena, C. (1959) 'Marriage and the family amongst East Indians in British Guiana', *Social and Economic Studies,* 8, pp. 226–58.

Steward, J.H. and Faron, L.C. (1959) *Native peoples of South America*. New York: McGraw Hill.

Stonequist, E. (1937) *The marginal man*. New York: Scribners.

Suarez, M.M. (1968) *Los Warao*. Departmento de Antropologia, Instituto Venexolano de Investigaciones Cientificas, Caracas.

Suarez, M.M. (1971) 'Terminology, alliance and change in Warao society', *Niewe West Indische Gids*, 48, pp. 56–121.

Swann, M. (1961) *The marches of El Dorado*. Penguin Books.

Thomas, C.Y. (1983) 'State capitalism in Guyana: an assessment of Burnham's co-operative socialist republic' in F. Ambursley and R. Cohen (eds.), *Crisis in the Caribbean*. Kingston, Port of Spain, London: Heinemann.

Turner, V.W. (1969) *The ritual process*. London: Routledge and Kegan Paul.

Turner, V.W. (1974) *Dramas, fields, and metaphors*. Ithaca and London: Cornell University Press.

Van Renselaar, H. and Hoetinik, H. (1968) 'Surinam and the Netherlands Antilles' in C. Veliz(ed.) *Latin America and the Caribbean*. London: Anthony Blond Ltd.

Ward, B.E. (1965) 'Varieties of the conscious model: the fishermen of South China' in M. Banton(ed.), *The relevance of models for social anthropology*. London: Tavistock.

Wilson, M. and Chaves, A. (1966) Amerindians. Unpub ms.

2   Reports and ordinances

Amerindian Lands Commission. (1969) Report by the Amerindian Lands Commission. Government Printers: Guyana.

British Guiana. (1910) Ordinance no.22 of 1910 (The Aboriginal Indian Protection Ordinance). Government Printers: British Guiana.

British Guiana. (1951) Ordinance no.22 of 1951 (The Amerindian Ordinance). Government Printers: Georgetown.

British Guiana. (1953a) Order no.59 of 1953. Government Printers: British Guiana.

British Guiana. (1953b) British Guiana, suspension of the constitution. London: HMSO.

British Guiana. (1962) Report of a commission of enquiry into disturbances in British Guiana in February 1962. London: HMSO.

British Guiana. (1966)- British Guiana (Guyana) development programme (1966–72). Government Printers: Georgetown.

Guyana. (1976) Act no.6 of 1976 (The Amerindian (Amendment) Act). Government Printers: Guyana.

Guyana Human Rights Association. (1985) Human rights report: 1985. Georgetown, Guyana.

International Commission of Jurists. (1965) Report of the British Guiana Commission of Enquiry. Geneva.

Knapp, S.C. (1966) Report on the Amerindians of Guyana and suggested development programmes. Government Printers: Georgetown.

Peberdy, P.S. (1948) Report of a survey on Amerindian affairs in the remote Interior, with additional notes on coastland population groups of Amerindian origin. Government Printers: Georgetown.

3   Newspapers

'Evening Post'. (Guyana)
'The Guardian'. (UK)
'Guyana Graphic'. (Guyana)
'Ratoon'. (Guyana)
'The Sun'. (Guyana)
'Sunday Graphic'. (Guyana)
'Sunday Times'. (UK)
'The Times'. (UK).

Index